ON OUR WAY BACK

STORY OF THE  SEASON 17/18

WORDS: TIM SPIERS   DESIGN: SIMON HILL

Express & Star

IN PARTNERSHIP WITH CLUB AND FANS

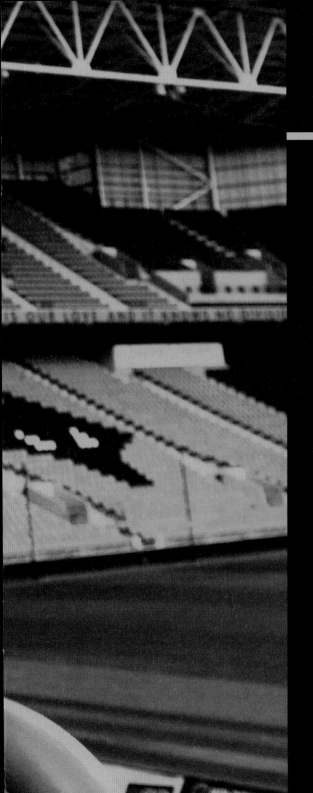

FOREWORD

THE 2017/18 SEASON WAS A VERY SUCCESSFUL ONE FOR THE CLUB. WE ACHIEVED OUR TARGET OF WINNING PROMOTION TO THE PREMIER LEAGUE WITH FOUR GAMES TO SPARE – A VERY IMPRESSIVE ACHIEVEMENT FOR NUNO, HIS STAFF AND ALL THE PLAYERS.

THE TEAM WAS VERY CONSISTENT THROUGHOUT THE CAMPAIGN AND THIS CONSISTENCY PROVED IMPORTANT DURING CRUCIAL MOMENTS. THERE WERE SOME SPECIAL VICTORIES WHICH HELPED US ON OUR WAY TO THE LEAGUE TITLE AND PROVIDED MEMORIES THAT I'M SURE WILL STAY WITH OUR SUPPORTERS FOREVER.

AS OWNERS WE INVESTED SIGNIFICANTLY INTO THE SQUAD AND WERE PLEASED TO SEE A NUMBER OF YOUNG SIGNINGS PLAY KEY ROLES DURING THE SEASON.

NUNO MUST BE PRAISED FOR MOULDING A SQUAD THAT PLAYED ATTRACTIVE, WINNING FOOTBALL AND CREATING A COLLECTIVE TEAM SPIRIT, WHILE OFF THE PITCH LAURIE, KEVIN AND ALL THE TEAM WORKED VERY HARD TO DELIVER SUCCESS.

THANK YOU TO OUR FANS FOR SUPPORTING US EVERY STEP OF THE WAY, FOLLOWING THE TEAM IN BIG NUMBERS ACROSS THE COUNTRY.

I ALSO ENJOYED THE EXPRESS & STAR'S DAILY COVERAGE OF WHAT WAS A SPECIAL SEASON.

WE NOW LOOK FORWARD TO CONTINUING THE CLUB'S GROWTH ON AND OFF THE FIELD IN THE PREMIER LEAGUE.

JEFF SHI
EXECUTIVE CHAIRMAN OF WOLVERHAMPTON WANDERERS FC

CONOR COADY

WHAT A FANTASTIC YEAR FOR WOLVERHAMPTON WANDERERS. AT THE START OF THE SEASON YOU COULD TELL THE BOYS WERE MOTIVATED TO DO SOMETHING SPECIAL – AND THAT'S HOW IT PROVED.

FROM THAT VERY FIRST GAME AGAINST MIDDLESBROUGH, IT WAS CLEAR WE HAD A TALENTED AND ORGANISED TEAM THAT COULD MATCH ANYONE IN THE DIVISION.

THERE HAD BEEN PLENTY OF CHANGE DURING THE SUMMER WITH A NEW HEAD COACH AND A LOT OF NEW PLAYERS BROUGHT IN BUT WE ALL GELLED QUICKLY DURING PRE-SEASON AND, AFTER THOSE FIRST FEW WINS, WE NEVER REALLY LOOKED BACK.

THERE WERE SO MANY HIGHLIGHTS AND THE BRISTOL CITY, MIDDLESBROUGH AND CARDIFF AWAY WINS PROBABLY STAND OUT BECAUSE THEY WERE SO DRAMATIC.

IN THE FINAL FEW WEEKS, WE HAD THE WIN AGAINST BIRMINGHAM AFTER SEALING PROMOTION AND A BRILLIANT DAY AT BOLTON WHERE WE SECURED THE TITLE AND I MANAGED TO FINALLY GET MYSELF ON THE SCORESHEET!

FROM A PERSONAL POINT OF VIEW, IT WAS AN HONOUR TO CAPTAIN THE TEAM ON MANY OCCASIONS AND OF COURSE LIFT THAT TROPHY WITH DANNY.

IT WAS A YEAR NONE OF US WILL EVER FORGET.

WHEN I JOINED WOLVES IN 2015 I SAID THE CLUB BELONGED IN THE PREMIER LEAGUE – SO TO PLAY A PART IN HELPING TAKE IT BACK THERE WAS VERY SPECIAL.

TIM SPIERS

YOU'RE NOT SUPPOSED TO STAND UP AND APPLAUD IN THE PRESS BOX. YOU'RE NOT SUPPOSED TO CHEER EITHER. OR SING, OR CHANT, OR CELEBRATE. IT WAS INCREDIBLY HARD FOR THIS WOLVES FANATIC-TURNED-'NEUTRAL' JOURNALIST TO AVOID DOING ANY OF THE ABOVE WHILE WATCHING NUNO ESPÍRITO SANTO'S WONDERFUL TEAM STORM TO THE CHAMPIONSHIP TITLE IN 2017/18.

As a fan it must have been the perfect campaign to witness; as a reporter it was a damn privilege. Wolverhampton Wanderers are a club going places in a hurry, but whatever happens in the next 10 years, the 2017/18 campaign will hold a special place in the hearts of the tens of thousands of supporters who lived and breathed it, as well as myself.

From day one, Wolves thrilled, impressed and amazed. It wasn't just the fact they won promotion, it wasn't just the fact they amassed one of the highest points tallies in the club's history – it was the fact they did it with such style, such panache, such verve, such swagger. There were passing moves, tricks, flicks and goals that took your breath away and, as a writer, it left you running out of superlatives at times. I've been lucky enough to do this job for three years but had previously followed Wolves as a fan since 1991. It goes without saying this was the finest football I've ever seen at Molineux, but when seasoned observers who were there in the glory days of Stan Cullis, Billy Wright and Peter Broadbent shared precisely the same sentiments, you knew you were witnessing greatness. It was often death by a thousand cuts but Wolves could be brilliantly devastating too. The strings to their bow were numerous; be it free-flowing passing moves, lightning-quick counter attacks, set-pieces, long range shots or *that* 35-yard volley.

There were stars all over the pitch. John Ruddy kept clean sheets in more than half the matches and was the hero at Cardiff. Willy

Boly was utterly imperious and yet delicately graceful at the same time, like a ballet-dancing doorman, while alongside him the ebullient and instantly likeable Conor Coady had the season of his life and wing-backs Matt Doherty and Barry Douglas performed with metronomic consistency. The fireworks came chiefly from Diogo Jota and Ivan Cavaleiro, two flamboyant exocets who laid on goals and assists galore. Helder Costa came to the party after Christmas and looked like his old brilliant self, while goals also came from Leo Bonatini and Benik Afobe.

Then there was the magician. Ruben Neves, aged just 21, did things with a football that many wouldn't even dream of. The ultimate string-puller with vision beyond the capabilities of most footballers, his campaign (and those six long-range goals) will never be forgotten.

Nuno brought it all together – his formation, his philosophy, his tactics, his mantras, his beard-stroking; a cult was born. The head coach makes no secret of finding his media commitments irksome but behind the scenes he was a different character altogether; amiable, polite and often sporting that trademark Cheshire Cat grin. The players were a pleasure to deal with and always open and welcoming, from conducting an unwanted interview after a (rare) defeat to sharing a beer during an unforgettable promotion party.

From Austria in July to Sunderland in May via thousands of miles travelling up and down the country, trying to work in a pitch-black car park in Hull after being thrown out the ground,

recording a podcast at 1am in a dingy Swansea hotel, getting lost in the streets of Southampton and nervously parking in a south London scrapyard at 10am on Boxing Day. The many long hours and days were worth it for a year that was an unforgettable adventure.

With match reports, videos, player ratings, stories, podcasts, live internet broadcasts, 24/7 tweeting, weekly press conferences, daily deadlines to meet and a massive readership to cater for it's an all-consuming job, but one that's made easy when an enchanting team produces such dreamy football, not to mention drama and scripts worthy of Hollywood. Midweek jaunts to Norwich and Hull just weren't as taxing when there was a golden reward at the end of the road. A word too for my good friend and colleague Nathan Judah, who presented every single video and podcast along the way, combining a newfound affection for Wolves (impressively setting Middlesbrough loyalties to one side) with his 'unique' sense of humour to great effect.

At Molineux, so often a pit of angst and frustration in recent years, this golden arena of collective obsession became a fortress. The place was transformed and it was a joy to be there. Games and goals will be etched in the mind forever – away days at Bristol City, Cardiff and Middlesbrough were as dramatic as they come, derby wins at home over Villa and Blues were so special and then came the icing on the cake against Bolton and Sheffield Wednesday. Memories to last a lifetime. Yes, 2017/18, what a season it was.

NUNO ESPÍRITO SANTO

"I like challenges" was the first public utterance Nuno made after being hired as Wolves boss. In other words: "Nuno had a dream".

If his dream was to produce one of the finest footballing teams ever seen at Molineux and conjure up a perfect season that no Wolves fan would ever forget, he certainly managed it. Rewind to June 1, 2017 though and, while there was excitement at Nuno's appointment, there was also trepidation at another summer of change.

Fosun had bought the club for £30million a year earlier and the first season was dogged by upheaval and a disappointing mid-table finish despite a big outlay on new signings, while two managers in Walter Zenga and Paul Lambert came and went. Fosun and Jeff Shi pledged they'd learned their lessons – they weren't wrong. The new boss arrived with a burgeoning reputation having enjoyed success on the continent with Rio Ave, Valencia and Porto and instantly carried an authoritative aura.

Like Fosun, set his sights high from the word go. "I'm looking forward to getting inspiration from those golden 1950s years – and making a new future," the 43-year-old said on the day he was unveiled. "I turned down Champions League clubs to be here – I believe in the project, I believe in the ideas."

Crucially – and unlike predecessors Zenga and Lambert – Nuno was a perfect fit to work alongside agent Jorge Mendes, his friend of 20 years. "I am a client of the best agent in the world," Nuno said. "He does his job. I do my job." Nuno was said to be 'cold and emotionless' at Porto but Wolves would instead get a fiery, intense, explosive character who formed an almost unique affinity with an adoring fanbase who sang his name week after week. Within months they forged a bond that's rare in football. But the Nuno love-in extended beyond a repertoire of songs, comedy merchandise or a

regular swooning on social media whenever the man spoke, as if he were a fabled philosopher. Indeed, it's difficult to recall a more universally popular Wolves manager in recent decades. It was the cult of Nuno.

The players respected him deeply. They trusted him, they took his ideas on board and they embraced his football philosophy. In contrast to his volatile touchline demeanour, Nuno made the training pitch a sedate environment where he would preach his mantras. "He's very relaxed and his demeanour's very relaxed," John Ruddy

would later say. "He tells you what he wants and he expects you to produce that. He can lose his temper when he needs to, like every manager, but he keeps you on that borderline in that you're not too comfortable and you're never too far ahead of yourself. That's a fantastic balance and his man-management is superb."

Back to June 1, though, when all this was in its infancy. "We believe our idea can succeed," Nuno said. "You just have to get the right recipe." That recipe was to mould a cohesive, consistent winning team with 12 new players

– many of them completely new to the English game – while adopting a new 3-4-3 formation and introducing an intricate style of football, with a huge emphasis on hard work, detailed preparation and constant professionalism. Here's how it happened...

SIGNINGS

Twelve new signings arrived in the space of 92 days as Nuno, Fosun and the Wolves hierarchy set about creating a team that could fight for promotion. Just a few players from the previous season – Matt Doherty, Danny Batth, Romain Saiss, Helder Costa, Conor Coady and Ivan Cavaleiro – would remain. Otherwise the squad was a blank canvas.

While their spending prowess seems almost limitless, Fosun invested wisely with an incessant focus on potential. The headline capture of Ruben Neves broke the Championship transfer record at £15.8million, yet Wolves' owners saw the 20-year-old as having big room for improvement and could be worth much more than that fee in years to come

Five players – Willy Boly, Diogo Jota, Leo Bonatini, Ruben Vinagre and Alfred N'Diaye, all aged 27 or younger – came in and a deal was put in place to buy each of them at the end of the season if they were a success. Again, Fosun were looking to the future.

There was also a fluid mixture of foreign, mostly Portuguese talents (six, to be precise) with a British steel core. The vastly experienced John Ruddy and Ryan Bennett added defensive nous from years with Norwich in both the Premier League and the Championship – and neither cost a penny. Perhaps the most left-field addition – in more ways than one – was the well-travelled Scot Barry Douglas, who joined from Turkish side Konyaspor for £1m.

Fosun weren't dying wondering – Bonatini's addition on August 1 was the 25th since the Chinese conglomerate's takeover a year earlier. With 135 transfer window days in that time it meant Wolves were buying or loaning a player roughly every five days. Moulding the new boys quickly would be crucial. There wasn't a moment to waste in pre-season.

PLAYERS IN

MAY 31 RYAN BENNETT (NORWICH, FREE)

JUNE 13 RODERICK MIRANDA (RIO AVE, £2.5M)

JUNE 20 PHIL OFOSU-AYEH (EINTRACHT BRAUNSCHWEIG, FREE)

JULY 1 BARRY DOUGLAS (KONYASPOR, £1M)

JULY 8 RUBEN NEVES (PORTO, £15.8M)

JULY 8 WILLY BOLY (PORTO, LOAN)

JULY 10 JOHN RUDDY (NORWICH, FREE)

JULY 11 WILL NORRIS (CAMBRIDGE, UNDISCLOSED)

JULY 20 RUBEN VINAGRE (MONACO, LOAN)

JULY 25 DIOGO JOTA (ATLETICO MADRID, LOAN)

AUGUST 1 LEO BONATINI (AL-HILAL, LOAN)

AUGUST 31 ALFRED N'DIAYE (VILLARREAL, LOAN)

PRE-SEASON

Pre-season comprised six games: four wins, two defeats, five goals scored and four conceded – it was a mixed bag in terms of performances but Wolves came to the boil perfectly with about an emphatic a 1-0 as you could get against Leicester, with the scoreline flattering the Premier League side.

In June, Austria offered luscious green surroundings and beautiful scenery with the 10-day trip providing an ideal opportunity for Wolves' many new players to get to know each other. In terms of fitness it was certainly very productive and the newly-appointed backroom

team were confident that they'd produced one of the division's fittest squads. Most importantly, though, a team and a spine formed throughout the six games and the many hours of relentless work on the training field. A new 3-4-3 formation began to click early on, with confidence gained by beating Bundesliga outfit Werder Bremen in the first game.

Defensively, Wolves looked organised and tough to break down and while creativity in the final third had been an issue, the Leicester victory felt like a breakthrough moment as new signing Diogo Jota began to warm up.

Ivan Cavaleiro stood out, having enjoyed a fine pre-season, while Barry Douglas and pass-master Ruben Neves were the pick of the new boys.

Looking ahead to the first game, Nuno pinpointed Molineux – not a happy stadium for the previous two seasons – as being crucial to Wolves' future gains. "The strength of the wolf is in the pack," Nuno said. "So we want Molineux to be our pack. We are happy with pre-season because it was tough work, good work, we tried to put things together."

The revelation of the summer was without doubt Conor Coady, who excelled from the word go in

his new sweeper role and quickly became the heartbeat of the team, not least with his noisy levels of communication, his shrill voice echoing around the Austrian hills.

A new team needed organising – and Coady and Danny Batth knew exactly how to do that. In the days leading up to the first game, Coady reflected the determined and confident mood in the camp when he said: "We don't want to carry on being a mid-table club. There's a fire in the belly – the boys want to go on and do something special."

JULY 12, 2017 WERDER BREMEN 0-1 WOLVES (DICKO, 50)

Wolves first half (3-4-3): *Burgoyne; Batth (c), Coady, Boly; Doherty, Price, Saiss, Douglas; Zyro, Enobakhare, Cavaleiro.*

Wolves second half (3-4-3): *John Ruddy; Bennett, Coady (c), Miranda; Doherty (Simpson, 59), Edwards, Saiss (Neves, 59) Deslandes; Ronan, Dicko, Mason.*

JULY 15, 2017 VIKTORIA PLZEN 1-2 WOLVES (DICKO 16, DOHERTY 31)

Wolves first half (3-4-3): *Ruddy; Bennett, Miranda, Boly; Doherty, Price, Edwards (c), Douglas; Mason, Dicko, Cavaleiro.*

Wolves second half (3-4-3): *Norris; Batth (c), Miranda, Boly (Coady, 60); Bennett (Simpson, 60), Neves, Saiss, Douglas (Deslandes, 60); Zyro, Enobakhare, Cavaleiro (Ronan, 60).*

JULY 18, 2017 JABLONEC 1-0 WOLVES

Wolves (3-4-3): *Norris (Burgoyne, 45); Batth (c) (Bennett, 60), Coady, Boly (Miranda, 60); Doherty (Simpson, 60), Neves (Price, 60), Saiss, (Edwards, 60), Douglas (Deslandes, 60); Enobakhare (Mason, 60), Dicko (Zyro, 60), Cavaleiro (Ronan, 60).*

JULY 22, 2017 SHREWSBURY TOWN 2-0 WOLVES

Wolves first half (3-4-3): *Ruddy; Miranda, Coady (c), Boly; Doherty, Neves (Saiss, 22), Edwards (c), Douglas; Ronan, Dicko, Cavaleiro.*

Wolves second half (3-4-3): *Norris; Bennett, Batth (c), Deslandes; Doherty (Simpson, 62), Price, Saiss, Douglas (Vinagre, 62); Zyro, Mason, Enobakhare. Subs not used: Burgoyne, Graham.*

JULY 25, 2017 PETERBOROUGH UNITED 0-1 WOLVES (SAMUELS 70)

Wolves first half (3-4-3): *Ruddy; Batth (c), Miranda, Deslandes; Doherty, Price, Ronan, Vinagre; Mason, Zyro, Cavaleiro.*

Wolves second half (3-4-3): *Burgoyne; Bennett, Coady (c), Boly; Graham, Edwards, Saiss, Douglas; Enobakhare, Mason (Samuels, 62), Jota. Subs not used: Simpson, Watt, McKenna.*

JULY 29, 2017 WOLVES 1-0 LEICESTER CITY 0 (CAVALEIRO 60)

Wolves (3-4-3): *Ruddy; Miranda (Batth, 68), Coady (c), Boly; Doherty, Neves (Price, 68), Saiss (Edwards, 68), Douglas; Enobakhare (Graham, 80), Cavaleiro (Zyro, 80), Jota (Ronan, 68). Sub not used: Norris.*

IT WAS AN UNFORGETTABLE SEASON FOR EVERYONE CONNECTED WITH THE CLUB, BUT AMID THE VICTORIES, THE FANTASTIC FOOTBALL, THE GLORY AND THE ECSTASY, THERE WAS A CONSTANT UNDERLYING SADNESS THAT ONE MAN WASN'T PART OF IT. CARL IKEME'S ACUTE LEUKAEMIA DIAGNOSIS IN JULY 2017 SHOCKED THE CLUB TO THE CORE. IKEME HAD BEEN PART OF THE FURNITURE AT MOLINEUX AND COMPTON PARK SINCE HE WAS A YOUNGSTER, PROGRESSING THROUGH THE ACADEMY AND THERE WAS MANY A TEAR SHED WHEN THE DEVASTATING NEWS WAS REVEALED. CARL IS A SOFTLY-SPOKEN GENTLE GIANT, ONE OF THE NICEST, GENUINE AND MOST HUMBLE GUYS YOU COULD WISH TO MEET – NOT JUST IN FOOTBALL, BUT IN LIFE – AND THE THOUGHT OF HIM GOING THROUGH SUCH AN ORDEAL AGED JUST 31 WAS DIFFICULT FOR EVERYONE TO PROCESS AT FIRST. THEN THERE WAS SUPPORT AND DEFIANCE – A LOT OF IT.

FANS, STAFF AND PLAYERS RALLIED IMMEDIATELY TO HIS AID AND A THEME TO THE SEASON SOON FORMED. MORE THAN £150,000 WAS RAISED FOR CURE LEUKAEMIA VIA A VARIETY OF CHARITABLE EXPLOITS AND, AT EVERY SINGLE GAME, CARL'S NAME WAS SUNG AND A FLAG BEARING HIS IMAGE PARADED BY FANS.

AT THE END OF THE CAMPAIGN THE GOALKEEPER RETIRED FROM FOOTBALL, BUT A FEW WEEKS EARLIER HE HAD ANNOUNCED HE WAS IN REMISSION – AND THAT WAS THE BIGGEST VICTORY OF THE SEASON. IT WAS ALL FOR YOU, CARL.

GAME BY GAME

sky BET CHAMPIONSHIP | EFL

SEASON 17/18

WHAT FOLLOWS IS OUR COVERAGE OF EVERY ONE OF WOLVES' 52 LEAGUE AND CUP GAMES, INCLUDING MATCH REPORTS AS THEY WERE PUBLISHED AT THE TIME, QUOTES FROM NUNO AND THE PLAYERS AND THE THOUGHTS OF OUR REGULAR 'FAN VERDICT' CONTRIBUTORS. THIS IS WOLVES' GLORIOUS 2017/18 SEASON, AS REPORTED IN THE EXPRESS & STAR.

WOLVES 1
(BONATINI 33)
MIDDLESBROUGH 0

"I'M HERE ON LOAN, I JUST WANT TO HELP. I HOPE MY FAMILY SEES MY GOAL"
LEO BONATINI

An opening-day win, a clean sheet, a debut goal and all watched by the fourth biggest attendance since Molineux was rebuilt – not a bad start Nuno. In years to come, this won't be one for the 'classic match' files. You never know, though, it might just be remembered as the start of something special. It's too early to tell if Nuno and his many new signings will bring success to a club that craves it so much – but optimism is certainly not in short supply in WV1.

Almost 30,000 very excited supporters are dreaming of a return to the big time – and after beating the team many expect to win the league this year, why shouldn't they? Wolves were solid if unspectacular here, efficient not exuberant. These are traits we should come to expect from a Nuno team (he possessed the best defence in the league as Valencia and Porto boss). They're also traits that Wolves have too often lacked since they returned to the Championship in 2014. But with organisation and discipline at the back and a dash of creativity up top, Wolves managed to see this one through despite Boro spurning two excellent chances.

A Brazilian striker on loan from a Saudi Arabian club took advantage of a Spaniard's mistake to give a Portuguese boss the perfect start to life in England. The Championship isn't what it used to be. It's evolved into a league of real quality, modern tactics and big-money purchases from home and abroad. Wolves have got to know the

division uncomfortably well over the years. But with a new continental system and playing style they hope to take advantage of its evolution. On this showing they might have a chance. The aforementioned Brazilian, Leo Bonatini, who only joined the club on Tuesday and is well short of match sharpness, made himself the hero of the hour, clinically taking advantage of Daniel Ayala's mishap. Wolves were nowhere near at their best here. Or, given that we hadn't even seen seven of these players in competitive action before Saturday, they weren't at the level we anticipate they can reach in the coming weeks and months.

They certainly never reached the heights of the free-flowing fast-paced attacking moves they put together against Leicester a week ago. Instead, this victory was built on the solid foundations of the past six weeks of training. Namely, the relentless work done on shape, discipline and positioning on the training ground. Boro couldn't find a way through the Wolves wall and failed to create a decent chance past the 75-minute mark. That's testament to the way Nuno has drilled Wolves' resoluteness into them. He's building from the back – and it shows. In a 46-game Championship campaign where the majority of matches will be settled by the odd goal it's a great trait to have.

For his first official XI as Wolves boss, Nuno handed debuts to no fewer than seven new signings. John Ruddy, Roderick Miranda, Willy Boly, Ruben Neves, Barry Douglas, Diogo Jota

and Bonatini all started. Chances were at a premium in the cagey opening stages although Wolves arguably played the better football, albeit with too many misplaced passes. Then on 33 minutes, out of the blue, came the breakthrough. An horrendous pass from Ayala across his own back line went straight to Bonatini who kept his cool and slotted past Darren Randolph to send a packed Molineux potty. The feverish atmosphere went through the roof with Nuno's name being sung loudly from all four corners.

Boro should have levelled just before half-time but £9million Denmark international Martin Braithwaite headed wide from eight yards, completely unmarked, with a Ruddy starfish jump putting him off. Wolves started the better after the break in search of a second goal. Substitute Bright Enobakhare dazzled his way past two defenders and side-footed goalwards with Randolph making a diving save, then Bonatini was played beyond the Boro back line by a gorgeous Romain Saiss pass but couldn't pick out Jota. Boro, who had been surprisingly lacklustre, began to improve and twice Ruddy had to deny Britt Assombalonga. Wolves began to sit deeper and Boro ramped up the pressure. Cyrus Christie went on a mazy run which ended with a lashed shot over the bar and there were hearts in mouths from a few throws and crosses in the final minutes. But they saw out four minutes of injury time without conceding a chance and the roar at full-time was deafening.

How promising that despite being shorn of so many creative talents (Ivan Cavaleiro and Helder Costa were missing through suspension and injury) Wolves still managed to beat a very expensively-assembled team that's just come down from the Premier League. Everyone knew it would be an emotional day at Molineux and it certainly didn't disappoint in that regard. At the

NUNO

I think it's three points we deserved, the boys worked well. We were ready but we're still not the final product. Every game is going to be better. This is what we want from the boys, always progress and make it better. Bonatini did a good job. He linked the game, dropped, combined and scored his goal. We're building up his fitness and must take care of that. It was fantastic to be at Molineux. Today was a special day for all of us.

FAN VERDICT – RUSS EVERS

Whilst it is very early days, Wolves seem to be living up to the hype. Ruddy was a rock on what was an emotional tribute day for the brave Carl Ikeme. Great touches from the club and the crowd and fair play to the Boro fans for their tribute. It's great to be a Wolves fan at the moment – long may it last.

forefront of everyone's minds was Carl Ikeme, whose video message before kick-off saw a few tears shed. It's been utterly inspiring to see everyone in the Wolves family unite to create so much love, affection and support for Wolves' number one. This and every win this season will be dedicated to Carl.

"THIS AND EVERY WIN THIS SEASON WILL BE DEDICATED TO CARL"

LINE UP

WOLVES (3-4-3):
RUDDY; MIRANDA, COADY (C), BOLY; DOHERTY, NEVES, SAISS, DOUGLAS; ENOBAKHARE (EDWARDS, 78), BONATINI (DICKO, 57), JOTA (GRAHAM, 83).

SUBS NOT USED: NORRIS, BENNETT, BATTH, RONAN.

MIDDLESBROUGH (4-3-3):
RANDOLPH; CHRISTIE, AYALA, GIBSON, FRIEND; DE ROON (FORSHAW, 65), CLAYTON, HOWSON (GESTEDE, 81); FLETCHER (BAMFORD, 57), ASSOMBALONGA, BRAITHWAITE.

SUBS NOT USED: KONSTANTOPOULOS, FABIO, FRY, LEADBITTER.

STAR MAN

ROMAIN SAISS
BROKE UP PLAY TENACIOUSLY AND SPRAYED THE BALL AROUND WITH CONFIDENCE. THIS WAS LIKE THE SAISS WHO ANNOUNCED HIMSELF WITH A MASTERCLASS ON HIS DEBUT AT NEWCASTLE LAST SEASON. HIS TARGET NOW IS TO REPRODUCE THIS LEVEL WEEK AFTER WEEK. A GREAT START (DESPITE SOMEHOW CONTRIVING TO SEND A SHOT 40 YARDS IN THE OPPOSITE DIRECTION TO THE GOAL).

TABLE

	TEAM	P	GD	PTS
1	BRISTOL CITY	1	2	3
2	QPR	1	2	3
3	CARDIFF	1	1	3
4	IPSWICH	1	1	3
5	NOTTM FOREST	1	1	3
6	PRESTON	1	1	3
7	SHEFF UTD	1	1	3
8	WOLVES	1	1	3

WOLVES
(DICKO 76)

1

YEOVIL
0

"IT'S A NICE FEELING TO SCORE AND WE'RE THROUGH TO THE NEXT ROUND"
NOUHA DICKO

New head coach, 11 new players, new formation, new playing style, renewed optimism in the stands – same old Wolves in the EFL Cup. Minnows Newport County, Barnet, Crawley and Cambridge and now League Two side Yeovil have all visited Molineux in the past two seasons – and been just about edged out by the odd goal on each occasion in what have largely been dull borefests. Wolves may have won this competition twice but the Wolves of 1997 to 2017 have been absolutely rubbish in this competition, let's be honest. Here they scraped past a team that was humiliated 8-2 at Luton Town just four days ago.

Wolves, of course, had the majority of the play, but by the 75th minute Yeovil had fashioned the best chance of the match as they briefly threatened to cause an upset at a quiet Molineux, with a sparse and bored crowd watching on. Did Nuno learn much from the game? Other than the fact his fringe players didn't really give him a selection headache for Saturday's trip to Derby, no. But Nouha Dicko gave a timely reminder of his goalscoring abilities with a snaffled winner 14 minutes from time. Indeed, that makes it two goals by strikers in successive games, an unheard of notion last season when goals from Dicko, Jon Dadi Bodvarsson and Joe Mason were rarer than Nuno shouting 'get it in the mixer, lads'. What an age we live in.

There were nine changes from the team that beat Middlesbrough 1-0 on Saturday, with only Willy Boly and Leo Bonatini keeping their places. Ruben Vinagre, an 18-year-old loanee from Monaco, was given his debut at left wing-back, while goalkeeper Will Norris and defender Ryan Bennett also came in for their first Wolves appearances. Yeovil, perhaps

surprisingly, made only three changes from their 8-2 shellacking at Luton and the priority for the League Two side was surely to, first and foremost, restore some pride after that defeat. Any Wolves fans turning up expecting a big win should have known better. Their recent record in the EFL Cup is poor to say the least, and even when they've beaten lower league opposition in the past two seasons it's been a tough watch, at best.

The first half was a frustrating one. Wolves produced some tidy build-up play – as you'd expect against a League Two team content to sit deep and defend – but the end product wasn't there. The best move they produced started with a Boly pass to Bonatini who fed Jordan Graham – he crossed for Bonatini who headed wide. Other than that, Connor Ronan sent a couple of pot shots wide and Dicko fired a shot on the turn over the bar from a Danny Batth knock-down. And that was it. In fact Yeovil produced the only shot on target of the opening 45 minutes when a rare venture forward ended with Otis Khan shooting straight at Norris. Jack Price, Dicko and Ronan came up with a few nice touches here and there but it was safe to say that no-one staked their claim for a place in the team to face Derby at the weekend. There were also a couple of hairy moments for Boly who looked more comfortable going forward with the ball than he did defending. At the other end the big centre-half met a Graham corner, heading it down into the ground and over the bar.

Wolves came out with renewed purpose after the break with the pacey and exuberant Vinagre in the thick of the action. He fired a shot into the side netting from a tight angle on the left, then sent in a low cross which the keeper spilled and Dicko just failed to get to the loose ball.

Graham whipped a free-kick into the corridor of uncertainty with all the zip of a Stuart Broad off-cutter, but no one could get on the end of it. Dicko then tried to take the initiative, crashing an excellently-struck 20-yarder inches over the bar. It was the kind of urgency Wolves had been sorely lacking and it was no surprise when Diogo Jota and Bright Enobakhare were sent on with just over 20 minutes left, with Dave Edwards and the tiring Bonatini withdrawn. However it was Yeovil who then fashioned arguably the chance of the night – substitute Sam Surridge was left completely unmarked between Batth and Boly but sent his 15-yard free shot just wide of the post. There was another hairy moment when a Batth pass only just reached Boly with a Yeovil attacker sniffing around.

Wolves were playing with fire – but with time running out Dicko broke the deadlock. Graham, a man whose middle name should be changed by deed poll to 'Assist', sent an outswinging corner towards Dicko and he couldn't miss with his close range header. For a man whose future at the club looks to be in doubt, it was a timely moment. The Mali international, now full of beans, then barged his way inside the box before firing low at the keeper as Nuno's boys threatened a second. Thereafter they did a quietly impressive job of seeing the game out, controlling possession and not letting Yeovil have a sight of goal. The EFL Cup hasn't been kind to Wolves for many years, but perhaps things will be different in this new regime.

NUNO

I was pleased for some moments, but I think we should do better. We have to prepare a squad for every situation, they have to be ready for any moment we decide to put them in to play. We need a full squad, everybody is important for us. Dicko worked very hard, in the first half he had a different task, playing with two strikers, we tried to bring more mobility.

FAN VERDICT – RUSS COCKBURN

Well if ever a game lived up to its billing it was this one. First round of the energy drink cup, a sparsely-filled Molineux, 200 Yeovil fans completing a sponsored 94-minute silence and playing a team that had eight put past them three days earlier. All the ingredients for a mundane affair that would probably be settled on penalties. Fortunately, we were spared that chore and, two games into Nuno's reign, we've won two without conceding. What's not to like?

LINE UP

WOLVES (3-1-4-2):

NORRIS; BENNETT, BATTH (C), BOLY; PRICE; GRAHAM, EDWARDS (ENOBAKHARE, 69), RONAN (SAISS, 81), VINAGRE; DICKO, BONATINI (JOTA, 69).

SUBS NOT USED: BURGOYNE, MIRANDA, COADY, DOHERTY.

YEOVIL (4-4-2):

KRYSIAK; ALFEI, N SMITH, DICKSON, JAMES; KHAN (OLOMOLA, 66), C SMITH (GRAY, 81), BAILEY, BROWNE; ZOKO (SURRIDGE, 55), SOWUNMI.

SUBS NOT USED: MADDISON, DAVIES, MUGABI, SANTOS.

STAR MAN

RUBEN VINAGRE

A POSITIVE PRESENCE DOWN THE LEFT FLANK AND LOOKED TO MAKE THINGS HAPPEN, PARTICULARLY AT THE START OF THE SECOND HALF WHEN HE LIFTED WHAT WAS BY THEN A FLAGGING TEAM PERFORMANCE. VIBRANT, ENERGETIC, QUICK AND CREATIVE. HE'S CERTAINLY RAW, AND AGED 18 YOU'D EXPECT THAT, BUT DEFINITELY HAS SOMETHING ABOUT HIM.

DERBY 0

WOLVES 2
(DOUGLAS 32, CAVALEIRO 75)

CHAMPIONSHIP: 12/08/17   ATTENDANCE: 27,757

"IT WAS A VERY CONVINCING PERFORMANCE. EVERYTHING SEEMS TO BE CLICKING"
BARRY DOUGLAS

You'd think Wolves fans would be used to setting themselves up for a fall by now, having experienced more false dawns than an Arctic winter.

Last season their team kicked off with a six-game unbeaten run and ended up in a relegation battle. Heck, back in 2011/12 they were briefly top of the Premier League with seven points from nine games – and contrived to win just three more games all season, totalling one of the worst top-flight points totals in living memory.

Three wins in a week with no goals conceded to begin the 2017/18 campaign though and the gold and black army are already starting to use the 'P' word. It's very, very early days and Wolves have achieved absolutely nothing. But going on the victories over Middlesbrough and Derby – two of the best teams on paper in the Championship – there's very little not to be delighted with so far.

"THE GOLD AND BLACK ARMY ARE ALREADY STARTING TO USE THE 'P' WORD"

Just don't ask Nuno Espírito Santo – who became the first Wolves manager since Ronnie Allen in 1965 to win his first three matches in charge – if he's 'delighted' with what he's overseen so far. The Wolves boss has his feet stuck so firmly to the floor they'd need prising off with a hammer and chisel. When an unsuspecting radio presenter asked him if he was delighted with what he'd seen at Pride Park, Nuno replied curtly: "No." 'Pleased' is his preferred adjective to describe his team's efforts – but whatever he says on the record he surely can't have envisaged the first competitive week of his tenure going so swimmingly. Nuno has built this team from the back with solid foundations – and five successive clean sheets including the back end of pre-season bodes very well for the coming nine months. That, more than an explosive forward line, is what grinds out results over a 46-game campaign and earns teams the 'P' word. And that's why this feels more tangible than the early-season excitement of 12 months ago.

Perhaps surprisingly Nuno stuck with the XI that beat Middlesbrough last weekend, choosing to leave the suspension-free Ivan Cavaleiro on the bench. The hosts made the better start with both ex-Molineux loanee Andi Weimann and perennial Wolves target Chris Martin heavily involved. Wolves were twice indebted to captain Conor Coady – who was the subject of a bid from Sheffield United in the week – for saving what looked certain goals.

After a second Weimann chance, the visitors burst into life, creating a succession of chances. Matt Doherty crossed to Leo Bonatini who turned not far wide at the near post, then Bonatini lashed threateningly into the six-yard box. Wolves were on top and on 32 minutes their pressure paid off – a Bright Enobakhare

cross towards Bonatini was blocked, it came out to Barry Douglas who struck low and true from 10 yards and it deflected off Richard Keogh into the net. Doherty and Douglas were proving very threatening on the overlap and Enobakhare and Diogo Jota were beginning to link productively with them.

Wolves were soon on the ropes at the start of the second half – but in the next few minutes they somehow contrived to spurn two of the most gilt-edged opportunities they could have wished for. First Jota was put clean through – he ran fully 50 yards but began to slow up before shooting, perhaps unaware of Andre Wisdom haring to catch him up and the defender got in a perfect sliding tackle in the nick of time. Then Bonatini played in Jota with a gorgeous pass – he struck the post from 15 yards, the ball came out to Bonatini who put it over the bar with the goal gaping.

Wolves were carving through Derby like a machete through cream cheese. Enobakhare's cute inside flick set Doherty into the box – he looked set to double the lead but sliced it into the side netting. Then, finally, came the second goal Wolves' play had so merited. Enobakhare played a crucial role, flying past his man and then feeding Jota who unselfishly teed up Cavaleiro for a tap in – and individual redemption after his sending off at the same ground just a few months earlier. Thereafter Wolves cruised it, with Jota and Enobakhare given standing ovations by the delirious away end.

It wasn't just that Wolves avoided their annual thrashing at Derby – it wasn't just that they won with plenty to spare. No, it was the manner in which they consistently sauntered through Derby's defence like a slalom ski champion. Some of the football they produced in the

NUNO

There's nothing to get excited about. We have two weeks gone, it doesn't mean anything. It's a good start and a clean sheet tells that our defence is progressing and getting better. It's about helping, balancing. I'm pleased. Just a final word for our fans – they were impressive. They made it feel like Molineux, coming here and supporting us, singing, it's very important to us so thank you to them.

FAN VERDICT – NATALIE WOOD

This was exciting to watch and every time we had the ball it felt like we could create something. We have had to put up with some awful football in recent seasons but this team feels like a breath of fresh air and have the potential to do really well this year. I haven't said this in a while but I'm already excited for the next game!

second half was heavenly. Everything suddenly clicked into place – Doherty and Douglas rampaged on the overlaps, combining beautifully with Jota and the excellent Enobakhare, who was given a serious show of faith to keep his place ahead of Cavaleiro. With Neves and the rejuvenated Romain Saiss pulling the strings and barely misplacing a pass, they really did look the real deal. Wolves just don't win at Derby. Three seasons ago it was a 5-0 shellacking, in 2015/16 it was a convincing 4-2 defeat and last season it was a very flattering 3-1 reverse. They also tend not to play incisive, piercing, beautiful football as well. Yes, something is stirring at Wolves. Long may it continue.

LINE UP

DERBY (4-3-3):
CARSON; WISDOM, KEOGH (C), DAVIES, FORSYTH; BUTTERFIELD (BRYSON, 62), HUDDLESTONE, JOHNSON; WEIMANN (ANYA, 71), MARTIN, RUSSELL (NUGENT, 62).

SUBS NOT USED: MITCHELL, BAIRD, PEARCE, BENNETT.

WOLVES (3-4-3):
RUDDY; MIRANDA, COADY (C), BOLY; DOHERTY, NEVES, SAISS, DOUGLAS; ENOBAKHARE (RONAN, 81), BONATINI (CAVALEIRO, 65), JOTA (DICKO, 86).

SUBS NOT USED: NORRIS, BENNETT, BATTH, PRICE.

STAR MAN

MATT DOHERTY
A KEY COMPONENT OF THIS VICTORY. CONSTANTLY PROVIDED AN OUTLET AND SENT OVER A SUCCESSION OF TEASING CROSSES WHICH WERE CRYING OUT FOR A FOX IN THE BOX TO TAP THEM HOME. COVERED SO MUCH GROUND UP AND DOWN THAT RIGHT FLANK. HE WAS A WINGER FOR LONG SPELLS BUT DID HIS FAIR SHARE OF IMPORTANT DEFENSIVE WORK TOO.

TABLE

	TEAM	P	GD	PTS
1	CARDIFF	2	4	6
2	WOLVES	2	3	6
3	NOTTM FOREST	2	2	6
4	IPSWICH	2	2	6
5	HULL	2	3	4
6	QPR	2	2	4

HULL 2
(DAWSON 27, MEYLER 90+9)

WOLVES 3
(NEVES 6, JOTA 43, DICKO 90)

CHAMPIONSHIP: 15/08/17 ATTENDANCE: 17,145

"IT'S A GOOD START, WE'RE HAPPY AND WE'RE PLAYING WELL. WE'LL TRY TO KEEP IT GOING"
DIOGO JOTA

Edge past Middlesbrough? Not bad. Convincingly beat Derby? That's quite impressive. Win both of those games and then go to Hull a few days later, come under big pressure and win yet again? Right ok, I think Wolves might be on to something here. Nuno Espírito Santo's team travelled to Hull and back and returned with all three points to continue their perfect start to the season. They did so thanks to two moments of pure brilliance from Ruben Neves and Bright Enobakhare, the former unleashing a 30-yard stunner and the latter once again adding end product to his raw talent when setting up Diogo Jota.

That's indicative of some of the level of quality Wolves are producing in the early days of Nuno's reign. But more impressive here was the second half rearguard action that denied Hull, a team considered among the promotion favourites who spanked Burton 4-1 here on Saturday, an equalising goal. Make no mistake, Wolves came under severe pressure from a very decent Hull side. In years past they'd have crumbled, without a shadow of a doubt. There's something different at play here. Wolves, from back to front, look very well equipped to make a big impact in this division. And, while the explosive football and moments of sheer artistry have got their supporters rubbing their eyes in disbelief, it's the defensive rigidity and discipline that bodes so well for the season ahead, starting at Molineux on Saturday when

Cardiff are the visitors for an early-season top-two showdown. 'Bring it on' will be the message from Wolves. Nothing is fazing them right now.

On a sunny midsummer evening Nuno had the luxury of naming the same XI for the third successive league game, meaning Ivan Cavaleiro again had to settle for a place on the bench. He was joined by Jordan Graham who, having being left out the squad at Derby, came in for Connor Ronan. Hull also named an unchanged side from the team that beat Burton 4-1 at the KCOM on Saturday. Abel Hernandez scored a hat-trick in that game and he partnered Fraizer Campbell up front. Hernandez began the game in confident mood, testing John Ruddy after just 15 seconds with a low effort from 18 yards. In fact the Tigers made the better start with Willy Boly having to deny a certain goal when just reaching Kamil Grosicki's pull-back ahead of the stretching Hernandez after the winger got around the back of Roderick Miranda.

But Wolves were in front after just six minutes – in the most spectacular way imaginable. Ruben Neves picked the ball up fully 30 yards from goal, set his sights, and planted the ball into the corner for what will be one of the goals of the Championship season. It seemed to shake Hull who struggled to keep possession and Wolves almost doubled their lead when a Neves corner to the back stick was somehow headed over by Miranda who got under the ball just a yard from

goal. The wing-backs Matt Doherty and Barry Douglas were causing the hosts problems and a final ball was all that was lacking. Wolves were looking vulnerable from set pieces though – and that's where Hull's equaliser came from.

Seconds after Douglas had cleared off the line from a flag kick, a short corner from the left was whipped in, Ruddy missed it with Hernandez pressurising, Neves cleared off the line but there was Michael Dawson to head home. It looked like it would be an uncomfortable end to the half – but another moment of brilliance saw them retake the lead. Enobakhare stormed past Max Clark down the right flank, got to the byline and played across goal where Diogo Jota slammed home from close range. Wolves hadn't reached the scintillating levels of football they'd produced at Derby but it was effective enough.

In the second half though, with perhaps fatigue a factor for both sides, the game slowed to a crawl. Romain Saiss, Neves and Jota were all deservedly booked for over-zealous challenges and Wolves struggled to make headway. They were very nearly pegged back when Campbell barged his way through the Wolves backline and drew a superb save from Ruddy. And then the hosts were just inches from an equaliser when a Hernandez header bounced off the crossbar with Ruddy beaten. Wolves were winning fewer 50/50s and the home crowd lifted the volume levels with Nuno's team on the ropes in what was becoming a stern test of their defensive credentials. Boly crucially headed a cross behind with Hernandez waiting. And in the process the striker was hurt, leading to a six-minute stoppage that quelled Hull's momentum.

The visitors took full advantage, sealing the deal when substitutes Cavaleiro and Nouha Dicko combined with the former sending the latter

"NEVES... FULLY 30 YARDS FROM GOAL PLANTED THE BALL INTO THE CORNER"

NUNO

Offensively we had moments of really good football and deserved the goals we got. All goals had the beauty that the fans come for. This is the moments to live in – to see the goal of Ruben, the magic of Bright, the space of Nouha, it's good football. I'm very happy. Nine points is the great reward we have for so many hours in pre-season working. The way the boys are so focused on their task, it's amazing. Nine points is a big reward for us.

FAN VERDICT – ADAM VIRGO

Sublime, sensational, breathtaking, mouthwatering and majestic – those are just five words describing Ruben Neves' wonder strike, never mind the 84 (+9) minutes that followed. After the final whistle had gone I was just thinking to myself, 'is this actually real, have we just played like that?'. You don't associate Wolves with football like this.

clean through and he made no mistake to send the away end into raptures. Hull managed to pull one back in the 99th minute, owing to a long stoppage when Hernandez was injured, via a David Meyler penalty when Doherty was judged to have fouled Clark, but it was too little too late for the Tigers.

LINE UP

HULL (4-4-2):
MCGREGOR; AINA, DAWSON (C), HECTOR, CLARK; BOWEN (LARSSON, 60), HENRIKSEN, CLUCAS, GROSICKI; CAMPBELL (DIOMANDE, 76), HERNANDEZ (MEYLER, 86).

SUBS NOT USED: MANNION, MAZUCH, WEIR, LENIHAN.

WOLVES (3-4-3):
RUDDY; MIRANDA, COADY (C), BOLY; DOHERTY, SAISS, NEVES, DOUGLAS; ENOBAKHARE (CAVALEIRO, 60), BONATINI (DICKO, 75), JOTA (BENNETT, 85).

SUBS NOT USED: NORRIS, BATTH, PRICE, GRAHAM.

STAR MAN

WILLY BOLY
LOOKING MORE AND MORE LIKE HE WILL BOSS THIS DIVISION. READS THE GAME SO WELL AND HAS THE PHYSICALITY TO BACK IT UP. WAS THE SCOURGE OF DANGER-MAN ABEL HERNANDEZ ON TWO OCCASIONS, WHEN TAKING THE BALL OFF HIS TOE WHEN A TAP-IN LOOKED CERTAIN, AND THEN GETTING A CRUCIAL HEAD ON A CROSS WHEN THE STRIKER WAS SET TO POUNCE.

TABLE

	TEAM	P	GD	PTS
1	CARDIFF	3	6	9
2	WOLVES	3	4	9
3	IPSWICH	3	3	9
4	MIDDLESBROUGH	3	2	6
5	NOTTM FOREST	3	1	6
6	LEEDS	3	1	5

WOLVES **1**
(BONATINI 67)

CARDIFF **2**
(RALLS 54, MENDEZ-LAING 78)

CHAMPIONSHIP: 19/08/17   ATTENDANCE: 27,068

"WE NEED TO LEARN TO STICK TO OUR OWN GAME PLAN – STICK TO WHAT WE KNOW"
CONOR COADY

You don't get many games like this in the Portuguese league. If Nuno Espírito Santo and his band of Portuguese superstars didn't know what the Championship was all about before this (and three wins suggested they had an idea), they certainly do now. Wolves have produced some beautiful football in the very early stages of the season, but this was all about brawn and bottle – and Wolves' bite barely made an imprint on a battle-hardened Cardiff side who bullied the home team into submission on a chastening afternoon.

The Bluebirds' two goals were both well-worked and easy on the eye, but in general they battered and harried Nuno's team, who were deservedly beaten. The Wolves boss knew how Cardiff would approach the game, but nothing could quite prepare the likes of Ruben Neves, Diogo Jota and Roderick Miranda for this. The latter had a nightmare against Junior Hoilett and was at fault for the first goal, while Willy Boly made an error for Cardiff's second and Romain Saiss was well below the standards he's set so far. Wolves duly missed their chance to top the table after four matches, with Neil Warnock's Cardiff

"THE VISITORS WERE BRUTISH – AND CERTAINLY NOT SUBTLE – BUT THEY WERE EFFECTIVE"

22

earning that early-season accolade instead. Wolves' winning run had to end sooner or later. It's how they react to this setback – and more importantly, how they learn from their mistakes – that will define whether this is a temporary blip.

At an overcast and healthily-stocked Molineux, Nuno stuck with the same XI that had served him so well in the opening two weeks of the season, naming an unchanged XI for the fourth league game in a row. The Bluebirds arrived with a clear game plan to stop Wolves getting into a passing rhythm and it certainly worked in the first half. Warnock's team prevented Wolves from playing out from the back, harangued them at every opportunity in possession and prevented them from breaking with constant niggly fouls. The visitors were brutish – and certainly not subtle – but they were effective.

Sol Bamba was presented with a golden early chance but somehow crashed his one-yard header off the bar from a corner. Bamba sent another free header wide and Hoilett tested John Ruddy from 20 yards, but Wolves held firm. At the other end they improved as the half went on. Bright Enobakhare looked like the most likely outlet for a goal – he curled a 20-yarder just over the bar and later turned, 35 yards from goal, rode a challenge and fired across goal and wide. Elsewhere Jota struggled to break free of Cardiff's shackles other than for one decent run and shot, but other than that Wolves looked toothless. They were also riled by Cardiff's rough treatment and the game became a scrap at times with challenges flying in and bookings being handed out by a referee who was struggling to keep a lid on proceedings.

The sparks even boiled over to the touchline when Nuno and Warnock practically locked foreheads when arguing over a Loic Damour

challenge on Saiss. It all made for a feisty and fascinating 45 minutes with the affronted home fans creating a feverish atmosphere and predictably booing Warnock – who even waved to the South Bank at one point – and the referee at half-time. The histrionics calmed down at the start of the second half – and there was nothing brutish about Cardiff's opening goal on 54 minutes. Hoilett sauntered inside from the left past Miranda and played to Joe Ralls who beat Ruddy at his near post.

Cardiff continued to look the more likely scorers. Kenneth Zohore twice tested Ruddy from a tight angle with Wolves' defence at sixes and sevens. It looked like it wasn't going to be Wolves' day – and then up popped Leo Bonatini to turn a Barry Douglas cross-shot home after good work from Ivan Cavaleiro and Jota. Molineux erupted and suddenly the momentum was with the home team who surged forward in the hope of a winner.

Wolves have spent £19million this summer – and £47m on transfer fees alone since Fosun bought the club last July. So there was a certain irony in the fact it was a guy they let go for free who scored the winning goal. Nathaniel Mendez-Laing only made one appearance in Wolves colours after coming through the academy ranks, but he returned to haunt his former club to take advantage of a Boly error and fire through Ruddy, who will have felt he should have saved it. And thereafter, despite their best efforts, Wolves couldn't muster an equaliser with substitute Nouha Dicko spurning their only opportunity when firing into the side netting.

Nuno steadfastly reiterated afterwards that he would never sacrifice his principles, never change his methods and never 'resort' to the football Cardiff play. That's an admirable stance, but in the beast that is the Championship will

NUNO
The referee must protect what people come to the stadium to see – they come to see football. Damour should have been sent off, there's no other kind of interpretation, I saw an elbow on the neck of Saiss. The ball was not there. I cannot change the way teams come to face us, I'm not concerned about that. I'm concerned about having an idea to deal with every moment in the game. The character we want to build is that when you're in front we have to score more to be comfortable.

FAN VERDICT - CHRIS HUGHES
After three games and three wins against much-fancied footballing sides we returned to earth with a bump louder than one of our flair players being decked off the ball. Cardiff came with a game plan to hassle us and stop our usual controlled, possession-based game and it worked a treat. In a way this could have been the result/performance we needed for Nuno to get a real understanding of what the Championship is all about.

it work? Their lack of a plan B was painfully evident here. And opposition teams will look at this game and say 'that's how to beat Wolves... rough them up and deny them space'. It's been a breathtaking start to the season but this was a reality check. If Wolves learn their lessons, this could perversely be a very welcome defeat in the long run.

SOUTHAMPTON **0**

WOLVES **2**
(BATTH 67, WILSON 87)

"THEY HAVE TOP PREMIER LEAGUE PLAYERS – WE WERE BRILLIANT, I WAS DELIGHTED WITH A CLEAN SHEET"
DANNY BATTH

And this was Wolves' second team... They say football's a squad game – well Wolves' looks pretty darn good at the moment. Wolves just don't do League/EFL/Milk/Carabao Cup wins. They certainly don't do them against teams in a higher division than them, with Premier League Coventry City (ask your parents, kids) their last victims some 22 years ago. Wolves reached the quarter-finals that year and have got nowhere near ever since. Well life feels pretty different under Nuno Espírito Santo.

The whole club has been revitalised in a very short space of time – witness the 1,500 who made the six-hour round trip to watch what they knew would be a second string side. Saints fielded a number of international players and several first-teamers, but Wolves deservedly beat them. They also, in spells, played the better football in what was certainly no smash-and-grab. The Championship may be the very clear priority, but if Wolves can put out a 'reserve' side and still beat Premier League opposition, long may their run continue.

Nuno sprang a big surprise with his line-up, handing Ben Marshall a start after six weeks out with a hip injury. Ivan Cavaleiro made his first start of the season, while French defender Sylvain Deslandes came in for his first senior appearance since April 2016. Also back for the first time since April 2016 was Michal Zyro, who

was named on the bench along with a host of under-23 youngsters. Southampton selected a strong-looking XI which included England international keeper Fraser Forster, former Chelsea midfielder Oriol Romeu, playmaker Dusan Tadic and prolific striker Charlie Austin. Wolves, backed by an impressive away following, may have had the far weaker team on paper but they started like a house on fire – and could have been 3-0 up inside 10 minutes.

All three chances fell to Nouha Dicko in a remarkable 90-second blitz and he should certainly have scored two of them. Jack Price sent him clear of the Saints defence with a lofted through-ball that the striker couldn't control. Then the impressive Ruben Vinagre played in Dicko who saw his shot from a tight angle saved by Forster. And then Cavaleiro tenaciously won the ball off Jeremy Pied in the box and squared to Dicko who scuffed his effort from a few yards out in what was a glorious opportunity spurned. Wolves had made a great start in possession with Cavaleiro and Vinagre combining nicely and Price looking to dictate play. But the hosts soon came into in and created a number of chances of their own before half-time, mostly from set-pieces as Wolves' zonal marking came unstuck yet again. Maya Yoshida sent a free header wide from a corner, then fellow defender Jan Bednarek headed straight at Will Norris, again

unchallenged. From the third free attempt Norris was forced to pull off a stupendous reaction stop at full stretch from another Yoshida header.

Tadic wasted a chance as glaring as Dicko's when he fired wide from six yards after Danny Batth failed to clear, with the Saints edging an entertaining first half but failing to break the deadlock. Mauricio Pellegrino's side matched Wolves with a three-at-the-back system which in particular lessened the attacking forays of Jordan Graham. Cavaleiro was Wolves' dangerman and Vinagre was lively behind him, teeing up Dicko for a half chance just before the break when the striker yet again peeled off his man but fired into the side netting. Connor Ronan replaced a rusty Marshall at half-time and the young Irishman made a sprightly start to the half, as did Graham, who essentially became a winger and caused havoc with a series of crosses on the overlap, while Ronan added some much-needed creativity but also some tenacity in midfield by winning the ball back on a number of occasions. For the first 20 minutes of the half, Wolves were the superior side, producing some excellent passing play with an admirably unswerving refusal to lump it long whatever the circumstance.

The game looked there for the taking – and on 67 minutes Batth took it. The captain rose highest to meet an inswinging corner and head past Forster,

sparking wild scenes in the away end behind that goal. Wolves fully merited the lead for an impressive, controlling second half display. Saints reacted by sending on attacking trio Nathan Redmond, Shane Long and Manolo Gabbiadini at an increasingly anxious St Mary's, while Zyro made his long-awaited comeback when he replaced Dicko and was promptly booked inside 30 seconds after an adrenalin-heavy late tackle. Then, just two minutes after coming on, Donovan Wilson became the second academy graduate to score on the night, taking a Zyro pass and beating Forster to put the icing on the cake for Nuno's team.

"THE GAME LOOKED THERE FOR THE TAKING – AND ON 67 MINUTES BATTH TOOK IT"

SOUTHAMPTON (4-2-3-1):
FORSTER; PIED, BEDNAREK (REDMOND, 73), YOSHIDA, MCQUEEN; ROMEU, STEPHENS; WARD-PROWSE, TADIC, BOUFAL (GABBIADINI, 76); AUSTIN (LONG, 76).

SUBS NOT USED: MCCARTHY, CEDRIC, BERTRAND, DAVIS.

WOLVES (3-4-3):
NORRIS; BENNETT, BATTH, DESLANDES; GRAHAM, PRICE, EDWARDS, VINAGRE; MARSHALL (RONAN, 45), DICKO (ZYRO, 75), CAVALEIRO (WILSON, 85).

SUBS NOT USED: BURGOYNE, JOHNSON, GONCALVES, ARMSTRONG.

STAR MAN

DANNY BATTH

HE'LL HAVE HAD HIS NOSE PUT OUT OF JOINT BY STARTING THE SEASON ON THE BENCH BUT THIS WAS THE PERFECT RESPONSE FROM THE CLUB CAPTAIN. ONE ERROR IN THE FIRST HALF WHEN HE DIDN'T CLEAR, LEADING TO A BIG CHANCE FOR TADIC, BUT OTHERWISE HE WAS EXCELLENT, PARTICULARLY IN THE LAST 20 MINUTES WHEN SAINTS UPPED THE PRESSURE AND THREW A SUCCESSION OF CROSSES INTO THE BOX WHICH OFTEN LED TO A BATTH CLEARANCE. SCORED HIS FOURTH GOAL SINCE APRIL 1 WITH A FINELY-TAKEN HEADER. NOTHING SILLY IN POSSESSION AND EVEN HAD THE CONFIDENCE TO SHIMMY PAST A CONFUSED CHARLIE AUSTIN WITH SOME STEARMAN-ESQUE SKILLS.

BRENTFORD

WOLVES

"WE'RE DISAPPOINTED NOT TO WIN BUT TO GRIND OUT A 0-0 DRAW AT BRENTFORD IS A POSITIVE"

JOHN RUDDY

Jeff Shi and Laurie Dalrymple frequented a local pub before kick-off to get a few rounds in for Wolves' travelling barmy army. Perhaps they knew what was coming, because the fans needed a couple of beers to get through an incredibly nervy final few minutes at an enthralled Griffin Park. This was a tight, tense affair which both sides will feel they should have won. And when all is said and done come May 6 when Wolves' 46th and last Championship game is over, they may look back on this as a decent point. Brentford are fooling no-one with their lowly early league position. They possess enough quality – and play good enough football – to finish at least in mid-table.

Depending on your disposition, you will feel Wolves showed resilience to grind out a point at a tight, compact ground where they have come unstuck in spectacular fashion in recent seasons – or you'll say this is exactly the kind of game Wolves should be winning if they've got any ambitions of finishing in the top two. On a warm London afternoon, there was one one alteration from the team that lost 2-1 at home to Cardiff last weekend, with Ruben Vinagre coming in for Barry Douglas who was struggling with a knock towards the end of that game. The fired-up hosts were the better team in the early stages, taking the fight to Wolves and winning more tackles and second balls.

Nuno's team weathered the early storm and began to play some nice stuff with Diogo Jota at the heart of most of it. He and Leo Bonatini, who was expertly linking the play, were combining to good effect, never more so than when the Portuguese man sent Bonatini clean through but he didn't get enough on his shot and Daniel Bentley made the save. That was the chance of the half for Wolves but they had a few other good moments, with Jota curling a 20-yarder wide and Vinagre showing plenty of attacking intent on the overlap including when he drilled at Bentley from a narrow angle. It was Brentford who shaded the first 45 though and they should have taken the lead six minutes before the break when their Jota hit the post from just 15 yards after the ball broke for him from a blocked shot. Wolves' passing fluency was lacking from midfield as they struggled to play their natural game on a tight pitch against motivated opposition, who were all over the visitors like a overeager dog chasing his master's leg.

Ivan Cavaleiro came on at the break for Bright Enobakhare, who had endured a poor half after taking a knock early on. The change didn't improve Wolves' fortunes though and Brentford again spurned a golden chance to take the lead, this time through Neal Maupay who horribly scuffed a six-yard volley. When Nuno's team did win it back they weren't moving the ball quickly enough, and were struggling to find space on a tight pitch, with Romain Saiss often overrun in midfield. Jota was by far their best outlet for a bit of magic and he embarked on another mazy run from deep before firing wide on the hour mark.

Their move of the match came not long after. Conor Coady intercepted and set Cavaleiro off in Brentford's half – he majestically picked out Vinagre on the left who got to the byline and crossed to the back stick where Cavaleiro headed into the side netting. Wolves were improving all the time, with Cavaleiro enjoying a productive half. Then Jota should have put Wolves ahead after Ruben Neves played him in, but shot too close to Bentley from 15 yards. With 15 minutes to go you couldn't call it. Romaine Sawyers sent a snap-shot over the bar and then Nuno sent on Nouha Dicko for Bonatini. Jack Price also entered the fray in place of Neves but Wolves couldn't get the breakthrough they wanted. Apart from a Matt Doherty shot which he crashed over the bar, it was Nuno's side who were on the back foot for the closing stages, with Brentford forcing a couple of corners. Then in stoppage time, Dicko just couldn't connect with Jota's pull-back and then Doherty and Coady saved Wolves couldn't get with last-ditch interceptions before Roderick Miranda criminally delayed his pass to Dicko as Wolves broke three-on-one in the last action of the game, with the striker flagged offside.

It was a farcical and frantic finish to a very decent football match that deserved a 2-2 scoreline rather than the goalless stalemate it

"THIS WAS A TIGHT, TENSE AFFAIR WHICH BOTH SIDES WILL FEEL THEY SHOULD HAVE WON"

NUNO

I'm not happy. We came here to try for three points. I think we had moments that we were close but also there were moments they were close. Once again I was concerned with the referee. They must protect football and be fair to both teams. I think the boys suffered. Contacts are sometimes made can cost you a game. Coady was fouled – you have to punish. It's got to be fair. I'm looking at the game, one point is good, keep building and working hard.

FAN VERDICT – CLIVE SMITH

How you rate our performance depends if you are a half full or half empty person. You can applaud the clean sheet and another point away from home or judge it as a failure to score and a missed opportunity against a winless side.

will be recorded as. It left Wolves with 10 points from their opening five fixtures – a thoroughly decent return especially considering the quality of opposition faced. After the international break next month's fixtures include the visits of Millwall, Bristol City and Barnsley to Molineux and trips to Burton and Sheffield United – on paper a far more appetising run that will reveal plenty about this team's promotion credentials. Wolves have come unstuck against unfashionable opponents on countless occasions in this division. Their mettle is about to be tested.

LINE UP

BRENTFORD (4-2-3-1):
BENTLEY; DALSGAARD, DEAN, BARBET (BJELLAND, 72), COLIN; YENNARIS, MOKOTJO (WOODS, 65); JOTA (JOZEFZOON, 65), SAWYERS, WATKINS; MAUPAY.

SUBS NOT USED: DANIELS, EGAN, CLARKE, CANOS.

WOLVES (3-4-3):
RUDDY; MIRANDA, COADY (C), BOLY; DOHERTY, NEVES (PRICE, 85), SAISS, VINAGRE; ENOBAKHARE (CAVALEIRO, 45), BONATINI (DICKO, 78), JOTA.

SUBS NOT USED: NORRIS, BENNETT, BATTH, RONAN.

STAR MAN

DIOGO JOTA

A CONSTANT THORN IN BRENTFORD'S SIDE. ON A NUMBER OF OCCASIONS HE EMBARKED ON A DAZZLING RUN OR PLAYED PIERCING ONE-TWOS. WOLVES' MOST CREATIVE PLAYER BY SOME DISTANCE. LIKE BONATINI HE SHOULD HAVE SCORED, BUT HE CAN BE VERY PLEASED WITH HIS DAY'S WORK. POSSIBLY THE STANDOUT PERFORMER IN THE EARLY WEEKS OF THE SEASON.

TABLE

	TEAM	P	GD	PTS
1	CARDIFF	5	8	15
2	IPSWICH	5	3	12
3	LEEDS	5	5	11
4	WOLVES	5	3	10
5	SHEFF UTD	5	1	9
6	NOTTM FOREST	5	0	9

WOLVES
(JOTA 10)
MILLWALL

1

0

"I BELIEVE IN MYSELF, IT WAS ONE OF MY BEST GOALS. WE HAVE AN EXCITING TEAM"
DIOGO JOTA

In previous eras and under previous managers, Wolves would have drawn this game. They dominated play, were by far the better side, but couldn't put Millwall away and you just know that most of Molineux were almost expecting a late equaliser – it would have been 'typical Wolves' to throw it away. We've seen it happen many, many times over in the 24 seasons they've spent at this level in the past three decades but, whisper it, this team look to be a different animal.

They exude an air of professionalism, they're unfazed and unperturbed. Things like a dodgy home record, or bogey teams, or 'traditional' cock-ups against teams they're expected to beat don't really matter to lads from Atletico Madrid and Porto. Their head coach, too, isn't particularly concerned with such trivial

"THIS GAME SHOULD HAVE BEEN PUT TO BED SEVERAL TIMES OVER"

matters. And it shows. So they saw this through relatively comfortably, albeit helped by a Millwall red card. However, what they aren't yet is clinical – and what they painfully lack is a prolific striker, something they may live to regret in the coming months.

This game should have been put to bed several times over but chances were spurned, notably two gilt-edged opportunities for Leo Bonatini. That's the negative. It feels harsh or even churlish to be critical after some of the glorious football Wolves produced here, spraying it around from back to front in what was a fine display of passing and movement. It's just that over a 46-game season in a division that somehow manages to get even more competitive year after year, the fine margins will matter and the fact Wolves don't appear to have a 20-goal-a-season man in their midst is a big oversight on their part. It wasn't for a lack of trying. On deadline day alone, a deal for Jurgen Locadia slipped through their fingers and moves were almost agreed for Stefano Okaka, Chris Martin and Loic Remy. But despite a deeply impressive transfer window, the inescapable truth is that Wolves failed to land the player they needed most of all.

Nuno made two changes from the side that drew 0-0 at Brentford two weeks ago, recalling captain Danny Batth in place of the injured Willy Boly and bringing in the fit-again Ben Marshall for his first league start of the season for Bright Enobakhare, who was joined on the bench by new midfielder Alfred N'Diaye. Millwall, who named ex-Wolves players Jed Wallace and George Saville in their starting XI, arrived at Molineux on the back of thrashing Norwich 4-0 last time out but it was the hosts who settled quicker – and took an early lead through a stunning strike. Diogo Jota exchanged passes with Bonatini, ran from deep and eschewed

options left and right before unleashing a 25-yarder that pinged into the bottom corner.

Nuno's team grew in confidence and would produce some excellent football for the rest of the half, enjoying the majority of possession – mostly in Millwall's half – that was a delight to watch. With wing-backs Matt Doherty and the impressive Ruben Vinagre essentially playing as wingers, Wolves had a front seven and all of them were involved in a succession of intricate passing moves. Even the back three were producing passes you'd expect from top quality midfielders. Indeed one gorgeous rake from Conor Coady set Doherty flying down the right and his low cross was turned goalwards by Bonatini, forcing keeper Jordan Archer to push past the post.

What was clear was that Wolves needed a second goal. They were given two warnings at the start of the second half when Batth produced his second important clearance of the match from an Aiden O'Brien cross and then Steve Morison sent a free 10-yard header over the bar after slack marking from Roderick Miranda, either side of a 20-yard Marshall rasper which stung the keeper's palms. A nasty over-the-top challenge from O'Brien on Jota, which earned a very deserved booking, saw the Molineux temperature rise and led to a succession of gritty tackles from both teams, before Wallace worked his way into a good position and dragged his shot wide in what was yet another moment that screamed 'Wolves you need a second goal pronto'.

The unlikely source of Romain Saiss's right boot very nearly provided it when his lovely 20-yard curler was tipped over the bar. And then O'Brien, just 10 minutes after his first yellow, handed Wolves a man advantage when

NUNO

Three points – very good, I'm happy. We had 70 per cent possession of the ball, it shows the ability of the team to control the game with the ball. If there's a 'but' – and there always is – we should transform this possession into more goals. We played good football but we can do better.

FAN VERDICT – ADAM VIRGO

I felt we were in control of the game from start to finish. We could have scored a couple more which would have been nice, but it's another three points and clean sheet. We were solid defensively and restricted Millwall from having any real chances. We weren't at our best by all means but we got the job done – these types of games aren't always easy.

he foolishly pulled back Doherty. Wolves looked to press home that advantage but other than a scuffed Bonatini shot they were still struggling to create. Bonatini really should have put the game to bed with 10 to go but shot at the keeper from 10 yards. In five minutes of added time, the finale became needlessly tense and John Ruddy had to produce a smart save – but Wolves saw it through. All in all, they enjoyed 70 per cent possession of the ball, produced a series of intricate passing moves between the lines and had an organised and resolute Millwall team on the back foot for most of the match. It was a team performance, Nuno's 'idea' writ large. And you still get the impression there's far more to come.

LINE UP

WOLVES (3-4-3):
RUDDY; BATTH (C), COADY, MIRANDA; DOHERTY, NEVES (N'DIAYE, 77), SAISS, VINAGRE; MARSHALL (ENOBAKHARE, 59), BONATINI, JOTA (CAVALEIRO, 87).

SUBS NOT USED: NORRIS, DESLANDES, PRICE, RONAN.

MILLWALL (4-4-2):
ARCHER; MCLAUGHLIN, WEBSTER, HUTCHINSON, MEREDITH (FERGUSON, 79); WALLACE (ONYEDINMA, 79), WILLIAMS, SAVILLE, O'BRIEN; GREGORY, MORISON.

SUBS NOT USED: KING, CRAIG, ROMEO, TUNNICLIFFE, COOPER.

STAR MAN

DIOGO JOTA
WHAT A GOAL. AS THIS IS 'WOLVES 2.0' WE CAN PERHAPS EXPECT TO SEE STRIKES OF A SIMILAR QUALITY THROUGHOUT THE SEASON, LIKE WITH RUBEN NEVES'S AT HULL. AS NUNO SAID AFTERWARDS, THIS WAS A 'MOMENT OF TRUE BEAUTY'. BUT EVEN ASIDE FROM THAT HE WAS A MENACE TO THE MILLWALL DEFENCE WITH SOME SUMPTUOUS CREATIVE PLAY, SETTING HIMSELF UP TO BE THE STAR OF THE SEASON AT THIS RATE.

TABLE

	TEAM	P	GD	PTS
1	CARDIFF	6	8	16
2	LEEDS	6	10	14
3	WOLVES	6	4	13
4	IPSWICH	6	2	12
5	SHEFF UTD	6	2	12
6	MIDDLESBROUGH	6	4	10

WOLVES 3
(BONATINI 28, JOTA 54, BATTH 85)

BRISTOL CITY 3
(FLINT 43, DIEDHIOU PEN 58, REID 82)

CHAMPIONSHIP: 12/09/17 ATTENDANCE: 23,045

"WE NEED TO KEEP IMPROVING, PERFORM THE SAME GOING FORWARD AND NOT CONCEDE SCRAPPY GOALS"
RODERICK MIRANDA

A member of the Jackson 5 was at Molineux to watch this thriller – and a victory for Wolves should have been as easy as ABC. Tito Jackson can come every week if Wolves games are going to be this entertaining. They went hell for leather with Bristol City in a six-goal thriller that had just about everything in front of a boisterous and enthralled Molineux crowd. Nuno's team had double the shots of Bristol City and, unlike their previous matches which have at times been a little staid, carved out a number of chances with some breathtaking football in what was a humdinger of a Tuesday night in the teeming rain.

Bristol City hadn't won on Wolves' turf since 1931 – 86 years and 25 matches ago. Back then Major Frank Buckley's secret weapon of choice was said to be injecting monkey glands into his players. Nuno's rather more orthodox version is work, work and then work some more, with no shortage of tactical nous and of course a heavy sprinkling of technical ability in the form of several gifted players lured from the likes of Porto, Benfica and Atletico Madrid. The fruits of his labour are already very evident but Wolves took their play to the next level at times here in front of their biggest midweek home crowd (23,045) for three seasons. They may not have won – and some shoddy set-piece defending, a feature of this season, played a big part in that (as well as some dreadful refereeing) – but this was a night that kept the feel-good factor going and showed again that Wolves have enough ingredients to do some real damage this season.

Nuno rang two changes from Millwall – in came Ivan Cavaleiro for his first league start of the season, while new Villarreal loanee Alfred N'Diaye was handed his full debut. Ben Marshall and Romain Saiss dropped to the bench where they were joined by Michal Zyro, in a league squad for the first time since April 2016. Wolves had produced a dominant display against the Lions which at times resembled a passing masterclass – and the first half here was no different. They picked up where they left off on Saturday with some deeply impressive one-touch passing and moving in the Bristol third. Debutant N'Diaye slotted nicely into midfield, adding physicality via his imposing frame but also a delicate touch. In fact it was N'Diaye who set up a deserved opening goal on the half-hour, making a great run into the box which was found by Ivan Cavaleiro and pulling back for Diogo Jota, whose tap goalwards was turned home by Leo Bonatini for his third goal in seven league games.

Wolves were well on top at this point and pinned the Robins back for most of the half, with West Brom loanee Jonathan Leko sporadically proving dangerous for the visitors in an otherwise dominant Wolves performance. Roderick Miranda had crashed a close-range shot over the bar from a Cavaleiro corner, Ruben Neves sent a 20-yard volley wide and Matt Doherty had the ball in the net from a great move but was flagged offside. Neves also pinged a 25-yard free-kick just over and Bonatini should have scored another on the stroke of half-time – he turned past the post from 10 yards after Jota's spectacular volley was saved. By then the score was 1-1. Some sloppy defending, including from Neves, in failing to clear a corner saw the ball drop to Aden Flint, whose deflected shot crept past a despairing John Ruddy dive. The fact Wolves were heartily applauded off, despite having just conceded a leveller, told you all you needed to know about their performance.

The perfect response to that equaliser would be to come racing out the blocks and take their performance up a notch – which is exactly what they did. Ten minutes of relentless pressure included another Neves free-kick, a goal-bound Cavaleiro shot which deflected over and then a gilt-edged chance for the same player who rounded the keeper but saw his effort cleared off the line. From the resulting corner the pressure paid off with a deserved goal when Bonatini flicked Cavaleiro's corner to Jota, who slammed home. Just four minutes later though, the visitors punctured the Molineux atmosphere with another equaliser. Ruben Vinagre handled a cross (although it looked ball-to-hand) and Famara Diedhiou slotted home the spot-kick. Wolves were absolutely adamant they should have had a penalty of their own when Danny Batth was pole-axed when going for a high ball. Referee Stephen Martin wasn't having it, although Nuno certainly was and he raced halfway down the touchline to remonstrate with the referee as Molineux reached fever pitch in what was a thoroughly enjoyable encounter.

Batth then somehow failed to connect with a superb Cavaleiro ball across goal, Jota slammed a 12-yard half-volley against the bar and Bonatini and Jota couldn't turn home Doherty's ball in the six-yard box as Wolves' evening turned from the sublime (football) to the ridiculous (misses). And then Wolves' inability to defend corners came to haunt them yet again. A header against the post came out to Bobby Reid, who tapped home and stunned Molineux with eight minutes to go. A wonderfully entertaining game of football played out in driving rain and a fantastic atmosphere had one more twist in the tail – substitute Marshall's corner was met by a powerful Batth header with 85 on the clock and it was 3-3 in what was the last real goalmouth action of a Molineux classic.

NUNO

It was a good game of football, it had a bit of everything, but we're disappointed with the result. That moment (Batth's equaliser) we showed character to fight back and put some justice in the result, this was very good, I thought we deserved to win. We made clear mistakes that produced the opponents' goal which we have to look at. It's clear. I don't want to judge the work of the referees, I know it's a tough job. But for me it goes beyond these decisions, it's the way they handle the game. Bristol started aggressively – I think there should be more protection to our players, the way they were kicked.

FAN VERDICT – ROB CARTWRIGHT

Bristol will look on this as their best-earned point of their season; for Wolves maybe a 'watershed' moment. The game should have been dead and buried before the first equaliser and to fall behind was a travesty. Two dubious penalty decisions went against us yet the crowd, appreciative of the skilful play and effort, kept with the team to the end. On another night we could have scored five or six quite easily. You could argue we are lacking a striker, but I think it is more about the need to get players into the six yard box quickly when we are on the attack, particularly a counter-attack.

LINE UP

WOLVES (3-4-3):
RUDDY; BATTH (C), COADY, MIRANDA (SAISS, 75); DOHERTY, NEVES (MARSHALL, 84), N'DIAYE, VINAGRE; CAVALEIRO (ENOBAKHARE, 76), BONATINI, JOTA.

SUBS NOT USED: NORRIS, DESLANDES, PRICE, ZYRO.

BRISTOL CITY (4-2-3-1):
FIELDING; WRIGHT, FLINT, BAKER, BRYAN; O'DOWDA, BROWNHILL (PATERSON, 77); SMITH, LEKO (TAYLOR, 68), REID; DIEDHIOU (PACK, 78).

SUBS NOT USED: STEELE, MAGNUSSON, ELIASSON, WOODROW.

STAR MAN

IVAN CAVALEIRO

IF NUNO'S PLAN WAS TO RILE CAVALEIRO BY MAKING HIM WAIT FOR HIS FIRST LEAGUE START SINCE APRIL LIKE A CAGED WOLF, IT CERTAINLY WORKED. THE PORTUGUESE WINGER HAS REGULARLY MADE AN IMPACT FROM THE BENCH OVER THE PAST MONTH AND HE EXTENDED THOSE CAMEOS TO A DEEPLY IMPRESSIVE 76 MINUTE PERFORMANCE HERE. PACEY, TRICKY AND INVENTIVE, HE GOT THE BALL ROLLING FOR THE OPENER WITH A WONDERFUL THROUGH-BALL FOR N'DIAYE AND HIS CORNER, ONE OF SEVERAL THAT WERE ON THE MONEY, LED TO JOTA'S GOAL. SHOULD HAVE SCORED HIMSELF BUT SAW A SHOT DEFLECTED OVER AND THEN HE DELAYED HIS NEXT EFFORT AFTER ROUNDING THE KEEPER. ALMOST ALL OF WOLVES' GOOD PLAY WENT THROUGH HIM AND HE LINKED UP PRODUCTIVELY WITH DOHERTY. RAN HIMSELF INTO THE GROUND TOO.

TABLE

	TEAM	P	GD	PTS
1	LEEDS	7	12	17
2	CARDIFF	7	5	16
3	SHEFF UTD	7	3	15
4	WOLVES	7	4	14
5	PRESTON	7	4	12
6	SHEFF WED	7	3	12

NOTTINGHAM FOREST **1**
(CARAYOL 75)

WOLVES **2**
(JOTA 47, 81)

"WE'RE VERY LUCKY TO HAVE DIOGO JOTA AT THIS CLUB – HE'S A GAME CHANGER"
CONOR COADY

CHAMPIONSHIP: 16/09/17   ATTENDANCE: 25,756

There's a reason why the majority of Wolves supporters shrug with general indifference when it comes to Jorge Mendes's involvement with their club. The rights and wrongs of the agent's strong influence on big decisions pales into insignificance for most on fairly straightforward grounds; ladies and gentlemen I present to you Exhibit A… Diogo Jota. Wolves haven't really tended to loan players from clubs like Atletico Madrid, well, ever. The fact Jota, Ruben Neves, Willy Boly and Ivan Cavaleiro play in gold and black is due to Football's Most Powerful Man™ – and it's safe to say Wolves wouldn't have attracted them to WV1 otherwise. Jota, in particular, is special. In fact he's arguably the most talented player Wolves have had since… Helder Costa, another Mendes man. The 20-year-old is arguably having more of an impact than Costa managed in such a short space of time last season. Four goals in three games during the past week have earned Wolves seven points and given their partying fanbase a new hero.

Costa took a little while to get going 12 months ago but Jota has hardly needed any time at all to get up to speed in the Championship, taking to the division like a duck to water despite being kicked all over the park by most opponents. This was a tight game that, as the cliché goes, looked as if it would be settled by the ball going in off someone's backside, or a bit of magic. It was the latter and Jota provided it with a deliciously cool finish after being set free by the increasingly impressive focal point of the team, Leo Bonatini. Earlier he reacted quicker than anyone to turn in

Cavaleiro's come-and-get-me ball into the box. It was a striker's instinct – and if Jota keeps this up then the fact Wolves failed to land a front-man in the transfer window will be less of an issue. Jota can do things that hardly anyone else in this division can. He is Wolves' magician and he cast a spell over Forest here in what was a superb result for many reasons.

A run of one win in four matches had threatened to quell the momentum generated in the early weeks of the season, if it had extended any longer. And there were times when it looked like Wolves wouldn't win here – some of their number were woefully off-colour in the first half and with 10 minutes to go Forest looked the more likely victors. That's the great thing about this team in the early days under Nuno, though – they possess the substance to back up the style. That means on days like this, when the free-flowing pretty passing is at a premium, they have the ingredients in their make-up to grind out a result, which bodes extremely well for the long months ahead.

Wolves, with Romain Saiss recalled in midfield instead of Alfred N'Diaye, started full of confidence and quickly played their way into a rhythm. Jota and Bonatini combined nicely on a couple of occasions and chances fell for Cavaleiro and then Jota, whose shots both found the keeper. But after a dreadful attempt from Jota, who spooned Cavaleiro's cut-back, Wolves' passing game fell apart and they produced their worst 20-minute spell since Nuno took charge, constantly giving the ball away with dreadful

sloppy passes. Fortunately for the visitors, Forest lacked the quality to take advantage with John Ruddy making comfortable saves from Kieran Dowell and Ben Osborn.

Whatever Nuno said at half-time – as it had against the Robins – did the trick as Wolves came flying out of the traps after the break. That man Cavaleiro upped his game to set up the opening goal inside a couple of minutes – his right-footed low ball from the right was ticklingly teasing and reached the centre of the six-yard box where Jota slid in to net his fourth of the season.

Forest sporadically tried to get back into the game. Liam Bridcutt cracked a free shot from 18 yards but, like all of Forest's other attempts up to this point, found Ruddy's arms. Then came another Forest shot that should have been straight at Ruddy – but an error from the keeper cost Wolves dear. Substitute Mustapha Carayol spotted him out of position and picked his spot perfectly from 25 yards. The City Ground erupted and Wolves, after looking so comfortable albeit without being at their best, were suddenly on the ropes. It looked like being a dicey final 15 minutes, but another moment of brilliance saw Wolves edge back in front with just nine to go. Bonatini brilliantly beat one player and then teed up the rampaging Jota despite being wiped out in the process by Matt Mills. Jota latched on to the pass and coolly slotted past keeper Jordan Smith in front of 2,000 delirious Wolves fans. Thereafter they saw out the remaining nine minutes – plus five added on – with relative ease for a fifth league win of the season.

Wolves only had 44 per cent possession of the ball, their lowest figure since Nuno took charge. And the sight of Neves hoofing the ball 50 yards upfield in the closing minutes was indicative of what was a functional, if unspectacular,

NUNO

Jota, like all the boys, is growing. It's a tough competition but we want the squad to progress in this way and each game is a chance to grow. The moments we're learning, like last week we had a big punch and mistakes. We didn't concede any situations like that here so that shows the growing. Leo Bonatini is a focal point and did a good job. He scored last week, he didn't score here, but his job was so important to create chances. It's about the team, it doesn't matter who scores as long as we take home the three points.

FAN VERDICT – ADAM VIRGO

Like many weeks this season, Diogo Jota is again my man of the match. Not only scored both of our goals but his all round play was just incredible to watch. You can tell he's played at Champions League level with how easy it is for him in the championship and the things he pulls off at times, it's a joke how good he is.

performance. On Tuesday night against Bristol City, Nuno criticised his team's poor 'game management' in twice letting a lead slip. Well, they learned their lesson quickly to see this one through and keep up their unbeaten away record. Wolves have got backbone in defence and magic up front. They also have a spot in the top two in the league, only behind Leeds on goal difference. At this very moment, things couldn't look much rosier.

"WHATEVER NUNO SAID AT HALF-TIME DID THE TRICK AS WOLVES CAME FLYING OUT OF THE TRAPS"

LINE UP

NOTTINGHAM FOREST (4-2-3-1):
SMITH; DARIKWA, MILLS (C), WORRALL, TRAORE; BRIDCUTT, MCKAY (CUMMINGS, 71); BRERETON (WALKER, 86), DOWELL (CARAYOL, 61), OSBORN; MURPHY.

SUBS NOT USED: HENDERSON, LICHAJ, FOX, BOUCHALAKIS.

WOLVES (3-4-3):
RUDDY; BATTH (C), COADY, MIRANDA; DOHERTY, NEVES, SAISS, VINAGRE (DESLANDES, 64); CAVALEIRO (MARSHALL, 62), BONATINI (N'DIAYE, 83), JOTA.

SUBS NOT USED: NORRIS, PRICE, RONAN, ENOBAKHARE.

STAR MAN

DIOGO JOTA
IN A TIGHT GAME HE WAS THE DIFFERENCE. FOUR GOALS IN THREE MATCHES – OR FIVE IN HIS PAST SIX – .WHO NEEDS A NEW STRIKER? MAKE NO MISTAKE WOLVES HAVE A VERY SPECIAL FOOTBALLER ON THEIR HANDS HERE. GREAT AWARENESS FOR THE FIRST GOAL (DARE I SAY A STRIKER'S INSTINCT) WHEN HE REACTED TO TURN IN CAVALEIRO'S CROSS. AND FOR THE WINNER HE HELPED CREATE IT HIMSELF, PLAYING A ONE-TWO WITH BONATINI AND THEN KEEPING HIS COOL TO BEAT THE KEEPER. THE GUY JUST GLIDES EFFORTLESSLY AROUND THE PITCH LIKE A PARTICULARLY SERENE SWAN. BEAUTIFUL TO WATCH.

TABLE

	TEAM	P	GD	PTS
1	LEEDS	8	11	17
2	WOLVES	8	5	17
3	CARDIFF	8	5	17
4	PRESTON	8	6	15
5	IPSWICH	7	4	15
6	SHEFF UTD	8	2	15

WOLVES
(ENOBAKHARE 98)

 1 (AET)

BRISTOL ROVERS

 0

"WE WANT TO KEEP THE CUP RUN GOING AND KEEP A WINNING FEELING AROUND THE SQUAD"

WILL NORRIS

These are heady days for Wolverhampton Wanderers. Forget the lofty league position, forget the ridiculous quality of some of their players, forget record signing after record signing, forget them playing some of the best football witnessed in years at Molineux – this is the one that should really make people stand up and take notice: they're in the fourth round of the EFL Cup. It's a feat they managed in 2011, 2010 and 2003 but on each of those occasions they were in the Premier League and skipped the first round. You have to go back to 1995 for the last time they progressed through three rounds of the competition, 22 years ago. It's a feat Mark McGhee, Colin Lee, Dave Jones, Mick McCarthy, Stale Solbakken, Kenny Jackett and Walter Zenga couldn't manage. But Nuno Espírito Santo, in his ever increasing list of achievements in just a few short months in WV1, has done it.

Ok, they beat Yeovil and now Bristol Rovers (as well as Premier League side Southampton) to progress to the fourth round, as you'd expect them to. And this was almost the opposite of a vintage performance (Rovers wasted a number of excellent chances). But the most impressive thing about this run to the last 16 is the use of squad depth (they made another eight changes here) – which bodes very well indeed for the long winter months when many of these players will be needed in the Championship. There weren't many standout performances in what was a very even game but the run will be doing the world of good to the likes of Jack Price, Bright Enobakhare and the excellent Will Norris. The keeper was required to make a number of fine saves, including pushing two shots on to the woodwork, while Enobakhare was finally a match-winner for Wolves after 30 appearances without a goal stretching back two years.

On another day, the impressive Rovers would have won it (it was a minor miracle they didn't score) but Wolves' game management has improved under Nuno. Make no mistake, though, if they want to take this run any further they'll have to play far better against what will be higher standard opposition in the next round (Rovers were the lowest-ranked side left). The fact Norris was by far and away their man of the match speaks volumes.

There were eight team changes, Nuno just keeping the same back three of Danny Batth, Conor Coady and Roderick Miranda. In came 19-year-old Danish youth international Oskar Buur Rasmussen – who joined on a free transfer last month after leaving AGF Aarhus – for a shock debut at right wing-back, while Michal Zyro made his first competitive start since April 2016. And it was Zyro, playing as a central striker, who was in the thick of the action early on and indeed went close on two occasions. The Polish forward whistled one over the bar from Ben Marshall's cute through-ball and then sent a great Sylvain Deslandes run-and-cross over from close range in what was a very decent opportunity.

At this point, the visitors were camped just outside their own box but as the half went on they grew in confidence and made it a very even first 45 minutes. Possession (54 per cent for Wolves) and shots (Wolves' eight to Rovers' seven) were both similar and the Pirates tested Norris more strenuously than Wolves managed with their keeper Sam Slocombe, with Liam Sercombe turning Miranda before producing a decent effort that Norris pushed wide. Zyro had another shot blocked, Ben Marshall's cross-shot was easy for Slocombe and Alfred N'Diaye lashed one into the North Bank but otherwise Wolves created precious little.

They didn't move the ball with enough pace in the Rovers third and there was little creativity from midfield or their wing-backs in what was a disappointing half for Nuno's team. Ironically, they could have done with a few cans of Carabao to lift the tempo. The energy levels didn't improve much immediately after the break but then Wolves came their closest yet to scoring when a first-time Enobakhare volley from Marshall's deep cross drew a superb save from Slocombe and then Batth headed the resulting corner over. Barry Douglas came on for his first appearance in a month replacing Deslandes on the hour as Nuno searched for more quality in the final third. Then a tiring Zyro was replaced by Cavaleiro up front and Connor Ronan came on for Marshall on 68 minutes. But the changes didn't make an impact. And then in stoppage time it opened up with Miranda's clipped shot bouncing off the crossbar and then Ellis Harrison firing wide from a good position for the visitors in what was the last chance of the 90 minutes.

Extra-time began with no action to speak of – and then Enobakhare finally broke the deadlock on 98 minutes. He took Douglas's low cross and beat Slocombe with a great finish from 15 yards. It was his first goal since his Wolves debut, 32 appearances ago in the same competition against Barnet in August 2015. Immediately sloppy Wolves were almost pegged back, having to rely on the excellent Norris to push a Rory Gaffney shot against the bar. And then, in the second period of extra-time, Norris produced more heroics when tipping Sercombe's thunderbolt over the bar before Dominic Telford sent a free header wide. Wolves were hanging on towards the end but saw it through to progress with Rovers earning a very late red card when last man Tom Lockyer brought down Donovan Wilson. It was a cruel end for Rovers – but Wolves are breaking a fair few hearts this season.

NUNO

The win is the most important thing and to be in the next round. It's important to manage all the squad, take a look at the under-23s and see what they have and try to help us in these moments. Two years (since Enobakhare's last goal) is too long, hopefully today gives him confidence. Seven clean sheets (from 11 matches so far) is good. This is what I'm saying every day, to get better, to correct things, good analysis and prepare well.

FAN VERDICT – HEATHER LARGE

Well, there is the easy way and then there is the Wolves way – we always have to make it more difficult for ourselves and this match was a prime example. But Will Norris was there to get us out of trouble with some fantastic saves and the visitors must have felt unlucky hitting the woodwork on more than one occasion. For large chunks of the game we controlled the play but too many times we gifted Rovers the ball far too easily. Thankfully, we were saved from ABBA penalties by Bright Enobakhare – we all knew he had it in him and it was a well-taken goal.

LINE UP

WOLVES (3-4-3):
NORRIS; BATH (C), COADY, MIRANDA; RASMUSSEN (WILSON, 90), N'DIAYE, PRICE, DESLANDES (DOUGLAS, 60); MARSHALL (RONAN, 68), ZYRO (CAVALEIRO, 68), ENOBAKHARE.

SUBS NOT USED: BURGOYNE, HAUSE, GIBBS-WHITE.

BRISTOL ROVERS (4-3-3):
SLOCOMBE; LEADBITTER (PARTINGTON, 97), LOCKYER (C), BROADBENT (MOORE, 105), BOLA; SERCOMBE, LINES, CLARKE; BODIN, HARRISON (GAFFNEY, 90), NICHOLS (TELFORD, 85).

SUBS NOT USED: SMITH, BROWN, SINCLAIR.

STAR MAN

WILL NORRIS

AN OUTSTANDING PERFORMANCE WHICH INCLUDED THREE MARVELLOUS SAVES. BRISTOL ROVERS WILL HAVE FELT GUTTED NOT TO WIN THIS TIE AND NORRIS WAS THE MAIN REASON THEY DIDN'T. PUSHED TWO ON TO THE WOODWORK AND THEN TIPPED OVER A 25-YARD RASPER FROM SERCOMBE OVER THE BAR. THREE WOLVES APPEARANCES IN THE CARABAO CUP FOR NORRIS AND NOW THREE CLEAN SHEETS. HE'S PROVING TO BE A MORE THAN ABLE DEPUTY TO JOHN RUDDY.

WOLVES 2
(ENOBAKHARE 80, N'DIAYE 90+3)

BARNSLEY 1
(JACKSON 90+1)

CHAMPIONSHIP: 23/09/17   ATTENDANCE: 28,154

"IT WAS INCREDIBLE TO SCORE IN FRONT OF 28,000 FANS, THEY REALLY HELPED US AFTER BARNSLEY SCORED"
ALFRED N'DIAYE

Look up 'functional' in the dictionary and it reads 'designed to be practical and useful, rather than attractive'. After a week in which Wolves failed to reproduce the easy-on-the-eye football that defined their opening month of the season – but still somehow managed to win all three matches – there surely can't be a more apt way to describe their recent performances. They began the campaign by dominating possession and shot statistics both home and away, reaching a high of 79 per cent of the ball against Yeovil in the Carabao Cup. Some of the sublime football on display was, by all accounts (including supporters who've been watching them for 60 years) the best witnessed by a Wolves team in a good long while. That's all changed in the past week. They registered 44, 52 and 50 per cent possession against Nottingham Forest, Bristol Rovers and Barnsley. The wondrous passing game has subsided and they're controlling far less of the game – but still coming up with the goods when it matters most. Another tick in the box for Nuno Espírito Santo.

In the Championship bear-pit, or indeed in any league, winning is all that matters. And in what will be a 50-game season for Nuno's team, there will be more occasions than not where they can't produce that attractive free-flowing passing game. Wolves relied on Diogo Jota's magic at Forest, Will Norris's superhero antics versus Rovers and here it was Alfred N'Diaye who produced a remarkable 10-minute substitute cameo to provide an assist and a goal. It was a crazy, preposterous end to a match that had barely flickered with excitement for the best part of 70 minutes. Wolves have made an unhappy habit of freezing in front of big Molineux crowds in recent years. But – and this is already becoming an oft-repeated cliché in itself just 12 games into the season – Wolves are a very different prospect these days.

Wolves, backed by a noisy and expectant home crowd, got into a rhythm early doors and created an early chance of note when Ivan Cavaleiro beat his man twice before crossing to the back stick where man-of-the-moment Jota ballooned a header over the bar. Barnsley grew into the game – Tom Bradshaw sent a free header too close to John Ruddy, while Adam Hammill was predictably lively on his return to Molineux and got his fair share of joy down that right flank. The visitors were giving as much as they were getting, with the Wolves performance going a little flat despite the big home crowd's efforts to rouse them. Sluggish Wolves then had a let-off with 30 minutes gone – Hammill's cross looked destined for Bradshaw's forehead before the striker appeared to get a push in the back from Danny Batth – but referee Jeremy Simpson waved away the penalty appeals. And that was that for a drab opening 45 minutes.

It was no surprise to see a change made at half-time – on came Barry Douglas in place of Ruben Vinagre at left wing-back – and the Scot almost made an immediate impact when his 12-yard effort was well saved by keeper Adam Davies. Nuno sent for Bright Enobakhare, with Cavaleiro replaced. Matt Doherty had become Wolves' creator-in-chief and his low cross was scuffed by Jota as the clock reached 70 minutes at an increasingly tense Molineux. Then Jota came alive to create the chance of the game, sending a through-ball into Leo Bonatini's path but from 15 yards the Brazilian blazed into the side netting.

With the ball swinging from end to end, it was anyone's guess as to who would break the deadlock. And then a masterstroke from Nuno – who eschewed the chance to send on Helder Costa with N'Diaye instead replacing Romain Saiss – led to Wolves taking the lead.

Within seconds of coming on N'Diaye got to the right byline and swung over a perfect cross for his fellow substitute Enobakhare who beat keeper Adam Davies with a perfectly placed left-footed volley.

Molineux went potty and the delight from his team-mates for Enobakhare was clear as he netted his second goal in five days, two years after his last strike. Wolves looked to play out time but Barnsley scored a deserved equaliser to seemingly break Wolves' hearts in the 91st minute. The old bugbear of failing to deal with set pieces cost Wolves as Adam Jackson lashed one home.

It looked for all the world that Wolves would have to settle for a point – but there was still time for a winner as that man N'Diaye slammed home the increasingly influential Bonatini's cross to secure a memorable win. It sparked goosebump-inducing scenes from a bumper crowd with even the normally restrained Nuno orchestrating the fans in celebration, all in front of the watching Fosun boss Guo Guangchang.

Barnsley burst Walter Zenga's bubble almost a year ago. The Tykes demolished Zenga's Wolves 4-0 here and the Italian lasted only five more weeks in the job. Wolves could have folded here. That they didn't is down to the attitudes Nuno has instilled into a team that looks increasingly equipped to challenge for promotion. But Wolves can't continue to trundle through games as they did here. Better teams – and Sheffield United at Bramall Lane on Wednesday look a decent example – will punish them. They were insipid, flat and complacent in the first half. Their Portuguese superstars Ruben Neves and Diogo Jota had off-days and Wolves lacked inspiration and creativity. Their character and determination got them through this one. But Wolves will need

NUNO

I'm delighted with three points, whether we deserved them is another question. I think we didn't play how we usually play – our mobility and the characteristics that we have, the creativity of changing the ball from one side to the other and creating the spaces – we didn't do it. Credit to Barnsley because they defended well but we must find solutions. During the second half there was a total change – we were what we want to be, this is the next step that we have to make for the next game, we want 90 minutes of consistency, possession – we must play for 90 minutes.

FAN VERDICT - CHRIS HUGHES

They say the hallmark of a great team is to win games when not at their best. Well, on this evidence, we are showing ourselves to be a good team. Did we expect a winner? Maybe not. But this is Wolves 2.0 and the game doesn't end until the ref blows that final whistle. To see the unbridled joy from all four sides of a packed Molineux, as well as from the XI on the field, when Alfred N'Diaye turned in Leo Bonatini's excellent cross to give us the winner brought a feeling that this is a club going places. Winning ugly is still winning and the points we accumulate from games like this could make all the difference come May.

more than that if the top-two spot that is now their very clear target is to be theirs come May.

LINE UP

WOLVES (3-4-3):
RUDDY; BATTH (C), COADY, MIRANDA; DOHERTY, NEVES, SAISS (N'DIAYE, 80), VINAGRE (DOUGLAS, 45); CAVALEIRO (ENOBAKHARE, 64), BONATINI, JOTA.

SUBS NOT USED: NORRIS, PRICE, MARSHALL, COSTA.

BARNSLEY (4-1-4-1):
DAVIES; MCCARTHY, JACKSON, LINDSAY, PEARSON; WILLIAMS; HAMMILL, MONCUR (MCGEEHAN, 82), POTTS (UGBO, 82), BARNES (HEDGES, 71); BRADSHAW.

SUBS NOT USED: TOWNSEND, MACDONALD, PINNOCK, THIAM.

STAR MAN

ALFRED N'DIAYE

THE KIND OF IMPACT SUBSTITUTION MANAGERS DREAM OF. TEN MINUTES, ONE ASSIST, ONE LAST-GASP WINNER – YOU CAN'T ASK FOR MUCH MORE THAN THAT. N'DIAYE SHOWED REAL QUALITY IN BOTH INSTANCES, PARTICULARLY THE ASSIST WHICH WAS A PERFECT LOFTED CROSS. HE HAD SHOWN A NUMBER OF ATTRIBUTES IN BOTH BOXES DURING HIS SMALL NUMBER OF APPEARANCES SO FAR. ONCE HE'S FULLY UP TO CHAMPIONSHIP SPEED, HE COULD BE SOME PLAYER.

TABLE

	TEAM	P	GD	PTS
1	LEEDS	9	12	20
2	WOLVES	9	6	20
3	CARDIFF	9	6	20
4	PRESTON	9	6	16
5	MIDDLESBROUGH	9	5	15
6	IPSWICH	8	3	15

SHEFFIELD UNITED ② (CLARKE 39, 58)

WOLVES ⓪

CHAMPIONSHIP: 27/09/17 ATTENDANCE: 25,893

"WE'LL HAVE SETBACKS, WE NEED CALM HEADS AND EXPERIENCE. WE'LL COME OUT FIGHTING ON SATURDAY"

DANNY BATH

A lot has changed at Wolves in the past three months – but some things will always stay the same. Leon Clarke only scored three goals in 32 appearances during his second spell with Wolves – here he scored two against them in 90 miserable minutes for Nuno Espírito Santo's team. There was an inevitability about in-form Clarke getting on the scoresheet but no one could foresee the drama that unfolded after just 15 minutes here. Conor Coady's early red card for pulling back – you guessed it – Clarke when through on goal changed the whole dynamic of what should have been a blood-and-guts top-end-of-the-table clash in the teeming Yorkshire rain. There were few arguments for the red but it all overshadowed the return of Helder Costa, who had been absent since March and missed Wolves' last 17 league games. Costa was given the hook shortly after Coady's red and Wolves only once looked like getting a result from this game thereafter. That came when they were awarded the most gilt-edged of all lifelines just after the break when 1-0 down but Ruben Neves missed his spot-kick and that was pretty much that for the night.

Wolves gave it a go for the final half-hour, playing three up front despite their man disadvantage, but there was no end product to speak of. With just 10 men against resurgent and highly-motivated opposition, backed by a vociferous home crowd, this was almost mission impossible. Saturday's trip to Burton now feels like a pivotal contest just before the international break, with the top 10 in the table becoming awfully congested. Nuno had selected Barry Douglas and Alfred N'Diaye, who both impressed off the bench in Saturday's 2-1 win over Barnsley, for the benched Ruben Vinagre and Romain Saiss, while Ivan Cavaleiro also dropped out as the boss named arguably his strongest XI of the season. Sheffield United were unchanged from the team that beat Sheffield Wednesday 4-2 on Sunday, meaning Wolves old boy Clarke started up front. Wolves got into a rhythm early doors and forged a good opportunity after nine minutes when Leo Bonatini nicked the ball off a defender and edged towards the box, but his shot was too close to keeper Jamal Blackman. The Blades responded with a chance of their own when Jack O'Connell's header from a corner was pushed wide by John Ruddy. It was an even start to what was shaping up to be a great contest – but then came the pivotal moment of the match.

Clarke was running through on goal and Coady, jostling with him, tugged him back. It wasn't a big impediment but the offence was clear and referee Peter Bankes had no hesitation in sending off Coady against his former club. From the resulting free-kick Paul Coutts sent a shot inches over – and that was just the beginning of the one-way traffic. Nuno shuffled his pack and sacrificed a gutted Costa, with Saiss replacing him in a 4-3-2 formation with Diogo Jota floating around Bonatini and tracking back when he could.

The rest of the half was almost exclusively played in Wolves' half. Nuno's team kept a good shape but the ball just wasn't sticking up front and kept coming back at that. Roderick Miranda made a magnificent block, Ruddy pushed a cross over his own bar, Clarke almost got a free shot from six yards and Chris Basham headed wide with Wolves sat deep and on the ropes, hoping to make it to half-time goalless. But then came the inevitable – a goal from Clarke. He met Enda Stevens' left-wing cross to drive home from close range in a goal that was all-too-simple from a Wolves perspective. All told there were no positive signs from a miserable first half in the torrential Sheffield rain with the hosts enjoying 59 per cent possession and nine shots to Wolves' two.

Nuno made a half-time change, replacing Bonatini with Bright Enobakhare as he sought more pace up front. Wolves began the second half with a positive mindset, playing further up the field and taking the game to the Blades – and it should have paid dividends almost immediately when Jota won a penalty when he was dragged back by Cameron Carter-Vickers. Up stepped Neves from 12 yards – but his penalty smacked against Blackman's left-hand upright. If Wolves needed confirmation it wasn't their night, that arrived eight minutes later when Clarke grabbed his second of the night, greeting Basham's free-kick with a bullet header that flashed past Ruddy.

Neves was given the hook for Cavaleiro as Nuno went for broke but despite some decent possession in the United third Wolves' lot didn't improve. They should have been further behind when David Brooks somehow stabbed wide from six yards. This came just after an N'Diaye 30-yarder almost reached the top tier behind Blackman's goal, which summed up Wolves' evening aptly. Thereafter they had a couple of dalliances in and around the Blades box

"WOLVES SLIPPED TO FOURTH IN THE TABLE. IT WAS A NIGHT TO FORGET"

NUNO

I'm disappointed, it's a bad result. The game started well but the red card, even though we stayed in the game and didn't allow them too many things apart from possession. There's nothing very positive from this game. We have to get up and show on Saturday that we really want to fight for each moment and each ball. The law is clear, if you're last man holding it means you don't want to try to play the ball, it's a red card. Football gives this opportunity – after one defeat you have a chance to go back and do it better. And win.

FAN VERDICT - RUSS EVERS

Bullied. Pure and simple. Leon Clarke, who always looked like the victim in a gold shirt, simply destroyed all three centre-halves, drawing Conor Coady into a 15th minute rash challenge for a red card and rising higher and stronger than a weak defensive line as we succumbed to another cross into our box. The ref had no choice with the sending off but after a brighter second half start he gave us a lifeline with a penalty that Ruben Neves couldn't convert. Our best football came when we were 2-0 down and Sheffield United became the latest big side whose power and passion we couldn't match.

with Danny Batth heading a corner wide and Jota unleashing a long-range thunderbolt that Blackman tipped over. But in truth the game was up on the hour mark as Wolves slipped to fourth in the table. It was a night to forget.

LINE UP

SHEFFIELD UNITED (3-5-2):
BLACKMAN; CARTER-VICKERS, WRIGHT (DUFFY, 56), O'CONNELL; BALDOCK, COUTTS, BASHAM, FLECK, STEVENS (LAFFERTY, 45); BROOKS, CLARKE (EVANS, 79).

SUBS NOT USED: MOORE, LUNDSTRAM, SHARP, CARRUTHERS.

WOLVES (3-4-3):
RUDDY; BATTH (C), COADY, MIRANDA; DOHERTY, NEVES (CAVALEIRO, 64), N'DIAYE, DOUGLAS; COSTA (SAISS, 19), BONATINI (ENOBAKHARE, 45), JOTA.

SUBS NOT USED: NORRIS, VINAGRE, PRICE, MARSHALL.

STAR MAN

JOHN RUDDY
WOLVES LOST 2-0 AND RUDDY WAS PROBABLY STILL THEIR BEST PLAYER, WHICH TELLS A STORY IN ITSELF. SOME GOOD SAVES IN THE FIRST HALF WHEN THEY WERE ON THE ROPES AFTER THAT COADY RED CARD. COMMANDED HIS BOX AND COULDN'T BE BLAMED FOR THE GOALS.

TABLE

	TEAM	P	GD	PTS
1	CARDIFF	10	8	23
2	SHEFF UTD	10	6	21
3	LEEDS	10	10	20
4	WOLVES	10	4	20
5	PRESTON	10	7	19
6	IPSWICH	9	6	18

BURTON 0

WOLVES 4
(JOTA 5, SAISS 11, VINAGRE 41, BONATINI 62)

CHAMPIONSHIP: 30/09/17   ATTENDANCE: 5,080

"WE WON AGAIN QUICKLY, THERE'S A LOT OF CONFIDENCE AND WE FEEL LIKE A TEAM NOW"
DIOGO JOTA

The country of Portugal is generally known over here for Nando's and Cristiano Ronaldo. Much more of this and it'll be famous for contributing to one of the most attractive football teams seen in Wolverhampton – and possibly even the West Midlands – in many a year. That's how good Wolves were here – some of the attacking play mustered up was nothing short of sensational. In what's believed to be a first in the club's 140-year history, more than half their line-up hailed from the same country other than Britain or Ireland. And all six Portuguese players on display – backed of course by their Portuguese head coach and his Portuguese backroom staff – made a big contribution to this extremely satisfying victory.

Wolves had been threatening to annihilate someone and it was Burton who were on the receiving end in a game that could – and should – have ended up 6-0 or 7-0 to Nuno's sublime side. Of course Wolves' spending in the past year outweighs that of the Brewers by about £50m – just 5,080 fans watched this game and Burton were a non-league club as recently as 2009. The difference between the stature and expectations of the clubs couldn't contrast more sharply – and anything other than a Wolves win would be been a big disappointment. But it should be remembered that Wolves lost here last season; in fact Burton took four points off them and were unbeaten at the Pirelli against Midlands teams in 2016/17. So it was no gimme. Nuno would no doubt have settled for a dour 1-0, with all the calls before the game being of 'bouncing back' from the 2-0 defeat to Sheffield United on Wednesday evening. Well, as Alan Partridge would say, they played liquid football in what was a resounding win.

Burton were lambs to the Wolves slaughter. Ivan Cavaleiro (who provided two assists and teed up three more clear-cut chances), Diogo Jota and Helder Costa linked and interchanged with the grace of ballet dancers. Behind them Ruben Neves controlled the orchestra like a master conductor and the defence kept things as solid as granite. It was a pleasure to witness. Two of the four goals were dreamy, particularly from Ruben Vinagre, who rubbed salt into the Burton wounds when he made it 3-0 just before the break. The manner in which Wolves briskly moved the ball from one end of the pitch to the other – often in the blink of an eye via just one or two passes – was devastatingly clinical. The movement, the trickery, the awareness, the precise passes at pace – Burton just had no answer.

At a damp and overcast Pirelli Stadium, there were four changes from the team that lost 2-0 at Sheffield United in midweek. In came Cavaleiro up front, Ryan Bennett at centre-half, Vinagre at left wing-back and Romain Saiss in central midfield, with Leo Bonatini and Alfred N'Diaye dropping to the bench. Conor Coady missed out through suspension and Barry Douglas, who looked to be hobbling in the closing minutes at Bramall Lane, wasn't in the squad. Wolves had been under par in terms of performances for a couple of weeks – but they more than made up for it here with a first 45 minutes that was stunning at times. The free-flowing football that defined their opening weeks of the campaign was back and better than ever.

They blitzed the Brewers from the get-go and were 2-0 up inside just 11 minutes. First Cavaleiro released Jota – who was the central forward of the Portuguese front-line – and he beat Bywater with a cool finish. Their second came from a Burton mistake, with Bywater dropping a free-kick on to Saiss's toe for his first ever Wolves

goal. And their third was a gorgeous move involving Cavaleiro and Vinagre, with the latter also netting for the first time in Wolves colours with a very smart 15-yard shot into the corner. Burton had enjoyed a productive 15 minutes or so when they began to win the physical battle, pushing Wolves deeper and testing John Ruddy on a couple of occasions (one save in particular was excellent), but otherwise this was a Portuguese pummelling.

Time and again Wolves broke at lightning-quick speed via just a couple of passes. Wolves were purring – Jota could have netted a couple more in what was a half reminiscent of some memorable away days in the early 2000s when Wolves steamrollered Stockport, Bradford and Walsall in the opening 45 minutes under Dave Jones. Understandably the tempo lessened after the break. Costa was replaced by Bonatini after a good 51-minute showing. Jota should have made it 4-0 but headed Bonatini's cross over – but Wolves didn't have to wait long as they made it a rout in blistering fashion on the break. Doherty and Cavaleiro combined and Bonatini crashed into the roof of the net.

The rest of the half was played out at a fairly sedentary pace as Wolves cruised to victory. Neves and Jota were rested (after Jota somehow headed over from close range) and thereafter chances were at a minimum until Danny Batth headed a Cavaleiro corner against the post with a minute to go, denying the Portuguese winger another assist. After no positives at Bramall Lane, there were no negatives at the Pirelli Stadium. There are many hurdles to overcome if Nuno is to repeat Jones's feat of winning promotion, but with almost a quarter of the season now gone, he couldn't have made a much better start.

NUNO

Everybody knows what it means to go with the result into the international break. I have a lot of experience of that and it's very important. We have some momentum and now some time to work with the players that are here. But we cannot ever 'go high'. Feet on the ground – Monday we go back to work. If you are a team that wants to succeed then every day you have to do something to make you better and try to achieve that maximum. I am enjoying it here very much. I think our fans enjoyed it and that is important for us. They were in there singing and supporting and it was a very good day for all of us.

FAN VERDICT – ROB CARTWRIGHT

This was the day – the day that everyone seemed to 'click' at the same time. No better bounce-back from Wednesday's low point. It was just a shame that it was against 'poor' opposition, as I think we would have beaten any team the way we played here. We completely controlled the second half. I cannot explain why we didn't score more than four, though this was another fine game with good build-up play. Leo Bonatini impacted the game just after coming on as a sub. He's such an intelligent player. All in all, it was a fabulous performance.

LINE UP

BURTON (4-4-1-1):
BYWATER; FLANAGAN (NAYLOR, 45), BUXTON (C), MCFADZEAN, WARNOCK; SCANNELL (VARNEY, 67), AKPAN (SORDELL, 58), MURPHY, DYER; ALLEN; AKINS.

SUBS NOT USED: RIPLEY, LUND, PALMER, BARKER.

WOLVES (3-4-3):
RUDDY; BENNETT, BATTH (C), MIRANDA; DOHERTY, NEVES (PRICE, 73), SAISS, VINAGRE; COSTA (BONATINI, 51), CAVALEIRO, JOTA (RONAN, 77).

SUBS NOT USED: NORRIS, DESLANDES, N'DIAYE, ENOBAKHARE.

STAR MAN

IVAN CAVALEIRO
WHEN CAVALEIRO IS AT HIS VERY, VERY BEST HE'S ARGUABLY WOLVES' MOST POTENT ATTACKING THREAT, EVEN MORE SO THAN JOTA AND COSTA. CONSISTENCY IS HIS PROBLEM – BUT ON DAYS LIKE THIS HE'S ALMOST UNPLAYABLE. TWO ASSISTS – ONE A GORGEOUS IMPROVISED FLICK TO SET JOTA CLEAR, THE OTHER A GORGEOUS IMPROVISED FLICK TO COMPLETE A ONE-TWO WITH VINAGRE – AND THEN HE PLAYED A BIG HAND IN THE FOURTH GOAL, SENDING POOR STEPHEN WARNOCK (CAN SOMEONE CHECK ON HIS WHEREABOUTS TODAY) INTO NEXT WEEK WITH A CASUAL CHANGE OF DIRECTION BEFORE PLAYING TO DOHERTY WHO TEED UP BONATINI. MAGNIFICENT.

TABLE

	TEAM	P	GD	PTS
1	CARDIFF	11	8	24
2	WOLVES	11	8	23
3	SHEFF UTD	11	5	21
4	LEEDS	10	10	20
5	BRISTOL CITY	11	9	20
6	PRESTON	11	7	20

WOLVES
(JOTA 55, BONATINI 71)
ASTON VILLA

2

0

"YOU CAN'T UNDERESTIMATE HOW MUCH THIS MEANS TO FANS WHO'VE BEEN THROUGH SOME TOUGH TIMES"
DANNY BATTH

Matt Doherty asserted in the build-up to this game that if Wolves could beat Villa with the swagger they'd shown when seeing off 'lesser' teams, it'd prove they were the real deal. After Steve Bruce's experienced, in-form team were convincingly beaten in a devastatingly clinical and deeply impressive performance, it's difficult to draw any other conclusion. Villa had won four on the spin, were unbeaten in eight and arrived at Molineux intent on frustrating Nuno Espírito Santo's side. Wolves have had a tendency to freeze on the big occasion in recent years. They also have a miserable record in games played after an international break. But any concerns about Wolves tripping up were completely unfounded.

Wolves not only won an important match against their local rivals, they did so in some style. They produced, yet again, some sensational football. A less organised and resolute defence than Villa's would have folded and been routed. Much of the pre-match talk centred around the clash of styles that would be on show, of a tight, cagey derby akin to an unstoppable force versus an immoveable object. That's pretty much how it played out, but Wolves were just too good. The sensational Diogo Jota scored one (his seventh of the campaign) and set up another to confirm his status as one of the best players in this league, if not the best. And at the moment Wolves are the best team – they're top of the league and having the proverbial laugh. Wolves have won more convincingly this season (the 4-0 demolition of Burton for a start) but to easily overcome a decent, organised team that was set up to frustrate them was something to behold. They hadn't beaten a top-10 side yet either, losing to Cardiff and Sheffield United and drawing with Bristol City.

The fit-again Barry Douglas and suspension-free Conor Coady replaced Ryan Bennett and Ruben Vinagre, who dropped to the bench. Villa's XI was as expected with Alan Hutton in for the suspended Neil Taylor. A fiery encounter was expected and – after the two teams walked out with sets of huge flames flanking them – it did not take long for referee Tim Robinson to dish out a yellow card. Villa's Robert Snodgrass was the culprit as, after 12 minutes, he bundled over Ivan Cavaleiro on the edge of the area. Wolves skipper Danny Batth headed wide following the resulting free-kick.

Both sides then made penalty appeals, which were ignored, and the hosts began to attack with more purpose – Jota looking dangerous every time he had the ball at his feet. Villa were defending their box well though, not presenting Wolves with any clear-cut chances from close range, so £15million man Ruben Neves tried his luck from 30 yards and forced Manchester United loanee Sam Johnstone to tip the ball just over. That was the last telling effort before the break but there was another booking, the visitors' Conor Hourihane receiving it.
Villa continued to sit back and invite pressure

– and Wolves punished them shortly into the second period. Unsurprisingly, it was Jota who scored the breakthrough goal. The Portuguese forward's first touch from Ivan Cavaleiro's pass wasn't actually that great but he then weaved his way past Ahmed Elmohamady before emphatically lashing the ball home past Johnstone, putting two Villa players on their backsides. Last time out it was Stephen Warnock left embarrassed on the ground, this time it was James Chester and Robert Snodgrass. Wolves are making fools of their opponents.

Villa just couldn't cope and soon enough Leo Bonatini, who replaced Helder Costa for the start of the second half, soon doubled Wolves' advantage. It was Jota who broke through the Villa backline before Hutton blocked his effort, with the ball falling kindly to Bonatini and he slotted in through the legs of Johnstone – 72 minutes gone. Snodgrass rattled the woodwork for Villa late on but a 2-1 scoreline would have been a miscarriage of justice. The full-time whistle was greeted like Wolves had won the league – the roof nearly came off Molineux, now a golden pit of euphoria.

As Nuno keeps telling us, Wolves are improving week by week, game by game. And to think there could be even more to come. Costa, Cavaleiro, Jota, Neves, Bonatini – all aged 23 or younger and all making such a big impact in this league. Then there's the fact that Vinagre (who excelled at Burton), Alfred N'Diaye (the hero versus Barnsley with a goal and an assist) and Bonatini (most goals and assists combined in the Championship) couldn't even make the starting XI.

Of those who did, Neves produced a midfield masterclass and Jota was the star, scoring the first and setting up the second, using his devastating pace to great effect on both

NUNO

The table doesn't mean anything, it's a good three points – it's good to be there but we have to sustain the performance which keeps you there in that position. Everybody is growing, anyone who comes in is taking their chance and we are growing together – it is all about the squad, it is not about just the team or the individual players, it is about the squad. We send a message to ourselves – we are back in work on Monday as we have a tough game next Saturday against Preston. We can still improve, there are details that we can improve and we will try to do that on Saturday, this is our day. I didn't quite know if it was the best performance. There is never perfection. The next thing is not to concede so many set pieces. I'm excited about the future. I enjoy the day to day work, it's very satisfying because we're building something together.

occasions. It had seasoned Wolves watchers dubbing it one of the best performances they'd seen at Molineux. Given the occasion, the rare full-house, the derby, the standard of opposition, it was hard to disagree. The whole thing was all watched by a modern stadium record at Molineux of 30,239, the biggest since the ground was developed in 1993 (and the largest since 1981). In that time the place won't have been much louder than it was on Saturday evening. And it's hard to think of a time when there'd have been more optimism. Wolves' fans feel their team could be on the verge of something big and there are few signs to the contrary. It's only October but Nuno's team just keep on delivering.

"A DEVASTATINGLY CLINICAL AND DEEPLY IMPRESSIVE PERFORMANCE"

WOLVES (3-4-3):
RUDDY; BATTH (C), COADY, MIRANDA; DOHERTY, NEVES (N'DIAYE, 80), SAISS, DOUGLAS; COSTA (BONATINI, 45), JOTA, CAVALEIRO (MARSHALL, 73).

SUBS NOT USED: NORRIS, BENNETT, VINAGRE, ENOBAKHARE.

VILLA (4-4-2):
JOHNSTONE; ELMOHAMADY, TERRY (C), CHESTER, HUTTON; SNODGRASS, HOURIHANE, WHELAN, ADOMAH (ONOMAH, 73); DAVIS (HOGAN, 64), KODJIA (O'HARE, 79).

SUBS NOT USED: STEER, SAMBA, DE LAET, BJARNASON.

STAR MAN

RUBEN NEVES
IF MONET WAS A FOOTBALLER HE'D BE RUBEN NEVES. THE PORTUGUESE MAESTRO USED THE MOLINEUX TURF AS HIS CANVAS AND PAINTED AN ABSTRACT PICTURE THEY SHOULD HANG IN THE TATE. COMPLETELY RAN THE SHOW IN MIDFIELD, HE'S SO CLEVER IN POSSESSION AND POSSESSES A PASSING RANGE THAT WOULDN'T LOOK OUT OF PLACE IN ANY OF EUROPE'S TOP LEAGUES. TESTED JOHNSTONE WITH A SWERVING 25-YARDER AND PRODUCED A MAJESTIC FLICK THAT GOT THE BALL ROLLING FOR THE SECOND GOAL.

TABLE

	TEAM	P	GD	PTS
1	WOLVES	12	10	26
2	CARDIFF	12	7	24
3	SHEFF UTD	12	6	24
4	BRISTOL CITY	12	9	21
5	PRESTON	12	7	21
6	LEEDS	12	6	20

CHRIS HUGHES

Where to start with that one? That was the most complete performance I've ever witnessed from a Wolves side. The whole team performed magnificently, Nuno played a blinder with team selection and substitutions, and the fans were vocal throughout. Do you change a side that won its last game 4-0? You do if you're Nuno. Despite a solid performance at Burton, Ryan Bennett was out for the returning defensive linchpin Conor Coady and, after putting in a marvellous, marauding display at Burton, so was youngster Ruben Vinagre in order to bring in the more experienced Barry Douglas at left-wing-back. Both choices were vindicated as Coady and Douglas excelled throughout. Nuno got his subs right too. At half-time, he introduced Leo Bonatini from the bench for Costa, who had seemed to try and force the issue a little too often in the first half rather than sticking to playing a patient, probing game, and this change turned the game. Suddenly we had a central focal point in Leo Bonatini, who wanted to drop deeper and pull John Terry or James Chester out of their defensive shell and leave gaps to be exploited. And boy did we exploit them! Jota had a decent first half but he took his game to another level after the break. Terry will be having nightmares for the rest of this week with flashbacks of our Portuguese genius repeatedly tying him in knots. Some Villa fans claimed Terry would have our attackers in his pocket on Saturday. After watching the game, you feel he could have had more pockets than a snooker table and still wouldn't manage to get Jota into one of them! Diogo Jota's finish for the opener was like a missile aimed squarely at the claims that Villa's four-game winning run proved they are one of the best sides in the division. He then moved through the Villa backline like a perfectly-balanced dancer, leaving three defenders in his wake, before a last-ditch challenge prevented him from launching another missile towards the Villa goal. However, the bargain Brazilian Bonatini was on hand to pick up the loose ball and double the lead. Game, set and match. Our artistry had outclassed their industry. Our brains had outsmarted their brawn. Our philosopher Nuno had out-thought their stoic Bruce. Everyone in the stands did their job in creating an atmosphere befitting of the football on display.

CLIVE SMITH

Wow – this Nuno chap keeps pushing the bar higher and higher. When did we last play that well at home? It looks like he knows what he's doing! A quarter of the season has gone and we look the real deal, passing the ball in the opponents' half like we have never seen before. Laurie Dalrymple has had the font changed on the back page of the programme and there is clarity to see the team there and on the pitch. Players know what they should be doing and today they all performed at a high level. Ruben Neves's peripheral vision is outstanding. He sees passes that only look possible after he has already played the ball. Steve Bull MBE is a legend, a cult hero and I love him to bits, always will. But Diogo Jota, less than 20 games I know, might be the best quality player I have seen in a Wolves shirt. At times he looks unplayable. It started away to Forest and has continued. We played excellently for the whole 90 minutes. Under pressure, we passed in neat triangles or squares with claret and blue blurs looking like piggy in the middle, rarely getting close to the ball. For once we looked the team with an extra man. There was prolonged applause at half-time and at the final whistle, I did not want to leave it had been so good. How have we got to be so good in such a short space of time? You look at the seven players on the bench and you are happy for any of them to come on. All the pieces in the jigsaw are in place. 'We need a goalscorer' – pah! What do we all know, eh? On paper it looked a tough game with Villa on a roll and a strong, experienced side with pace in attack. The pressure was on with the carrot of top place hanging over us and a large, expectant crowd. In possession though we looked relaxed while the pressure and intensity was applied in getting the ball back when we did not have it. In open play, Villa hardly had anything of note close to goal. Set pieces looked their only possible chance but our defending was more than competent too. Roderick Miranda, Conor Coady and Danny Batth all did well, again. Against a lively frontline they all played well. Miranda was probably the pick. Neves and Romain Saiss were totally in control of midfield. Hunting the ball down, collecting it, distributing it to a gold shirt. Sounds easy – it worked a treat. Saiss looks fitter, has more stamina and covers more of the pitch than he ever used to. Leo Bonatini played the second half and just fitted in perfectly. Open for passes, he played a constant give-and-go game. A clinical finish sealed the result. Jota was a joy to watch. His balance and ability to turn away from, often two, players is like Sergio Aguero or Alexis Sanchez. Let's hope nobody else notices.

"I'M EXCITED ABOUT THE FUTURE"

NUNO

WOLVES ③
(CAVALEIRO 44, BONATINI PEN 59, 63)

PRESTON NORTH END ②
(HUGILL 65, COADY OG 76)

CHAMPIONSHIP: 21/10/17　**ATTENDANCE: 27,352**

"AFTER THE GAME OUR PLAYERS HAD THEIR HEADS DOWN – WE KNOW WE NEED TO IMPROVE"
LEO BONATINI

There's more than one way to skin a cat, as Nuno's versatile team are proving. In Wolves' three successive wins they've blitzed Burton in a demolition derby, outmanoeuvred Villa in a tactical chess match and now seen off Preston in what was – quite literally at times – a brutish boxing match. There was no knockout blow from Wolves here though. They landed a couple of lusty blows midway through the contest but ended up punch-drunk on the ropes in the final rounds and only just about edged it on points. This was a surreal afternoon at Molineux, with a stinker of a first half preceding a thrilling second period which contained four goals, a red card, two melees and a grandstand finish. And the whole shooting match was depressingly dominated by a referee who miserably failed to keep a lid on what was always going to be a tempestuous affair, what with Preston's penchant for fouls and bookings (they top the league table for both) and Wolves' pleasing and new-found refusal to be bullied.

Steve Martin was the man in the middle. You might remember him from such poor refereeing performances as last month's visit of Bristol City, when he again managed to irk both managers. Martin's film star namesake got his big break in the 1979 comedy The Jerk – and this felt like a remake. A succession of Preston fouls went unnoticed or unpunished, while the visitors complained about the penalty decision that put Wolves 2-0 ahead and an alleged elbow by Leo Bonatini. Martin's deficiencies, though, shouldn't detract from what was a poor Wolves performance and a fortunate victory. Nuno said his team would need to be patient in this game – he wasn't wrong.

This was the league's unstoppable force in second-top scorers Wolves versus the immovable object of the league's meanest defence in Preston. And in truth there was little between the two teams in terms of chances and play. Not that they were alike in style – if Wolves resemble a classical symphony when in full flow Preston are unashamed late 1970s punk – there's nothing subtle about their approach and they gave Wolves a hell of a game here.

In came Leo Bonatini after scoring twice off the bench in Wolves' last two matches, with Helder Costa dropping to the bench. The visitors arrived having only lost once this season – and the reasons behind that were evident in a largely frustrating half for Wolves. Undoubtedly the hardest-working team Wolves have faced so far, Preston harassed and harried them with a very effective high pressing game that Nuno's team struggled to cope with. They consistently won the ball back in the Wolves half and, try as they might, the hosts just couldn't get their usual slick passing game going.

Ref Martin didn't help Wolves' cause, setting the tone early on by allowing Josh Earl to escape without a booking when he wiped out Matt Doherty. Thereafter an irate Nuno and his backroom team grew more and more irritated by what they perceived to be rough tactics from the opposition – who have conceded more fouls and earned more yellow cards than any Championship team.

The crowd raised the noise level as the fouls continued, but it all masked what was a lifeless Wolves performance particularly in the final third where there was no urgency or creativity to speak of. Yet Wolves still went into the break 1-0 up when, just before half-time, Ivan Cavaleiro turned in Barry Douglas's cross after good work from Doherty in the build-up. The pattern of play continued in the second half but then two goals in three minutes from Bonatini saw Wolves take complete control of the game. First he converted from the spot after Doherty was bundled over by Josh Harrop and then the in-form Brazilian was in the right place as the ball hit him from Diogo Jota's saved shot and rolled over the line. Molineux went absolutely berserk and a cry of "We're Wolverhampton, we're top of the league" echoed round the stadium. Preston must have been wondered how on earth they'd gone from drawing 0-0 and the better team to 3-0 behind in the space of 19 minutes. But they responded with a goal of their own just two minutes later when Jordan Hugill edged ahead of Danny Batth to nod a cross past John Ruddy.

And then, after Bonatini and Cavaleiro had enjoyed standing ovations, Preston pulled another back when Tom Barkhuizen's ball inside was deflected off Conor Coady for an own goal with 14 minutes to go. Molineux was hosting a party just a few minutes earlier but now there was tension in the air. However, despite a frantic finale during which Alan Browne was sent off for two bookings – although bizarrely he left the field before actually being shown the card owing to the ref having to deal with the third melee of the match and had to return from the dressing room to be ceremonially sent off – Wolves saw it through, with Batth and Miranda making crucial blocks and Alfred N'Diaye doing a great job of breaking up play. It was tension personified but Molineux erupted with joy and relief as the final whistle finally blew. A number of challenges were thrown their way in a rugged opposition and a dodgy referee, but they came through it with another three points. Yet another positive sign in what's become a dream first three months of the season for the convincing table-toppers.

NUNO

I'm pleased with three points, it's important. What can't make us totally pleased is the performance. This was not the best performance we've had. The first half, there was too much stopping and holding. We achieved three goals at home but we must manage better the final minutes and not concede these situations. The mistakes can cost you. It's a difficult job (being a referee). It's unfair for me to be judging all the situations but what I saw was too much holding of our players. It must stop and he must punish these moments. Holding is not part of football. We stood up (to the physical challenge) but it's not about that, it's about the law. I'm not complaining about the gameplan of our opponents–it's my job to find solutions.

FAN VERDICT – NATALIE WOOD

The match was the definition of a Championship game. Preston came with a very clear game plan, they were physical and hard-working. I dread to think what the average heart rate was around the ground during the last 10 minutes – but it wouldn't be a Wolves game without the stress! Ultimately it was another three points. Not every game is going to be a walk in the park and there is no doubt Preston will be right up there at the end of the season. It wasn't a great performance by any means but the work rate right up to the final whistle was fantastic and hopefully there's a chance to correct some issues before an easy trip to Manchester City on Tuesday...

LINE UP

WOLVES (3-4-3):
RUDDY; BATTH (C), COADY, MIRANDA; DOHERTY, NEVES, SAISS, DOUGLAS; CAVALEIRO (ENOBAKHARE, 75), BONATINI (COSTA, 75), JOTA (N'DIAYE, 82).

SUBS NOT USED: NORRIS, BENNETT, PRICE, MARSHALL.

PRESTON (4-2-3-1):
MAXWELL; FISHER, HUNTINGTON, DAVIES, EARL; PEARSON, JOHNSON; BARKHUIZEN, BROWNE, HARROP (MAVIDIDI, 61); HUGILL.

SUBS NOT USED: WOODS, BOYLE, GALLAGHER, HORGAN, ROBINSON, HUDSON.

STAR MAN

LEO BONATINI
LIKE A FRY-UP AT WETHERSPOONS, EVERYONE STARTED OUT WITH PRETTY LOW EXPECTATIONS FOR BONATINI BUT HE'S DELIVERED THE GOODS, HIT THE SPOT AND GOT THE JOB DONE TIME AND AGAIN. SEVEN GOALS IN 13 LEAGUE APPEARANCES IS A FANTASTIC RETURN FOR A PLAYER WHO DIDN'T HAVE A PRE-SEASON AND IS IN A NEW LEAGUE AND COUNTRY. COMBINE HIS FOUR ASSISTS WITH THOSE SEVEN GOALS AND YOU'VE GOT THE MOST EFFECTIVE CHAMPIONSHIP PLAYER BY A DISTANCE (JOINT SECOND ARE SIX PLAYERS WHO'VE CONTRIBUTED TO EIGHT GOALS, INCLUDING JOTA). IT'S FOUR GOALS IN HIS LAST THREE, TOO, INCLUDING TWO FROM THE BENCH WHICH SHOWCASED AN EXEMPLARY ATTITUDE DESPITE BEING PERHAPS UNFAIRLY DROPPED. HIS GOALS ASIDE, BONATINI'S LINK-UP PLAY WAS OF A VERY GOOD STANDARD YET AGAIN.

TABLE

	TEAM	P	GD	PTS
1	WOLVES	13	11	29
2	CARDIFF	13	8	27
3	SHEFF UTD	13	7	27
4	LEEDS	13	9	23
5	ASTON VILLA	13	6	22
6	BRISTOL CITY	13	6	21

MANCHESTER CITY 0 (CITY WIN 4-1 ON PENS)

WOLVES 0

CARABAO CUP R4: 24/10/17 ATTENDANCE: 50,755

"WE DID OURSELVES PROUD. THE LADS MADE SOME UNBELIEVABLE BLOCKS AND A DRAW WAS FAIR"

WILL NORRIS

It wasn't supposed to be like this. Manchester City had won their last 11 matches in all competitions. Yes they made nine changes like Wolves, but they could call upon 'reserves' like Gabriel Jesus (£27million), Raheem Sterling (£50m), Claudio Bravo (£17m) and Eliaquim Mangala (£32m). Wolves brought in Ryan Bennett (free) and Jack Price (academy graduate). The hosts also fielded one of the world's finest strikers, Sergio Aguero, who needed one goal to become the club's all-time record goalscorer. The first 10 minutes suggested it would be a long night for Wolves – well, it was, but only because they took City all the way to extra time. In doing so they became the first team to stop free-scoring City from finding the net in 90 minutes since Manchester United in April – Pep Guardiola's team had scored 57 in 17 matches since. This was an organisational masterclass orchestrated by Nuno Espírito Santo; Wolves produced a phenomenal display of deeply impressive defensive discipline, focus and concentration to keep City at bay for so long – and they could so easily have won it inside 90 minutes.

Nuno's boys created not one, not two, not three but four wonderful opportunities to score. Three fell Bright Enobakhare's way (the other was Helder Costa) but each shot was infuriatingly too close to Bravo. Enobakhare's most glaring opportunity came in stoppage time at the end of 90 minutes and he looked close to tears when replaced by Leo Bonatini minutes after spurning it. The youngster did superbly to get into the right positions, outmuscling Mangala twice, but that crucial composure was lacking. There were heroes out there for Wolves, every single player gave every ounce of sweat imaginable to keep the City hordes at bay. Will Norris was outstanding in goal and the back three of Kortney Hause, Conor Coady and Danny Batth were nothing short of exceptional. City had all the ball but Wolves had a gold and black wall. That they lost on penalties won't detract from an heroic display – they managed what no Premier League team has managed this season and kept City at bay. Indeed Bravo was very much the standout performer for the home side, which showed you just how well Wolves had performed.

Nuno made nine changes from the team that beat Preston 3-2 on Saturday with only Coady and captain Batth keeping their places. Hause made his first appearance of the season after injury, while Ryan Bennett was utilised as a right wing-back. However, with City fielding the likes of superstars Aguero, Jesus and Sterling, Wolves' usual 3-4-3 formation soon became 5-4-1. Pep Guardiola's team dominated possession (73 per cent) and play for the first half an hour but an organised, rigid and most importantly composed Wolves backline meant clean-cut chances were rare. Aguero was the obvious dangerman but he wasted a glorious opportunity early on when firing a free shot wide. The Argentine also tested the commanding Norris with a 20-yard curler, sent a close range volley past the post and lashed a half-volley whistling over. It was one-way traffic.

Sterling was getting plenty of joy down the right, getting in behind Ruben Vinagre on a number of occasions with the youngster struggling to cope, meaning Ben Marshall switched flanks to help out. But other than Sterling prodding wide from an Ilkay Gundogan pass, that was it in terms of chances for the rest of the half. Wolves weren't hoofing it clear, far from it. They chipped to the flanks where possible and Enobakhare looked to hold it up. They grew in confidence and, after Bennett has tested Bravo with a header, Enobakhare got the better of a dithering Mangala and was clean through – but Bravo saved with his boot. The youngster grimaced in anguish.

If anything, Wolves' defensive grip tightened after the break and they looked menacing going forward through Enobakhare and Alfred N'Diaye. The first 20 minutes of the second period yielded few chances and the 6,000-strong barmy army started to dream of a famous result. Then came a second fantastic chance for Wolves. Marshall slipped in Costa with a perfect pass – the Portuguese winger was 10 yards out, but couldn't chip over the advancing Bravo. It was heart-in-mouth time at the other end when a shocking Norris clearance dropped at the feet of Aguero, but the keeper made a great recovery to palm the ball clear.

The hosts began to push Wolves deeper but Norris was in outstanding form, blocking and catching everything that came his way. Wolves broke when they could and in injury time, after 10 minutes of severe City pressure, they broke and should have won it. Connor Ronan played in the superb Enobakhare, who was the furthest man forward but still in his own half – he hared to the City box but shot straight at Bravo. The whistle blew and Enobakhare looked inconsolable.

"THAT THEY LOST ON PENALTIES WON'T DETRACT FROM AN HEROIC DISPLAY"

NUNO

It's over now, finished, the door is closed on the Carabao Cup. Let's take the positives, we did a fantastic competition, won at Southampton, fought against Yeovil and Bristol Rovers and against Manchester City, but it's over. It gives us the hunger to go to QPR and fight for what we want.

FAN VERDICT - ROB CARTWRIGHT

We've always had a fantastic club, with fantastic fans. Now we have a fantastic team with a manager to match. I expected us to play the 'reserves' as is the norm now in cup games. I also expected Nuno to prepare his team to fully compete with the best team in UK – I didn't expect a clean sheet; nobody did to be fair. The Man City fans we walked around the stadium with before the game were sure it was going to be 10-0 or more, reminding us that Stoke were on the end of seven goals recently. Big shout out to Will Norris. He's going to be some keeper. He dealt with everything City could throw at him. Well-protected by his fantastic defence, but that's four League Cup games now and four clean sheets.

Extra-time was nondescript bar a Leroy Sane shot which whistled wide. And so it went to penalties – they were taken in front of the end where the hoarse Wolves supporters were housed, but City soon took charge when Coady and N'Diaye were denied by Bravo and then Aguero won it with a dink. Brave Wolves had finally succumbed, but could hold their heads oh-so high.

LINE UP

MANCHESTER CITY (4-3-3):
BRAVO; DANILO (WALKER, 103), MANGALA, ADARABIOYO (STONES, 90), ZINCHENKO; BERNARDO SILVA (SANE, 95), TOURE, GUNDOGAN; STERLING, AGUERO (C), JESUS (DE BRUYNE, 83).

SUBS NOT USED: MORAES, DELPH, NMECHA.

WOLVES (5-4-1):
NORRIS; BENNETT, BATTH (C), COADY, HAUSE, VINAGRE; MARSHALL (RONAN, 73), PRICE, N'DIAYE, COSTA (CAVALEIRO, 79); ENOBAKHARE (BONATINI, 90).

SUBS NOT USED: BURGOYNE, DOHERTY, MIRANDA, DESLANDES.

STAR MAN

KORTNEY HAUSE
FIRST GAME SINCE MAY... IN FRONT OF 50,000 PEOPLE... AGAINST AGUERO, JESUS AND STERLING... AND HAUSE WAS A COLOSSUS. NOTHING FAZED HIM, HE WAS COOL UNDER PRESSURE AND THREW HIS BODY ON THE LINE TO STOP A COUPLE OF CERTAIN GOALS. HAUSE HAD A HABIT OF DOING THIS LAST SEASON TOO, CASUALLY DROPPING INTO THE TEAM AT STOKE AND LIVERPOOL AWAY TO COMPLETELY BOSS THE OPPOSITION. A RIDICULOUSLY MATURE PERFORMANCE FROM THE 22-YEAR-OLD WHO SHOWED NUNO EXACTLY WHAT HE'S CAPABLE OF.

QUEENS PARK RANGERS 2
(WASHINGTON 41, SMITH 81)

WOLVES 1
(BONATINI 43)

CHAMPIONSHIP: 28/10/17   ATTENDANCE: 16,004

"WE HAVE GOT THAT TARGET ON OUR BACK, THAT'S THE EXPECTATION WE HAVE TO DEAL WITH"
JOHN RUDDY

A year ago today Wolves were a club in turmoil. Managerless after the sacking of Walter Zenga, 17th in the table following a bore 1-1 draw at Blackburn and fully 17 points behind league leaders Newcastle with just 15 matches gone. Twelve months on they're second in the Championship with 29 points from only 14 games. They've just produced their worst performance of 2017/18 – yet still came up with occasional moments of spellbinding football and on another day could easily have won. That's progress. Indeed, despite a wholly indifferent display they still played better than in half of their games last season.

That's not to say that Wolves don't deserve criticism for this untimely defeat, which saw them drop to second in the Championship owing to Sheffield United's win over Leeds on Friday night. Their passing game was way off, with terrier-like QPR severely restricting their space. Wolves like to lounge around in first class these days but this was a crammed rush-hour tube journey with no room to breathe. Ian Holloway's team were winless in seven but they clearly raised their game a few notches here with the league leaders in town. And on a tight pitch they stopped the supply to Wolves' wing-backs, with Matt Doherty (so influential against Preston) rendered anonymous and Barry Douglas continuing his poor recent form.

There was a physical presence too, which has already become Wolves' bugbear this season. QPR handed it out and Wolves didn't cope as well as they'll need to over the course of a brutish and relentless six months ahead. They failed, again, to deal with a tall, strong striker, namely Matt Smith who twice got the better of Roderick Miranda, including for the winning goal. With Willy Boly, Kortney Hause and Ryan Bennett all now fit to feature, Miranda's place must be vulnerable.

Diogo Jota and Leo Bonatini, whose partnership has become telepathic with the pair laying on a hatful of goals for each other, tried to get Wolves going with the former brilliantly teeing up the latter twice – once for the equaliser and once with a sumptuous dummy and pass on the hour mark, which Bonatini should have buried. But elsewhere no-one did themselves justice. Nuno's substitutions, for once, made no impact with a worryingly off-colour Helder Costa still a shadow of the player he was last season despite this being the sixth appearance since his comeback.

Nuno stuck with the same XI that beat Preston 3-2 last weekend, meaning Danny Batth and Conor Coady both started despite playing for 120 minutes at Manchester City in midweek. QPR came into the game in dreadful form having gone winless in seven but Holloway's team edged a first half low on quality. Utilising a 4-3-3 system the hosts rapidly closed Wolves down, denying them any space and disrupting their preferred smooth passing game.

Wolves began to step up the tempo towards half-time but then on 41 minutes they were behind – Massimo Luongo raced in to tackle Romain Saiss as the Moroccan received the ball 25 yards from goal and the ball dropped to Conor Washington who edged ahead of Batth and clipped over John Ruddy. However, far from knocking the stuffing out of Wolves it brought them – or more specifically Jota – to life when he embarked on a sensational jinking run down the left flank. QPR's defenders couldn't get near him and Jota scythed inside before teeing up Bonatini who finished from close range. It was the moment of magic Wolves had been lacking and yet another productive link-up between Jota and Bonatini who have developed an excellent understanding in the opening months of the season.

Jota was Wolves' dangerman and he was heavily involved when they should have taken the lead on 62 minutes, linking up magnificently with Bonatini yet again, exchanging dummies and a one-two before Bonatini blazed over from six yards. It would have been a goal of the season contender and there were audible purrs in the press box. But the hosts continued to pose danger at the other end and 6ft 6in substitute Smith easily rose above Miranda to head just wide, before Ruddy spilled a cross on the edge of his own area and Coady had to clear off the line after Washington lobbed it goalwards. The game was becoming stretched and with 15 minutes to go you couldn't pick a winner. Jota looked set to score after being picked out by substitute Bright Enobakhare but fired straight at the keeper. And it was QPR who won it, the dangerous Smith beating Miranda again to head home a cross after Wolves failed to clear their lines. There were no chances forthcoming in the final nine minutes, plus five added on, and Wolves crashed to their third defeat of the season.

The hosts produced double Wolves' number of shots (16 to eight) and played with more purpose and drive. Wolves didn't come across as complacent, but they were bullied into submission. They would love to have responded by passing QPR off the park – Nuno attempted to lead his orchestra but there was a loud barking dog outside who kept putting them off. Fine margins ultimately decided it – had Bonatini's chance gone in, or Cavaleiro been awarded a penalty, Wolves may have won when playing badly, as they've done on a number of occasions already. Wolves have come so far in the past year. If in a year's time they're to go a lot further, then this proved they're far from the finished article yet.

NUNO

It wasn't only our missed chances but the mistakes we made that put QPR in the game. We have to look at both ends of the pitch. QPR is a different team, we knew how they were and were able to control that situation and put our idea into the game. But every game is a different challenge and circumstances that we have to take care of. We were not the team that we should be – a team that wants to come and play 90 minutes high intensity, fight for every moment. That's the only way to win. What was missing was being effective. We had good moments of building and creating chances and should be effective.

FAN VERDICT – CLIVE SMITH

Just the result we needed to stop anyone getting carried away. We were poor; our worst performance of the season. Whereas the Cardiff brutality and Conor Coady red card were mitigation for previous defeats, at Loftus Road we collectively played poorly. QPR pressed us, forced us deeper and we failed to keep possession and play our quick accurate passing. Our work rate was good without the ball but our attacks were stifled as our passes were frequently intercepted. Ruben Neves, Matt Doherty and Romain Saiss found some space on the ball early on, but that was soon closed down and balls played into their box were scarce. We lacked finesse or creativity and frankly the first 40 minutes was quite a slog and far from an enjoyable watch.

LINE UP

QPR (4-3-3):
SMITHIES; BAPTISTE, LYNCH, BIDWELL, ROBINSON; SCOWEN, COUSINS (WSZOLEK, 66), LUONGO; FREEMAN (FURLONG, 90+1), SYLLA (SMITH, 66), WASHINGTON.

SUBS NOT USED: LUMLEY, MACKIE, NGBAKOTO, WHEELER.

WOLVES (3-4-3):
RUDDY; BATTH (C), COADY, MIRANDA; DOHERTY, NEVES (MARSHALL, 84), SAISS, DOUGLAS; CAVALEIRO (COSTA, 57), BONATINI (ENOBAKHARE, 70), JOTA.

SUBS NOT USED: NORRIS, BENNETT, BOLY, N'DIAYE.

STAR MAN

DIOGO JOTA

WOLVES MOST LIKELY OPTION FOR A BIT OF MAGIC, WHICH HE DULY PROVIDED FOR THE GOAL WHEN HE WENT ON A SEARING RUN DOWN THE LEFT WHICH QPR JUST COULDN'T HANDLE. SUBLIME LINK-UP WITH BONATINI FOR A GREAT CHANCE IN THE SECOND HALF. HE LATER SHOULD HAVE DONE BETTER WHEN PLAYED INTO THE BOX BY ENOBAKHARE BUT SHOT STRAIGHT AT THE KEEPER. LOOKED FRUSTRATED WITH HIS TEAM-MATES AT TIMES.

TABLE

	TEAM	P	GD	PTS
1	SHEFF UTD	14	8	30
2	WOLVES	14	10	29
3	CARDIFF	14	8	28
4	BRISTOL CITY	14	7	24
5	LEEDS	14	8	23
6	ASTON VILLA	13	6	22

NORWICH 0

WOLVES 2
(BOLY 18, BONATINI 72)

CHAMPIONSHIP: 31/10/17 **ATTENDANCE:** 26,554

"THE BOYS WERE OUTSTANDING. IT'S THE STANDARD WE'VE SET SO WE NEED TO KEEP IT NOW"
CONOR COADY

In a weird way, maybe it would be good if Wolves could lose more often. They've accrued a few beneficial knacks under Nuno Espírito Santo and one of them is they react superbly well to defeats. Their two previous league losses this season (to Cardiff and Sheffield United) were followed by convincing away wins at Southampton in the Carabao Cup and Burton Albion. And here they recovered from arguably their worst performance of the season just four days ago to produce one of their best in a convincing outmanoeuvring of a very capable Norwich side on their own turf.

The Canaries may have hit the post early on and caused Wolves a few problems, but this scoreline flattered Daniel Farke's team. Wolves were domineering from front to back. Their sturdy defence made a number of excellent blocks, meaning ex-Norwich keeper John Ruddy enjoyed a comfortable return to his old stomping ground. In contrast to Saturday their wing-backs were so effective going forward and up front they dazzled via Diogo Jota in particular but also Ivan Cavaleiro and Alfred N'Diaye who enjoyed a great game on his return to the side. They say all promotion-chasing sides should avoid two defeats in a row. Wolves, like with a lot of things under Nuno, are pretty good at that.

The head coach made three changes from the team that lost at QPR, showing his ruthlessness with captain Danny Batth and fellow defender Roderick Miranda dropped from the squad, while Romain Saiss missed out through suspension. In came N'Diaye, former Norwich defender Ryan Bennett for his second league start for the club and Willy Boly for his first appearance since August 26 due to a hamstring injury. After a scrappy start both teams opened up and

created a number of chances in what was an entertaining first half between two attacking, attractive sides.

Norwich were within inches of taking a 14th minute lead when Wolves' Achilles heel – defending set pieces – nearly cost them again when Marley Watkins glanced a free-kick against the post. But the chance seemed to spark Nuno's team into life. They breezed through the gears causing no end of problems for the home defence and could easily have scored four times in the next 15 minutes. As it was they had to settle for one – Boly's first goal for the club. It came from the third of three successive corners when the big centre-half was left unmarked to head Barry Douglas' inswinger past Angus Gunn from just a couple of yards. Just before then Matt Doherty had seen a ferocious goal-bound effort blocked and Ruben Neves produced a gorgeous 20-yard pearler which Gunn tipped wide.

After the goal rampant Wolves continued to threaten in what was a real purple patch. Leo Bonatini should have picked out Ivan Cavaleiro when latching on to a loose backpass, but tried to round the keeper and fire from a tight angle, which went comfortably wide. Then a superb block denied Jota from point blank range after good work from Doherty. In fact everyone played well in what was an impressive team performance in the first half. Douglas looked back to his early season form, an up-for-it Cavaleiro occasionally sauntered past defenders, N'Diaye added a physical presence in midfield and a sturdy back three restricted Norwich's attempts with plenty of support as Wolves defended in numbers.

Norwich sporadically posed danger, mostly through livewire James Maddison who ran menacingly from deep on a number of

occasions. And then just before the break defender Timm Klose was allowed a free header from a corner, but sent it wide. Considering the standard of opposition it was one of the most impressive halves of Wolves' season so far and they continued in the same vein after the break. They should have doubled their lead inside two minutes after breaking three-on-two, but N'Diaye's 15-yard shot was too weak after he was teed up by Cavaleiro.

N'Diaye was again in a great position a couple of minutes later but couldn't connect with Jota's low ball from just six yards out, with Klose putting him off. Norwich may have hit the post early doors but all told Wolves should have been out of sight at this point and their profligacy was almost punished when Watkins got above Coady to meet a cross but headed at Ruddy. Jota teed up his partner in crime Bonatini on the hour mark after a scintillating run but the Brazilian prodded past the onrushing keeper and wide as Wolves wasted another good opportunity. Then, after Coady got in the way of another shot from danger-man James Maddison, Wolves sliced Norwich open only for Ivo Pinto to throw himself in front of Jota's shot from just eight yards with most of the crowd expecting the net to bulge.

With 18 minutes to go Wolves finally made their dominance count. Doherty and Bennett worked brilliantly to keep a free-kick alive with the latter lobbing towards Bonatini who expertly drilled a volley into the far corner from 12 yards. Thereafter, they saw out the game with relative ease, defending deeply and frustrating the hosts who barely had a sniff of goal, leading one disgruntled home fan to yell "this is f***ing boring". For table-topping Wolves it was anything but.

NUNO

I'm happy with the performance of the boys, definitely. First, the reaction – it was important to bounce back from what happened the previous game. It's important in these moments of the season how you perform and when. It must be every game and at every stadium. The first step the boys did is to assume the last game was not 'the way'. We took this step together, got up together and stood up together, it was good. We have to know that we're not going to win every game, this is the truth about football, so a reaction, not so much is to stand up and say I want to believe in my idea, the way I play, the way I train, I think and I see. This was the message – let's be ourselves.

FAN VERDICT – ROB CARTWRIGHT

As away days go, this one is right up there. Never mind the second 3am return home in a week. It was well worth it. We could fill a whole Express & Star supplement on 'what we love about Nuno'. For starters, I like the way he responds to a defeat. Sensible in post-match interviews; raises the bar for his players; determination to put it right and uses his squad to good effect. Three times now we have bounced back with a fine away win, with three clean sheets. The man is a genius and his showing of appreciation to supporters at the end of games reinforces that we are all in this together. We are top of the league. The games can't come quick enough. Three whole days until the next one.

LINE UP

NORWICH CITY (4-2-3-1):
GUNN; PINTO (C), HANLEY, KLOSE, HUSBAND (STIEPERMANN, 60); REED, TRYBULL (ZIMMERMANN, 65); VRANCIC, MADDISON, MURPHY (JEROME, 60); WATKINS.

SUBS NOT USED: MCGOVERN, MARTIN, HOOLAHAN, CANTWELL.

WOLVES (3-4-3):
RUDDY; BENNETT, COADY (C), BOLY; DOHERTY, NEVES, N'DIAYE, DOUGLAS; CAVALEIRO (ENOBAKHARE, 61), BONATINI (PRICE, 75), JOTA (COSTA, 84).

SUBS NOT USED: NORRIS, HAUSE, VINAGRE, MARSHALL.

STAR MAN

LEO BONATINI
JUST SHADES THE DESTROYER N'DIAYE FOR MAN-OF-THE-MATCH. BONATINI BECAME THE FIRST WOLVES PLAYER SINCE HENRI CAMARA IN 2004 TO SCORE IN FIVE CONSECUTIVE LEAGUE GAMES. OF HIS THREE CHANCES TO SCORE AT CARROW ROAD THE GOAL WAS ARGUABLY THE MOST DIFFICULT, BUT HE EXPERTLY GUIDED HIS VOLLEY INTO THE CORNER. NUNO PRAISED HIS WORK RATE AFTERWARDS. THAT'S NINE GOALS FOR THE SEASON NOW, A PHENOMENAL START FOR THE PREVIOUSLY UNKNOWN AL HILAL STRIKER. IN FACT OF ALL WOLVES' KEY PLAYERS SO FAR THIS SEASON YOU WONDER WHERE THEY'D BE WITHOUT BONATINI IN PARTICULAR, ESPECIALLY AS THERE'S NO OBVIOUS BACK-UP WERE HE TO HAVE BEEN A FLOP. MORE THAN JUST HIS GOALS, HIS ALL-ROUND GAME MAKES/ALLOWS WOLVES TICK IN THE FINAL THIRD.

TABLE

	TEAM	P	GD	PTS
1	WOLVES	15	12	32
2	CARDIFF	15	10	31
3	SHEFF UTD	15	7	30
4	BRISTOL CITY	15	9	27
5	DERBY	14	6	25
6	LEEDS	15	7	23

WOLVES 2
(SAISS 9, BONATINI 26)

FULHAM 0

"I'M VERY HAPPY BECAUSE I DON'T SCORE A LOT OF GOALS! I'M CONFIDENT FOR THE SEASON"
ROMAIN SAISS

CHAMPIONSHIP: 03/11/17 ATTENDANCE: 24,388

Wolves last won a Championship match in November back in 2008 – you just knew that barren run wouldn't last long under Nuno Espírito Santo. They ended a quirky and miserable sequence of 19 matches (12 defeats and seven draws) without a November victory at this level – and did so with impressive ease. Perhaps we should rename this Nunovember, because on this form the rest of the month won't be a problem either. This was supposed to be a pass-fest between two teams that love to play it on the floor, so it was ironic Wolves' two goals came from set pieces. Romain Saiss and man-of-the-moment Leo Bonatini were the beneficiaries of whipped deliveries from the trusty left boot of Barry Douglas in what was otherwise a fairly unremarkable encounter.

Wolves played on autopilot for long spells in what was, for the first hour, a notable drop down from the dominant display they produced at Norwich on Tuesday. Then with Fulham offering a minimal threat they ramped it up for a sumptuous 20-minute spell which had Molineux purring. But ultimately all that mattered was they registered their fifth win in six games and extended their lead at the top of the Championship to four points ahead of the weekend's fixtures. We knew there'd be goals – there had been 29 in the previous six meetings between the two teams – and two was enough for Nuno's men who went into the international break on a high. They've already accrued 35 points from just 16 matches. Wolves were on 35

points from 33 matches in 2016/17 – yet another indicator of just how different things are in WV1 this season. In front of the television cameras this sent out a message for the watching nation – 'catch us if you can'. They're going to take some stopping.

The unlucky Alfred N'Diaye made way despite his dominant midfield display at Norwich, with Saiss coming back in after suspension. Former Wolves midfielder Kevin McDonald captained Fulham on his return to Molineux as the Cottagers looked to improve on a poor run of recent run of form that had left them rooted in the obscurity of mid-table. However it was table-toppers Wolves who took the game to the visitors from the off, starting like a train in the first five minutes, hunting the opposition in packs and racing forward at speed.

After Ruben Neves sent a 35-yarder not far wide, they took the lead in the ninth minute when an inswinging Douglas corner was met by Saiss at the near post and he beat David Button with a fine header. It was poor defending from the visitors but Saiss took the goal well – his second for the club. Fulham had a plan to quell Wolves' threat from the flanks, with wingers Neeskens Kebano and Floyd Ayite constantly tracking wing-backs Douglas and Matt Doherty to make their defence a back six. And for the most part it worked – aside from a Diogo Jota shot which flashed across the face of goal Wolves created nothing from open play. Indeed the visitors should have levelled when

John Ruddy allowed a free-kick to slip through his fingers and, of all people, McDonald horribly misjudged a lob which ballooned over with an open goal at his mercy.

When Wolves made them pay, it was from yet another set piece – the fourth goal in a row (including the two at Norwich) they netted via a potent Douglas free-kick or corner. This time it was a free-kick from the right flank and Bonatini glanced home at the near post for his seventh goal in six consecutive league games – and his 10th of an unexpectedly fantastic start to the season, making him the league's top scorer. Thereafter the whole thing went a little flat, both on and off the field, with Nuno visibly frustrated at his team's performance, which wasn't a patch on what they'd produced at Carrow Road. They were coasting, though.

The teams exchanged chances at the start of the second half with Bonatini stabbing wide after a gorgeous Ivan Cavaleiro flick and then Ayite firing past the post from a good position for Fulham. Then Wolves took total control of the match as they moved through the gears with what was occasionally spellbinding football. Chances fell to Cavaleiro, who flashed one wide, Bonatini, whose header was brilliantly saved and Jota, who had a goal-bound effort blocked by Ryan Fredericks. The Molineux crowd lapped it up and sang Nuno's name almost throughout – a day after the boss reaffirmed his commitment to the club amid links with the vacant Everton job. Bonatini went close again, this time with a great effort from a diving header from Doherty's cross. And then the final 10 minutes were a easy enough as Wolves saw the win through with ease in what was another impressive display of their promotion credentials.

NUNO

For a third game in a week it was incredible – there was no time to totally recover and the boys go and work the way they did, so we must be proud. The word 'comfortable' doesn't exist in football even when we are 2-0 up. We were always focused, balanced and switched on. That allowed us to get some good counters and maybe produce enough to arrive at another goal. (Douglas's) free-kicks are one of the things we work on but the game goes beyond those situations and I think we created enough of them to score. Bonatini is a quality player but his work is more than just the goals. He works for the team and he's the first defender we have.

FAN VERDICT – RUSS COCKBURN

Nothing better than a Molineux stroll under the floodlights to welcome in the international break. Whilst Fulham are not in a great run of form at present, they do have players that can hurt you, so this could have been a potential banana skin. Not for this team, not for Nuno. Ruben Neves and Romain Saiss controlled the centre of the park with ease, allowing the three magicians up top to do their stuff. Like many times this season, I don't think any of the starting XI performed under a 7/10, which says a lot about our consistency. Star man was a certain Mr Neves. When he's on form, Wolves are on form and he appears to have re-discovered his early season tempo with back-to-back impressive performances.

"THIS SENT OUT A MESSAGE FOR THE WATCHING NATION – CATCH US IF YOU CAN"

LINE UP

WOLVES (3-4-3):
RUDDY; BENNETT, COADY (C), BOLY (N'DIAYE, 79); DOHERTY, NEVES, SAISS, DOUGLAS; CAVALEIRO (ENOBAKHARE, 75), BONATINI (MARSHALL, 87), JOTA.

SUBS NOT USED: NORRIS, BATTH, VINAGRE, COSTA.

FULHAM (4-5-1):
BUTTON; FREDERICKS, ODOI, REAM, SESSEGNON; KEBANO (MOLLO, 53), NORWOOD, MCDONALD, JOHANSEN, AYITE (SOARES, 63); FONTE (KAMARA, 70).

SUBS NOT USED: BETTINELLI, KALAS, EDUN, CISSE.

STAR MAN

RUBEN NEVES
NEVES SHOWED EXACTLY WHY HE'S JUST BEEN CALLED UP TO THE FULL PORTUGAL SQUAD. WHAT A PERFORMANCE. TECHNICALLY THE GROUNDSMAN IS IN CHARGE OF THE MOLINEUX PITCH BUT IN REALITY HE'S JUST BORROWING IT FROM NEVES. THE GUY IS TUNED DIFFERENTLY TO OTHER FOOTBALLERS – IT'S LIKE HE'S IN ANOTHER DIMENSION (AS STRANGER THINGS FANS WILL APPRECIATE) WHILE THE REST OF THE MERE MORTALS PLAY ON EARTH. PLAYS PASSES THAT OTHERS DON'T SEE. AND YOU JUST KNOW HE'S GOING TO SCORE A WONDERGOAL SOON – HE TRIED HIS LUCK FROM INSIDE HIS OWN HALF – IF THAT HAD GONE IN NONE OF US WOULD HAVE BEEN ABLE TO CLOSE OUR JAWS YET. WHAT IS HE DOING AT WOLVES?

TABLE

	TEAM	P	GD	PTS
1	WOLVES	16	14	35
2	CARDIFF	15	10	31
3	SHEFF UTD	15	7	30
4	BRISTOL CITY	15	9	27
5	ASTON VILLA	15	8	26
6	DERBY	14	6	25

READING **0**

WOLVES **2**
(CAVALEIRO 16, DOHERTY 88)

CHAMPIONSHIP: 18/11/17   ATTENDANCE: 20,708

"IT WAS HARD WORK BUT WE BELIEVE IN EACH OTHER – WE THREW OUR BODIES IN THE WAY"
MATT DOHERTY

Time and again, questions are being asked of this Wolves team – and time and again they're coming up with the right answers. On the balance of play, this should have been a draw all day long. In fact, on the number of chances created, Reading edged it – and had Wolves on the ropes for long spells. With five minutes to go, Wolves' 1-0 lead looked as brittle as a tea-dunked digestive – then they promptly went up the other end and scored, as if to ask what everyone was so worried about.

Nuno Espírito Santo's team just don't do late calamities. They possess the resilience to complement their sensational attacking flair – and the two facets were both witnessed in tandem at the Madejski. On the one hand, it was Wolves' superior quality in the final third that won them this tight encounter – Ivan Cavaleiro's outrageous audacity in rolling the ball past befuddled keeper Vito Mannone with the underside of his boot displayed the uninhibited panache we've come to expect from Wolves' forward players this season. Then Helder Costa began to resemble, well, Helder Costa, when he gleefully skipped past a couple of challenges with the joyful abandon of a galloping gazelle before teeing Matt Doherty up for the clinching second goal.

But, on the other hand, it was ample defending of the last-ditch variety that ultimately earned the three points. This was take-your-girlfriend-home-to-meet-the-parents style defending, as opposed to the frisky weekend away that was happening at the other end of the pitch. It was no nonsense, by the book, get the job done defending. Subtle, it wasn't.

Kamikaze-style blocks were produced by Ryan Bennett, Conor Coady and the magnificent Willy Boly, who could write a manual of how to defend in the Championship defending despite only having played eight games in the league. If 'winter is coming', to coin the Game of Thrones phrase, then Boly is Wolves' impenetrable wall whom not even the Icelandic Night King Jon Dadi Bodvarsson could pass.

You know things are going Wolves' way when neither Bodvarsson nor David Edwards, who was rightfully afforded a fantastic reception from the visiting supporters when he belatedly entered the fray as a substitute, can reignite the curse of the ex-Wolves player.

The hosts actually started full of confidence – and shaky Wolves could have conceded twice inside the opening 10 minutes. First John Ruddy unconvincingly fumbled a long-range John Swift shot on to the post with just 45 seconds on the clock. Then Coady played a backpass to the keeper and Mo Barrow charged down his clearance, with the ball narrowly bouncing wide. It was a sloppy start from Nuno's team but they gradually got into a rhythm – and were ahead on 16 minutes. Cavaleiro cut inside from the left and played to Diogo Jota, whose return pass to his fellow Portuguese forward was sumptuous and cut through a motionless Reading backline, allowing Cavaleiro the luxury of rolling the ball on his studs as he gorgeously went round Mannone and tapped home. It was the kind of goal that epitomised Wolves' confidence – and quality – this season and sent an army of 4,000 travelling fans potty.

Cavaleiro and Jota were clearly in the mood, with the two players combining delightfully on occasion and wing-backs Ruben Vinagre and Doherty providing a good outlet whenever Wolves piled forward. Reading though began the second half as they had the first period, on the front foot, and Boly and Ruben Neves both made crucial blocks. Liam Moore nodded a clever free-kick into the six yard box where Conor Coady crucially dived in to head clear. Then Romain Saiss and Neves got in a right muddle to lose possession, allowing Sone Aluko a free 20-yard shot which Ruddy saved. The home side ramped things up and only a stunning Ruddy save denied Barrow from point-blank range, with Aluko drilling the rebound inches wide.

Vinagre almost cost his team with some lunacy in his own box, trying to take a player on, but Wolves escaped when Ruddy blocked the resulting shot. It was a minor miracle that Wolves were still ahead – but with two minutes to go they broke and sealed the win. Costa, just on as a sub, produced some dazzling footwork down the right and the ball eventually came to Doherty, who buried a left-footed finish past the keeper.

Playing below your best and winning is so often the habit of a successful team – and Wolves keep doing it. They've produced some spellbinding performances of free-flowing football so far this season – this definitely wasn't one of them. The phrase 'muck and nettles' probably isn't in Nuno's vocabulary – it's something his predecessor Mick McCarthy, the last Wolves manager to achieve promotion from this division, would have said. Much more of this and the Portuguese head coach may want to start adopting it – but ultimately all that mattered here was that Wolves won three points to return to the top of the table.

Home games against Leeds United and Bolton Wanderers this week offer a presentable opportunity to cement that position at the top of the table. Wolves are showing no signs of falling, no matter how high the hurdle.

NUNO

Reading are a team that cause us a lot of problems, but a team that changed their shape to play against us. We had to find solutions – one of them was to defend well. The boys did well. When you see a player throwing his body in front of the ball, or putting his face there, that's commitment. We had solutions, it's all about solutions. We found solutions to unbalance them and play our game. Doherty is doing a good job. He's a player that is growing with sustained performances game after game, hard work in defence. That position is demanding physically and mentally. He's doing well and it's a good prize for him.

FAN VERDICT - RUSS EVERS

So two degrees, pitch black, driving rain and mid November – that'll stop 'em. Wrong! For all of the possession and intent that Reading showed – and to their credit, it was a lot on both counts – this game was won on five or six team moments as Nuno calls them and some individual brilliance. The moves for both of our goals were sublime and superbly finished by Ivan Cavaleiro and Matt Doherty. The lead was preserved thanks to heroic defending and, ultimately, two or three world class saves by John Ruddy. Looking good, ay it?

LINE UP

READING (3-4-3):
MANNONE; MCSHANE, MOORE, ILORI (EDWARDS, 30); BACUNA, SWIFT, VAN DEN BERG, GUNTER; BEERENS (BODVARSSON, 81), KERMORGANT (ALUKO, 66), BARROW.

SUBS NOT USED: CLEMENT, BLACKETT, JAAKKOLA, RICHARDS.

WOLVES (3-4-3):
RUDDY; BENNETT, COADY (C), BOLY; DOHERTY, SAISS, NEVES, VINAGRE; CAVALEIRO (N'DIAYE, 79), BONATINI (ENOBAKHARE, 72), JOTA (COSTA, 85).

SUBS NOT USED: NORRIS, BATTH, MIRANDA, PRICE.

STAR MAN

WILLY BOLY
HIS BEST PERFORMANCE IN A WOLVES SHIRT. HE WAS ABSOLUTELY EVERYWHERE, MAKING AN ENDLESS SUCCESSION OF HEADERS, INTERCEPTIONS, BLOCKS, TACKLES AND CLEARANCES INCLUDING ONE OFF THE LINE. LITERALLY THREW HIMSELF AT THE BALL ON A FEW OCCASIONS TOO. AND THEN ON THE OFFENSIVE HE CAN STROLL OUT WITH THE BALL PAST HALFWAY WITH THE CLASS OF A SEASONED CENTRAL MIDFIELDER. ONE OF A FEW WOLVES PLAYERS WHO ARE PUTTING THEMSELVES IN THE 'TOO GOOD FOR THE CHAMPIONSHIP' BRACKET.

TABLE

	TEAM	P	GD	PTS
1	WOLVES	17	16	38
2	SHEFF UTD	17	12	36
3	CARDIFF	17	11	34
4	BRISTOL CITY	17	10	31
5	ASTON VILLA	17	8	29
6	MIDDLESBROUGH	16	8	26

WOLVES
(DOUGLAS 15, CAVALEIRO 26, JOTA 72, COSTA PEN 76)

LEEDS
(ALIOSKI 48)

"EVERYONE IS GROUNDED. WE CAN'T GET AHEAD OF OURSELVES OR BE COMPLACENT"
BARRY DOUGLAS

CHAMPIONSHIP: 22/11/17   ATTENDANCE: 28,914

They turned on the Christmas lights in Wolverhampton before this game – and Wolves lit up Molineux with a resounding and at times breathtaking performance. The two games between these clubs last year had serious ramifications. Days after Leeds' 1-0 win at Molineux, Walter Zenga was sacked, while Wolves' win at Elland Road put a huge dent in Leeds' play-off hopes. This victory won't have the consequences of those matches, but in its own small way it will carry importance for a number of reasons, not least for the fact that at 2-1 up, Wolves looked a little fragile – before duly taking advantage of a Leeds red card to ram home their dominance.

In front of a huge Molineux midweek crowd of almost 29,000 – the biggest midweek gate here since 2004 – Wolves turned on the gas. At times in the first half they toyed with Leeds like a lion pawing at a helpless, injured stoat. It almost seemed unfair on the visitors, who were clueless as how to quell the onslaught of delicious football Wolves were producing. It felt like it should have been for an adult audience only. And following a brief spell after half-time when Leeds scored and threatened an unlikely comeback, Wolves ramped it up yet again and scored twice in four minutes to seal the points in style. Only once this

"WOLVES ARE GOING TO TAKE SOME STOPPING"

season have Wolves scored first and not gone on to win (the 3-3 against Bristol City) and aside from that short Leeds spell it was one-way traffic.

A number of players impressed – Ivan Cavaleiro was majestic, Ruben Neves imperious and Barry Douglas continued his brilliant form with a goal to add to his three assists in his last three appearances. But all over the pitch Wolves were a class above a team that began the evening in seventh place. It's been said before and it'll undoubtedly be said again – Wolves are going to take some stopping.

Nuno made one change from the team that beat Reading 2-0 and it was an expected one, with the suspension-free Douglas replacing Ruben Vinagre. Leeds had a familiar face in goal in the form of Andy Lonergan, who played 14 times for Wolves last season. The visitors impressively beat Middlesbrough on Saturday but Wolves came into this game on the back of three successive 2-0 wins and they were simply too good for the Yorkshire side in a dominant first-half performance. For a spell of around 20 minutes, Wolves were unplayable – they breathtakingly caressed the ball around the Leeds half at considerable pace and with spellbinding movement. Puppet master Neves pulled the strings and Cavaleiro had the beating of defenders at will, showcasing his immense technique with a display of confidence and skill.

Goals came from Douglas, who whipped a free-kick past Lonergan at his near post from the right of the box (from almost the exact position he'd teed up Leo Bonatini's header against Fulham) and the on-fire Cavaleiro. The Portuguese's goal was a thing of beauty. Bonatini set the rampaging Matt Doherty free – he played to Cavaleiro, who gorgeously turned his man and

fired past Lonergan from the edge of the box. Minutes later he nearly scored another when played in by Diogo Jota, deliciously prodding goalwards but just wide, while Bonatini had almost netted when Cavaleiro turned provider to cross towards the near post. It was dreamy football from Nuno's team, who are quite something to behold when they're in this mood.

The home fans were giving it the 'ole' from the half-hour mark before singing "West Bromwich Albion, we're coming for you". On this showing Wolves will be aiming higher than that. They kindly let Leeds have the ball for a spell towards half-time but aside from a couple of regulation parries John Ruddy wasn't troubled and Wolves were rightly given a rousing ovation as the half-time whistle blew. It was set up to be a cakewalk in the second half – but Leeds blew the game wide open from nowhere just three minutes after the break. It had some competition but Ezgjan Alioski's rocket of a first-time volley from a floated Samuel Saiz pass was the goal of the game and shocked the packed home crowd. It shocked the team too. Wolves hadn't conceded for 326 minutes and now they couldn't string two passes together, with Leeds enjoying their best spell of the game.

Then, just as it looked like we had a real game on our hands, an act of utter stupidity from Ronaldo Vieira handed Wolves the initiative when he was given a second yellow card for foolishly lunging in on Jota.

On came Helder Costa in place of Cavaleiro and the winger injected yet more life into Wolves' play, beating a defender with some wonderful football as he picked up where he left off at the Madejski on Saturday. It was all Wolves again – and they went in for the kill to finish the contest with two goals in four minutes. First Jota

fabulously dinked over Lonergan after Bonatini played him in and then Costa scored his first goal since April from the penalty spot after the keeper had fouled Bonatini. The final minutes were a procession. Much more of this and Wolves' promotion bid will be too.

LINE UP

WOLVES (3-4-3):
RUDDY; BENNETT, COADY (C), BOLY; DOHERTY, SAISS (N'DIAYE, 80), NEVES (PRICE, 80), DOUGLAS; CAVALEIRO (COSTA, 69), BONATINI, JOTA.

SUBS NOT USED: NORRIS, BATTH, MIRANDA, ENOBAKHARE.

LEEDS (4-2-3-1):
LONERGAN; AYLING, COOPER (C), JANSSON, BERARDI; VIEIRA, PHILLIPS; HERNANDEZ (O'KANE, 69), ALIOSKI, SAIZ (DALLAS, 77); ROOFE (EKUBAN, 69).

SUBS NOT USED: WIEDWALD, PENNINGTON, ANITA, SHAUGHNESSY.

STAR MAN

IVAN CAVALEIRO
WHEN HE'S IN THE MOOD THERE ARE FEW BETTER IN THE DIVISION THAN CAVALEIRO AND HE REALLY TURNED IT ON IN THE FIRST HALF. ONE SUBLIMELY TAKEN GOAL WHEN HE LEFT THE LEEDS DEFENDER SEEING STARS WITH A NAUGHTY TURN AND FINISH FROM THE EDGE OF THE BOX. ALMOST SCORED A FEW MINUTES LATER AND HE ALSO LAID ON A GOOD CHANCE FOR BONATINI. WITH COSTA STARTING TO MAKE AN IMPACT FROM THE BENCH CAVALEIRO NEEDS TO KEEP PERFORMING – AND THE STIFF COMPETITION WILL ONLY BENEFIT THE TEAM IF IT MAKES HIM PLAY LIKE THIS

TABLE

	TEAM	P	GD	PTS
1	WOLVES	18	19	41
2	CARDIFF	18	12	37
3	SHEFF UTD	18	11	36
4	ASTON VILLA	18	9	32
5	BRISTOL CITY	18	9	31
6	MIDDLESBROUGH	18	9	29

WOLVES 5
(BOLY 13, BONATINI 25, CAVALEIRO PEN 62, 82, JOTA 87)

BOLTON 1
(BUCKLEY 74)

CHAMPIONSHIP: 25/11/17   ATTENDANCE: 27,894

"THIS IS THE BEST SQUAD I'VE EVER BEEN INVOLVED WITH. THE QUALITY AND TOGETHERNESS IS SUPERB"
JOHN RUDDY

Before this month began, Wolves hadn't won a Championship match in November since 2008. Their record in second tier matches since then read 'played 19, won 0, drawn 7, lost 12'. Wolves aren't really "Wolves" though these days are they? Under Nuno – in Nunovember – they've played four games, won all four, scored 13 goals and conceded only two. Any slight trepidation about this match (Bolton being a bit of a bogey team and having gone unbeaten in seven) evaporated inside the first half an hour when Wolves went 2-0 up and never thereafter looking in any danger of not winning. They were at least one class above the Trotters, whose task was merely to try and keep the score down, which they were managing until the final eight minutes when sumptuous finishing from Ivan Cavaleiro and Diogo Jota exerted Wolves' utter dominance. Wolves barely had to break out of second gear – they moved forward at will with the aforementioned Portuguese forwards on great form and always looking like they had something special in them.

Imagine what the scoreline could have been if Wolves were anywhere near their best? Fans of a gold and black persuasion are having to get used to several hitherto dormant emotions and sensations this season – supporting a team that plays spellbinding, creative, pacey, passing football is definitely a new one. Watching their team barely get out of second gear and still thrash a team that was unbeaten in seven games 5-1 was another to add to the list – as was seeing Wolves win in November.

Wolves were unchanged while Bolton named no fewer than four ex-Wolves men in their squad. Ex-captain Karl Henry, right-back Mark Little and one-time loanee David Wheater all started and Adam Le Fondre was named among the substitutes. It took Wolves only 13 minutes to break the deadlock and, when it came, it was breathtakingly simple, with Barry Douglas providing his seventh assist of the season when sending a corner on to Willy Boly's head and he did the rest. If the first goal was industrial then the second was artistry. Ruben Neves released Jota with a pass to die for – Jota beat the keeper and Bonatini finished it off, heading over the line. Thereafter Wolves couldn't have been more comfortable if they were wearing slippers and playing on a pitch of feathers, but in the final minutes of the half the contest became needlessly tetchy – and both head coaches paid the price.

A running battle between Jota and Wheater culminated in the Bolton man crashing through the back of Jota – both benches went up. Phil Parkinson erupted and had to be held back from confronting Nuno and, after an ensuing melee that saw security staff wade in, Parkinson and Nuno were sent to the stands. After 15 minutes to calm down, the second half started a more sedate pace and Wolves were in control without seriously testing keeper Ben Alnwick. In the absence of much goalmouth action, the home fans entertained themselves, singing about Nuno's whereabouts and asking for a wave, but the head coach's location remained unknown. And then, on 62 minutes, Wolves sealed the points. Romain Saiss was taken out in the box for a clear penalty, which was clinically dispatched by Cavaleiro for his third goal in three games.

A cakewalk should have followed but Wolves sloppily allowed Will Buckley to reach a through-ball and poke past John Ruddy for a consolation with 15 minutes to go, shortly after substitute Helder Costa had almost made it 4-0 with a low shot well saved by Alnwick. Normality resumed eight minutes from time when Cavaleiro scored again, taking Costa's pass and curling beautifully past the keeper. There was time for a fifth when Ruddy superbly cleared into the rampaging Jota's path – there was never any doubt he'd beat Alnwick when racing through, and he duly did.

The back three and the two wing-backs all contributed, Neves led the orchestra and even Ruddy came up with an assist, while Costa enjoyed a third successive productive substitute appearance, taking his tally to two assists and a goal in just 44 minutes of action in seven days – but still he can't get in this team. Up front, Bonatini scored his 11th goal in 19 league appearances. It's worth contrasting that with Wolves' striker woes over the past couple of seasons; since January 2016, six strikers – Nouha Dicko, Adam Le Fondre, Bjorn Sigurdarsson, Jon Dadi Bodvarsson, Paul Gladon and Joe Mason – netted 13 goals in 138 league appearances. Almost everything about the club has been transformed in such a short space of time – and everything about this team screams promotion. You can try to pick faults or look for chinks in Wolves' armour but all you'll come up with is a short period of sloppiness and complacency during which Bolton scored a consolation goal. Leeds managed a similar spell and a goal on Wednesday night. But on both occasions Wolves won with plenty to spare – an ominous sign for their Championship rivals. Their lead is a healthy one and it's going to take a major dip in form for that gap to be closed.

Five wins in a row, eight wins in nine matches, successive home wins of 4-1 and 5-1, top scorers (eight more than the next best side) with 40 goals, the most clean sheets in the league and a lead of four points – Wolves are in dreamland. Long may it continue.

LINE UP

WOLVES (3-4-3):
RUDDY; BENNETT, COADY (C), BOLY; DOHERTY (VINAGRE, 88), SAISS, NEVES, DOUGLAS; CAVALEIRO (N'DIAYE, 85), BONATINI (COSTA, 72), JOTA.

SUBS NOT USED: NORRIS, BATTH, PRICE, ENOBAKHARE.

BOLTON (4-2-3-1):
ALNWICK; LITTLE, BEEVERS, WHEATER, ROBINSON; HENRY, PRATLEY (C) (LE FONDRE, 78); AMEOBI (NOONE, 63), VELA, ARMSTRONG (BUCKLEY, 63); MADINE.

SUBS NOT USED: HOWARD, BURKE, DARBY, CULLEN.

STAR MAN

IVAN CAVALEIRO
THE ONE THING CAVALEIRO HAS LACKED AT WOLVES HAS BEEN CONSISTENCY – ON HIS DAY HE'S UNSTOPPABLE BUT THAT DAY HAS ONLY COME AROUND EVERY THREE OR FOUR GAMES. WELL THIS IS THREE PERFORMANCES IN A ROW NOW THAT HE'S SERIOUSLY TURNED ON THE JUICE. HELDER COSTA'S RETURN TO FITNESS WON'T BE A COINCIDENCE – CAV KNOWS HE HAS TO PERFORM TO KEEP HIS PLACE AND HE'S DOING EXACTLY THAT. TWO GOALS TOOK HIS TALLY TO FOUR IN THREE MATCHES AND HE COULD HAVE HAD A COUPLE MORE. OOZED CONFIDENCE. BOLTON'S DEFENDERS RESEMBLED THE CHUCKLE BROTHERS TRYING TO CATCH A WILD OSTRICH.

TABLE

	TEAM	P	GD	PTS
1	WOLVES	19	23	44
2	CARDIFF	18	12	37
3	SHEFF UTD	19	11	37
4	ASTON VILLA	19	11	35
5	BRISTOL CITY	19	10	34
6	DERBY	18	9	32

BIRMINGHAM CITY　**0**

WOLVES　**1**
(BONATINI 8)

"I'M SO HAPPY TO SCORE 12 GOALS BUT I'M HAPPIER THAT WE'RE TOP OF THE LEAGUE"
LEO BONATINI

For a while this resembled anything but a West Midlands derby. Wolves produced, in patches, the kind of football rarely seen in these parts, with silky, sumptuous play that had Blues surely fearing a heavy defeat. Then came a second half which felt much more familiar – rugged tackles, a tight 45 minutes of few chances, a boisterous atmosphere and a red card – and still Wolves came out of top. They've come through some stern tests this season and, despite the fact Blues couldn't muster a single shot on target, this was another one.

Nuno Espírito Santo's team were beautiful to watch at times in the first 45 minutes but the second half was a different story and they had to grind this one out. Despite a couple of relatively minor scares they did so with relative comfort, particularly after Harley Dean's red card, with John Ruddy remaining untested behind an impenetrable defence that has conceded only two goals in six matches. A sold-out away end saw, not for the first time, their team produce a victory that had all the hallmarks of a promotion winner – playing below their best and winning.

Alfred N'Diaye got the nod over Jack Price to replace the suspended Ruben Neves in the only change from the team that beat Bolton 5-1 last weekend. There were 28 points between the

"WOLVES PLAYED LIKE ROLLS ROYCE... BLUES WERE A CLAPPED OUT ROBIN RELIANT"

sides at the start of play and it certainly showed during a dominant first half performance from Wolves. They began on the front foot, striking fear into the Blues defence with some attractive movement particularly from Diogo Jota, Ivan Cavaleiro and Leo Bonatini. It only took them eight minutes to break the deadlock when Bonatini fired his 12th goal of the season over the line – well, just over the line – with Blues keeper David Stockdale producing an admirable effort to deny him after saving first from Cavaleiro and then from Jota. Blues' only tactics in the early stages appeared to be 'kick Jota' (you wouldn't have been surprised to read that in big red letters on the home tactics board) and Marc Roberts was very fortunate to avoid a red card for a horrendous tackle from behind.

Nuno and his staff were understandably livid but Roberts, who had caught Jota off the ball a few minutes earlier, escaped with a yellow. Cavaleiro was picking up where he'd left off against Bolton and tested Stockdale from 18 yards before firing over from long range, while the rampaging Matt Doherty almost picked out Bonatini with a low cross. The home supporters soon grew agitated with what was a very evident gulf in class and the Blues team responded with fear, regularly giving the ball away.

Indeed, the biggest difference between the sides was how they kept possession. Wolves played like a smooth ride in a Rolls Royce with heated seats and a cup holder – Blues were a clapped out Robin Reliant with a dodgy exhaust and a radio stuck on Country Music FM. Everything was going wrong for Blues, who were booed off at half-time. There was a notable improvement at the start of the second half from the hosts who, with the introduction of Stephen Gleeson, began to keep possession albeit without threatening the Wolves goal in what was a very flat 15 minutes.

Bonatini teed up Jota in a rare Wolves attack and then Helder Costa was introduced in place of Cavaleiro as Nuno tried to get his team going again. Blues' fans tried to do that with their team, raising the noise volume tenfold after what had been a deathly-quiet opening hour other than boos and howls of frustration. The action on the pitch was minimal in what had become a bitty contest – and then, minutes after his introduction, Costa should have doubled Wolves' lead but tried to drift past keeper Stockdale instead of shooting and the keeper blocked.

N'Diaye was then perhaps lucky to stay on the field after an altercation where he appeared to push his forehead towards Maikel Kieftenbeld, but the referee gave a booking. Wolves had created the half's only two chances but Nuno won't have been happy with their performance – they were sluggish and slow and offered a way back into the game for Blues. Better teams would have punished them but Blues, despite a bit of rabble rousing from what was now a fired-up crowd and team, still only offered crosses and set pieces as a threat.

Nuno looked to get a grip in the form of Price, who replaced Bonatini with 15 minutes to go, with N'Diaye moving up front, and Price did what fellow Compton Park academy graduate Gleeson had done earlier, adding calmness and poise to his team's midfield. Wolves were beginning to look assured again and Dean's red card, for foolishly interrupting another Jota/Roberts flashpoint by pushing the Wolves man to the floor, ensured it was a comfortable final few minutes as Nuno's team made it six wins in a row at the home of their local rivals.

NUNO

We knew it'd be a tough game but we deserved the win and we deserved the clean sheet because we defended very well as a team and didn't concede chances at all. From my point of view we should have done better when we have so many chances but creating them is hard so being effective will come naturally. It was a tough week – so long without competition, knowing to come for a derby but we were there from minute one. Birmingham really wanted to win so it was a tough fight. We fought for every ball. I'm looking at the next game against Sunderland. We only think about the next game. I think the midfield worked well, there were many situations which required a lot of running, covering and balancing. We did well.

FAN VERDICT – NATALIE WOOD

A bad performance had to happen at some point – just a shame it had to happen on TV and in a local derby, but even with some absolutely disastrous second-half displays we still managed (somehow) to walk away with three points. In the first half we were in control, looked confident and relaxed. However, in the second half we were a different team. We looked complacent, could hardly complete a pass for most the half and, to be honest, looked very, very lazy. It really showed how important Neves has become, without him we were struggling to get any width and it all looked very one dimensional, but ultimately three points in the bag and on to the weekend.

LINE UP

BLUES (5-3-2):
STOCKDALE; NSUE, ROBERTS, MORRISON (C), DEAN, GROUNDS; KIEFTENBELD, N'DOYE (DAVIS, 80), JOTA (GLEESON, 45); BOGA, JUTKIEWICZ (ADAMS, 68).

SUBS NOT USED: TRUEMAN, COTTERILL, MAGHOMA, GALLAGHER.

WOLVES (3-4-3):
RUDDY; BENNETT, COADY (C), BOLY; DOHERTY, SAISS (ENOBAKHARE, 80), N'DIAYE, DOUGLAS; CAVALEIRO (COSTA, 60), BONATINI (PRICE, 75), JOTA.

SUBS NOT USED: NORRIS, BATTH, MIRANDA, VINAGRE.

STAR MAN

DIOGO JOTA

JOTA WOKE UP ON DECEMBER 4TH A YEAR OLDER – HE'LL WAKE UP ON DECEMBER 5TH LOOKING AND FEELING ANOTHER FIVE YEARS OLDER. THE 21ST BIRTHDAY BOY TOOK AN ALMIGHTY BATTERING HERE, THE FOOTBALLING EQUIVALENT TO 12 ROUNDS WITH MIKE TYSON. HE WAS THE VERY CLEAR TARGET FOR BLUES' KICK-HAPPY MIDFIELDERS AND DEFENDERS, PARTICULARLY FORMER WAKEFIELD AND WORKSOP TOWN DEFENDER MARC ROBERTS WHO SEEMED TO THINK HE WAS BACK IN THE NON-LEAGUES TRYING TO KICK LUMPS OUT OF 'THE FOREIGN LAD'. JOTA, WHO WAS MAGNIFICENT AT TIMES WHEN PRODUCING HIS SILKY FOOTWORK TO GREAT EFFECT, MUST BE HIGHLY COMMENDED FOR NOT RISING TO THE BAIT – OR SHYING AWAY.

TABLE

	TEAM	P	GD	PTS
1	WOLVES	20	24	47
2	CARDIFF	20	16	43
3	BRISTOL CITY	20	11	37
4	SHEFF UTD	20	9	37
5	ASTON VILLA	20	11	36
6	DERBY	20	9	35

WOLVES 0
SUNDERLAND 0

"IT WAS FRUSTRATING BUT IT SHOWS OUR STANDARDS – WE'RE FRUSTRATED WITH A DRAW AND A CLEAN SHEET"
CONOR COADY

A dedicated group of staff worked through the night to get this game on amid heavy snow and freezing temperatures – Nuno and 27,000 Wolves fans may have wished they hadn't bothered. After all that back-breaking labour from a team of 11 ground staff, the 11 guys on the pitch contrived to produced Wolves' first Molineux blank since April. It ended a run of six consecutive wins home and away – and six victories in a row at Molineux.

The final whistle was greeted by silence, as well as a gentle sigh of indifference, rather than the raucous cheers and 'top of the league' chants everyone has become spoiled by in recent weeks. This had to happen at some point – it's just a shock to anyone who's seen Sunderland this season that it was the Black Cats who ended Wolves' hot streak and became just the third team to stop them scoring this season.

Wolves, with Neves replacing N'Diaye in midfield, began as they needed to, on the front foot, but despite a couple of minor scares, the Black Cats defended with organisation and discipline – in sharp contrast to their blunder-laden opening months to the campaign. With Coleman's team sitting so deep it was mostly left to Neves to try to pick apart the cyan-shirted defenders, but with so many digging a trench in front of keeper Robbin Ruiter, he was mostly restricted to those familiar quarterback-style passes out wide. It was a half riddled with frustration – and one of the worst 45 minutes seen from Nuno's team this season. There was no lack of effort from the home team but they could certainly be accused of a lack of urgency and creativity.

The whole thing was summed up on the stroke of half-time when Bonatini shanked a 15-yard shot nearer the corner flag than the goal. The half-time whistle drew a muted response, while the away fans sang "top of the league, you're having a laugh," which was rich from them, albeit fair based on that 45 minutes. Wolves upped the tempo at the start of the second period with Douglas's 20-yard free-kick clipping the top of the bar and Bonatini seeing a shot blocked.

Remarkably, it took until the 56th minute for either side to muster a shot on target. That honour fell to Lewis Grabban whose long-ranger was gobbled up by Ruddy. Then, just after the hour, came what should have been a pivotal moment. Lee Cattermole, booked just a minute earlier, foolishly went flying in on, yes, Jota, and was rightly shown a second yellow and a red card. Wolves had produced 13 shots (none on target) to Sunderland's one at this point but most of those efforts were woefully substandard and with 20 minutes to go a slight air of desperation crept into their play.

It was attack versus defence but Wolves couldn't blow the Sunderland house down. Their end product was bang average, with Cavaleiro shanking two crosses when well placed and Neves blazing two more shots comfortably off target. The pattern was a familiar one for the dying minutes. Sunderland gave up all hope of attacking and sat in their own box. Costa had a shot – blocked, Boly had a shot – blocked. Then Jota finally threaded one through the defence but his curling effort was well saved. The pressure was ramped up in five minutes of stoppage time but that clear-cut chance never arrived and Molineux was plunged into silence at full-time.

So what went wrong? Well for a start, Sunderland must be commended for a impressive defensive display of discipline, organisation and concentration. Chris Coleman has taken them back to basics to grind out a few much-needed results. The visitors broke on occasion in the first half, but after Lee Cattermole's red card they gave up any notion of attacking. The man disadvantage didn't phase them and their keeper Robbin Ruiter wasn't forced into a save of real note. Sunderland's official man-of-the-match poll didn't even have Ruiter as one of its three choices, which tells you something about the accuracy of Wolves' 23 shots.

Nuno's team dominated possession (72 per cent) as well, but time and again they made poor decisions in promising areas. There's no stat for 'poor end product' but that was Wolves' biggest problem here. Work-rate? Not an issue. But creativity was in short supply and once the impenetrable Sunderland wall sat even deeper after Cattermole's red it simply frustrated an increasingly frantic and decreasingly-sophisticated Wolves even further. The whole thing was a bit of a write-off, with Coleman becoming one of few managers to out-fox Nuno tactically. The Wolves head coach's subs didn't work (the unpredictable youngsters Bright Enobakhare and Ruben Vinagre were oddly snubbed) and there was no Plan B.

One to chalk off as 'one of those days'? After the season they've had so far and the magnificent recent run of victories, you can let them off. On the one hand that's two games in a row Wolves have been well below their best, on the other they've still earned four points and two clean sheets and sit eight points clear of third. However full your glass is, there are a couple of warning signs to be heeded. Blues and Sunderland are two of the league's worst sides, but that can't be said of Sheffield Wednesday (a), Ipswich (h), Millwall (a) and then third-placed Bristol City (a) to come before the year ends. They'll have to play considerably better than this if their handsome lead is to remain intact.

NUNO

It is disappointing because it is not the result we wanted but frustration? No, it is part of football. Victories are hard to achieve and we work hard to achieve that. The boys did everything. They kept trying. There was only one team looking for the three points. Our fans must realise that we need them to keep pushing to the end. I thought we created enough. The high standards will always be there because we are a team that wants to grow and improve and be able to deal with every situation. One of them is this: nine players behind the ball, not wanting to play, we have to deal with that. On another day things will be different.

FAN VERDICT – HEATHER LARGE

On a day when we would have gladly welcomed a few goals to celebrate just to warm ourselves up in the freezing temperatures, we were instead left watching a game that was, on the whole, slightly underwhelming. There was some of the style of the new era Wolves team we've come to know and love but we found it very tough against a very defensive Sunderland side that was clearly aiming for a point. While it wasn't the result we wanted, it's certainly not a disaster because we're still top of the league with a healthy lead.

LINE UP

WOLVES (3-4-3):
RUDDY; BENNETT, COADY (C), BOLY; DOHERTY, SAISS (N'DIAYE, 68), NEVES, DOUGLAS (COSTA, 75); CAVALEIRO; BONATINI, JOTA.

SUBS NOT USED: NORRIS, BATTH, PRICE, VINAGRE, ENOBAKHARE.

SUNDERLAND (5-4-1):
RUITER; LOVE (GALLOWAY, 80), BROWNING, O'SHEA, WILSON, MATTHEWS; GOOCH (EMBLETON, 90), CATTERMOLE, GIBSON, HONEYMAN; GRABBAN (VAUGHAN, 84).

SUBS NOT USED: STEELE, BEADLING, ASORO, MCGEADY.

STAR MAN

RUBEN NEVES
A CLASS ACT. CONTROLLED THE TEMPO AND PRODUCED A VARIETY OF PASSES TO TRY TO UNPICK THE SUNDERLAND BACK LINE. A CHEST AND VOLLEY OUT TO DOHERTY WAS BEFITTING OF A GRANDER STAGE. WITH THE BLACK CATS SITTING SO DEEP NEVES WAS ABLE TO VENTURE FURTHER FORWARD THAN NORMAL AND IT FELT LIKE HE HAD MORE SHOTS THAN DURING THE REST OF HIS WOLVES APPEARANCES COMBINED. SADLY, THOUGH, ALMOST EVERY SINGLE ONE WAS WAY OFF TARGET, WHICH FOR A PLAYER OF NEVES' TECHNIQUE AND SKILL WAS DISAPPOINTING, BUT OTHER THAN HIS FINISHING, HE WAS EXCELLENT.

TABLE

	TEAM	P	GD	PTS
1	WOLVES	21	24	48
2	CARDIFF	20	16	43
3	BRISTOL CITY	21	12	40
4	DERBY	21	12	38
5	ASTON VILLA	21	11	37
6	SHEFF UTD	21	8	37

SHEFFIELD WEDNESDAY 0

WOLVES 1
(NEVES 34)

CHAMPIONSHIP: 15/12/17   ATTENDANCE: 23,809

"EVERY TEAM WANTS TO BEAT US AND IT'S DIFFICULT BUT WE CAN DO IT"
ROMAIN SAISS

Functional, adjective; designed to be practical and useful rather than attractive. One moment of brilliance aside from their record signing, this was Wolves at Hillsborough. For the third game running Nuno Espírito Santo's team were well below the very high standards they've set in the past few months. However, for the third game running, they also didn't concede a goal – and for the second game in three it took a solitary strike to win all three points. The sign of champions? Wolves keep being called the Manchester City of the Championship but in truth their early success this season has been defined by remarkably consistent and organised defending, as a unit. Yes, they possess the magic and the flair going forward but when that isn't in great supply, as it wasn't here and as it often won't be during a 46-game season, they rely on being superbly well-drilled and organised. They kept their 12th clean sheet in 22 matches tonight. And if this is Wolves' bad patch, you reckon they might still do ok this season...

As well as being functional, they're also history boys. For the first time in Wolves' 140-year history they have won four away games in a row without a conceding a goal. They've also become the quickest Championship team to reach 50 points since, well, Wolves, in their title-winning 2008/09 season. And perhaps most ludicrously of all, they've already won as many games (16) as they managed in the whole of last season. Diogo Jota may have been off the pace, Romain Saiss a shadow of the player he's been this season and Wolves' passing game was haphazard to put it kindly – but they won. And to be honest, if they continue doing so, nothing else matters.

There was one enforced change from the team that drew 0-0 with Sunderland with Ruben Vinagre replacing the injured Barry Douglas

at left wing-back. The hosts were deprived of no fewer than nine first team players including Fernando Forestieri, so often the scourge of Wolves in recent years, as well as ex-Wolves striker Steven Fletcher, George Boyd, Sam Hutchinson and Barry Bannan. Wednesday came into the game winless in five and in 15th place in the table, with under-fire boss Carlos Carvalhal watching from the stands after an FA charge. Meanwhile, Wolves were seven unbeaten and brought the best away record in the league to Hillsborough.

But in the opening 30 minutes, there was little to separate the two teams in what was a scrappy and dull opening in freezing Yorkshire. Wolves couldn't get their passing game going at all, failing to generate any tempo or rhythm, while Wednesday's main tactic of targeting Vinagre and swinging crosses into the box was fruitless. Nuno's team, as in their last two encounters, didn't look themselves and they should have been punished on 21 minutes when Adam Reach skewed horribly wide from a great position, before John Ruddy saved a glancing Joost van Aken header. A stoppage to allow Leo Bonatini treatment for an injured shoulder came at the right time – and then Ruben Neves came to the party with the game's first moment of genuine quality to open the scoring. Ivan Cavaleiro's cleared free-kick dropped nicely for the Portuguese midfielder whose calm, side-footed 20-yard finish into the bottom corner was befitting of a much grander stage – a moment of genuine beauty from a class act.

Wolves should have taken charge but they continued to look jittery. Ruddy came for a free-kick and was in no man's land but the ball was bundled wide, while Ryan Bennett became needlessly embroiled in a running battle with Jordan Rhodes during which he fouled the striker

twice in 30 seconds and appeared to knee him in the thigh. The home fans bayed for blood but the referee dished out only a yellow card. Nuno will have asked for more tempo from his team – and to cut out the sloppy passes – but if he did they didn't listen, with Wednesday starting the second half stronger.

A couple of Owls corners were dealt with before Neves was in the right place at the right time to intercept Gary Hooper's header back across goal with Rhodes lurking for a tap in. Going forward Wolves continued to lack the vibrancy and creativity we've become accustomed to this season but they still forged a couple of chances, namely for Saiss who sent a header wide and Bonatini who rolled an effort just past the post on the turn. At the other end, substitute Lucas Joao sent a six-yard header over but was penalised for a foul, before Nuno called for captain Danny Batth to try and shore things up with Bennett going to right wing-back and Matt Doherty switching flanks.

Wednesday now had two big target men up front in Joao and fellow sub Atdhe Nuhiu, with their intentions clear, while Wolves were resorting to hoofing it clear (yes you did read that correctly) in what was the most 'typical Championship' encounter Nuno's team had been involved in this season. They started to better cope with Wednesday's aerial bombardment – and with five minutes to go their cause was given a helping hand when Morgan Fox was sent off for a second booking. Wolves looked to exploit the gaps and Cavaleiro fired just wide but thereafter it was a fairly comfortable final few minutes as Nuno's versatile team extended their unbeaten run to eight matches.

NUNO

We deserved it because to defend the way we defend against such a difficult situation that Sheffield created in the second half takes a lot of quality and character, so well done to the boys. I think John Ruddy didn't make a save. It shows a lot about the way they defend, the way they put their bodies in front of the ball and our goal, it shows a lot. It's not all about talent and quality. What supports everything is the way that you have a clean sheet, the way you support each other and react to loss of possession, the way you keep your shape and run back. This is football. It's going to be a tough, tough period. We will try to achieve what we try every game – fight, enjoy and win.

FAN VERDICT – NATALIE WOOD

"Well it wasn't pretty but it was effective" – a summary by a fan leaving the game just about summed it up. Compared to recent months the past few games have been disappointing but the results are still coming in. The first 30 minutes were so scrappy that I think many of the away end were wondering why we had paid £33 each in the freezing cold on a Friday night. There was a lack of intensity and creativity. However after 30 minutes Wolves came alive, especially a certain Mr Neves who seemed like he had lost his way slightly recently. His goal was beautiful. Maybe a little shake-up in the team might not be the worst thing just to get things kick-started again during this busy period.

LINE UP

SHEFFIELD WEDNESDAY (4-4-2):
WILDSMITH; PALMER, LOOVENS (C), VAN AKEN, FOX; WALLACE, BUTTERFIELD (JOAO, 63), JONES, REACH; RHODES (NUHIU, 63), HOOPER.

SUBS NOT USED: KEAN, VENACHIO, ABDI, PUDIL, MATIAS.

WOLVES (3-4-3):
RUDDY; BENNETT, COADY (C), BOLY; DOHERTY, SAISS, NEVES, VINAGRE (BATTH, 66); CAVALEIRO (N'DIAYE, 90+1), BONATINI (COSTA, 72), JOTA.

SUBS NOT USED: NORRIS, MIRANDA, GIBBS-WHITE, ENOBAKHARE.

STAR MAN

WILLY BOLY
WOLVES WITH BOLY – PLAYED 13, WIN PERCENTAGE 76, GOALS CONCEDED SIX. WOLVES WITHOUT BOLY – PLAYED NINE, WIN PERCENTAGE 66, GOALS CONCEDED 11. THE STATS DON'T LIE – WOLVES ARE A BETTER TEAM WITH BOLY THAT WITHOUT. HE'S A COLOSSUS. GAVE THE BALL AWAY TOO FREQUENTLY HERE BUT AS NUNO SAID AFTER HIS EXCELLENT CLEARANCE UNDER HIS OWN BAR WAS AS IMPORTANT AT NEVES' WINNING GOAL.

TABLE

	TEAM	P	GD	PTS
1	WOLVES	22	25	51
2	CARDIFF	21	16	44
3	BRISTOL CITY	21	12	40
4	DERBY	21	12	38
5	ASTON VILLA	21	11	37
6	SHEFF UTD	21	8	37

WOLVES 1
(CAVALEIRO 40)

IPSWICH TOWN 0

CHAMPIONSHIP: 23/12/17   ATTENDANCE: 30,218

Though they might not have been at their fluent best of late, Wolves just continue to rack up points at a rate deflating to their promotion rivals. This latest victory was the eighth in nine Championship games for Nuno Espírito Santo's men and extended their lead at the top of the table to a yawning seven points, while their advantage over third-placed Bristol City grew to 10.

It also represented, just for good measure, a first victory over former boss Mick McCarthy and a first over the Tractor Boys in 11 years. It all means that midway through the season, Wolves are on pace to beat Reading's record Championship points haul of 106. Concerns over a recent lack of fizz in the final third only serve to prove just how high expectations have been raised.

True, a return of just three goals in the last four games represents something of a dry spell for the division's most potent attack. But as has

"IT IS THEIR DURABILITY WHICH IS PERHAPS THE MOST PLEASING AND IMPORTANT QUALITY"

been the case in three of those four games, one goal is more often than not going to be enough when you also boast the Championship's meanest defence. The most telling statistic concerning Wolves at present is the run of four consecutive clean sheets, stretching back to November. Only Leeds and Bolton have found a way to penetrate the backline of Nuno's team during their current nine-game unbeaten run – and they were both thrashed. For all the plaudits which have rightly been heaped on this team for the quality of football they have produced, it is their durability which is perhaps the most pleasing and important quality.

Barry Douglas replaced Ruben Vinagre in the XI but Wolves started slowly and it said everything about the rather subdued start that their best effort of the opening quarter was directed toward their own goal, when Conor Coady played a return pass which goalkeeper John Ruddy almost contrived to let through into the net, stumbling over the ball before recovering to clear as Ipswich striker Joe Garner bore down on goal.

Diogo Jota had the home side's first serious effort in the right direction, a well struck half-volley which Bartosz Bialkowski saved diving to his left. Otherwise things were desperately flat, with Ipswich content to sit deep, while Wolves worked to find an opening. It took until the 34th minute for the first clear-cut chance to arrive. Willy Boly's ball over the top was chested down by Jota but the Portuguese forward was denied a likely opener by Myles Kenlock, who dived in to block the shot.

For 39 minutes, the visitors executed their gameplan to near perfection. All it needed, however, was one moment of hesitation to create some rare space for Ivan Cavaleiro, who did not

pass up the opportunity to fire home his seventh goal of the campaign when he curled a fine finish into the bottom corner from Jota's cross.

Ipswich had offered virtually nothing to that point but came close to leveller when Kevin Bru crossed for Martyn Waghorn and the striker rushed a half-volley wide of the post. Suddenly, Wolves found themselves on the back foot. Coady needed to be alert to clear a dangerous Gavin Ward cross at the near post, while Bru curled a long-range effort straight into the arms of Ruddy. As the visitors tired, Wolves threatened to add further to their lead. Helder Costa hooked a volley over the bar, while Douglas pulled a free-kick inches wide and Romain Saiss headed off target when it looked easier to score, but it mattered not when the final whistle blew.

Wolves are a team with a number of stars, but it was the central midfield pairing of Neves and Saiss who stood out – both barely wasted a pass during the 90 minutes despite the sea of blue shirts in front of them. Cavaleiro also impressed with his willingness to run the channels and display the physical edge which, 12 months ago, was missing from his game.

Such willingness will be crucial for the tough challenges which still lie ahead for Wolves – the next game at Millwall being a prime example. At present, however, it is difficult to make a case for them faltering too much. Of the last 10 teams to lead the Championship at Christmas, only one has failed to finish the season inside the top two. Mean in defence and ruthless in attack, Wolves are close to being the perfect machine.

"WE'VE GOT TO KEEP GOING, WE WANT TO WIN EVERY GAME. NO ONE IS GETTING CARRIED AWAY"

CONOR COADY

NUNO

It is a good moment for us, let's enjoy it. It was a tough game. We knew before the game Ipswich would be tough. We anticipated and prepared well. Now it's time to recover from this game and enjoy our Christmas. We will be back to work to prepare for Millwall and we will be ready. We knew the schedule before the competition started and we have prepared well. A 46-game season is a hard competition but the players can do it – and even more. It requires a lot of hard work. We still have space to go even better.

FAN VERDICT – RUSS COCKBURN

All I want for Christmas is to be top of the Championship, 10 points clear of third and playing some delightful football. Thanks to Nuno Santo, Christmas wishes do come true. This was relatively comfortable as far as 1-0 wins go. A masterclass in shape, organisation and defensive responsibilities stifled the rare Ipswich attacking forays and gave us the platform for our more creative players to do just enough to win the three points. In just six months, Nuno's managed to shape a team that is defensively sound, pleasing on the eye and is strolling what is considered to be one of the toughest leagues in the world. He has done this by combining international flair with domestic talent and the result is a joy to behold.

MILLWALL 2
(GREGORY 13, COOPER 72)

WOLVES 2
(JOTA 45+4, SAISS 56)

CHAMPIONSHIP: 26/12/17   ATTENDANCE: 13,121

"WE KNEW IT WOULD BE A BATTLE – WE ROLLED OUR SLEEVES UP AND EARNED A POINT"
MATT DOHERTY

Four goals, loads of chances, endless tackles, numerous bookings, a touchline barney and a penalty appeal – Wolves may not have got the result they came to London for but this was great Boxing Day fare at a rambunctious Den. This end-to-end encounter saw Wolves at their best (albeit briefly, with some wonderful passing from Ruben Neves and a scorching strike from Romain Saiss) and worst (set pieces were a problem again and Millwall's rough tactics worked a treat). They conceded their first goal for 389 minutes and could have let in a couple more. They also lacked their usual control, although to be fair to the hosts they made Wolves work tremendously hard for the point they earned here.

The Lions lived up to their name and wimpering Wolves struggled to cope, particularly in the first half, but still regularly created chances and a draw was a fair result. It means Nuno's team keep up their unbeaten record, which stretches back 10 matches. However, there will be a concern ahead of Bristol City away on Saturday with Ivan Cavaleiro and Willy Boly having gone off injured. The Ashton Gate trip looms large – if Wolves can get through that unscathed, things will look very pretty indeed.

From the team that beat Ipswich, Nuno made one change, handing Helder Costa a first start since Villa at home in October, with Leo Bonatini dropping to the bench. There were a couple of familiar faces in the Millwall XI with Jed Wallace and George Saville facing their former club. Wallace had said after Wolves' win

over the Lions at Molineux in September that it would be a different story at the New Den – and so it proved in one of the most entertaining first halves of Wolves' season. The snarling hosts were feral from the off, chopping and cutting away at Wolves' midfield with Saville and Shaun Williams launching into challenges. Millwall looked intent on getting an early goal, breaking forward in big numbers in the opening minutes and – after Matt Doherty had forced a good save from Jordan Archer – they got their reward when Wallace broke at searing pace and fed Lee Gregory who sidefooted past Ruddy.

It was a deserved lead and Wolves took a while to adjust to what was a ferocious bombardment of tackles and closing down from Neil Harris's team. At one point Saiss tried to move Wolves on in midfield and was instantly surrounded by four opposition players, while there was a brief melee of three crunching tackles in five seconds from the hosts. It looked unlikely that Millwall could keep up the tempo and indeed Wolves did start to get their passing game going, with Matt Doherty and Barry Douglas regularly making overlaps on the flanks to help prise Millwall open.

Before then, Wolves were lucky not to be 2-0 down with Aiden O'Brien volleying wide from six yards, but thereafter Nuno's team started to be themselves. Helder Costa, who was looking like the old Costa, curled a couple of decent efforts wide before shooting too close to Archer after being played in by a gorgeous Neves pass – not the first he'd offered in the half. The hosts still threatened at the other end and on 45 minutes

defender Jake Cooper headed a corner into the side-netting.

It was another let off – and within seconds Wolves took full advantage when Costa danced his way to the byline and crossed low for Diogo Jota – anonymous up to this point – to slam home. During all this Cavaleiro was down injured just outside the Millwall box, something Nuno appeared to be arguing with his counterpart Harris about, and the Portuguese forward was withdrawn at half-time with Leo Bonatini coming on.

The timing of the goal was crucial and, despite Millwall enjoying the better of the start of the second half, Wolves would soon exert their authority and take the lead. Saiss's third goal of his Wolves career was by far his best – a 25-yard belter that was too good for a flailing Archer – after great work from Costa. That was the cue for 10 minutes of overdue control from Wolves, who finally slowed down the pace of the game.

They then suffered their second injury blow of the match when Boly was withdrawn with a tight hamstring. The Frenchman has been crucial since returning from injury with Wolves only conceding three goals in 10 appearances. Four minutes after his withdrawal Millwall were level – a corner wasn't cleared and Cooper, who had threatened twice from set pieces already, nodded home. From there it was anyone's game. Jota had a strong penalty appeal turned down, but both teams had to settle for a point from a blockbuster Boxing Day clash. After the rather sedate wins of recent weeks, this was a game to relish, a completely different challenge for Nuno's team to face – yet again they came through it unbowed.

"WOLVES TOOK A WHILE TO ADJUST TO WHAT WAS A FEROCIOUS BOMBARDMENT OF TACKLES"

NUNO

It was an entertaining and well-disputed game, a lot of fighting for the ball. It's a tough stadium, one of the toughest in the competition. We were able to equalise the intensity of the game and had good chances. We keep on fighting and keep on going. Just look at Millwall's points – 27 points (in total) and 21 are at home. We showed we are ready for every type of game and situation. I want to thank the fans – it was fantastic support and on Saturday we will need them again.

FAN VERDICT - RUSS EVERS

Perhaps earlier in the season we may have lost this one against a big – in some cases huge – side who fought, kicked and battled their way through the 90 minutes. Millwall seemed to have done their homework as they concentrated on lumping high balls into our box at every opportunity for the Jurassic Park-like figures to win 95 per cent of the headers. On the floor, we played well in parts and ok in others, deserving a point but, in the cold light of South Bermondsey, perhaps no more than that. But the unbeaten run goes on and proves we have learned a lot about the physical side of the game. Onwards and still upwards.

MILLWALL (4-4-2):
ARCHER; MCLAUGHLIN (ROMEO, 52), HUTCHINSON (C), COOPER, MEREDITH; WALLACE, SAVILLE, WILLIAMS, O'BRIEN (TUNNICLIFFE, 82); GREGORY, ELLIOTT (MORISON, 60).

SUBS NOT USED: MARTIN, CRAIG, THOMPSON, ONYEDINMA.

WOLVES (3-4-3):
RUDDY; BENNETT, COADY (C), BOLY (MIRANDA, 68); DOHERTY, SAISS, NEVES, DOUGLAS; COSTA (N'DIAYE, 80), CAVALEIRO (BONATINI, 45), JOTA.

SUBS NOT USED: NORRIS, BATTH, VINAGRE, ENOBAKHARE.

STAR MAN

RUBEN NEVES
HAS THERE BEEN A BETTER PASSER OF THE BALL AT WOLVES IN THE PAST 40, EVEN 50 YEARS? THIS REPORTER HAS BEEN WATCHING WOLVES SINCE 1991 AND APART FROM NENAD MILIJAS, WHO WAS MORE INCONSISTENT THAN NEVES (ALTHOUGH PLAYING AT A HIGHER LEVEL) THERE'S NO-ONE WHO COMES CLOSE. NEVES WAS NEVER GOING TO WIN THE PHYSICAL BATTLE AGAINST A FERAL AND PSYCHED-UP MILLWALL BUT WHAT HE DID DO WAS ADMIRABLY COMPETE. THEN WHEN GIVEN THE CHANCE, HE SPRAYED THE MOST DIVINE PASSES TO SET DOHERTY AND COSTA IN ON GOAL, WHILE A 50-YARD PING TO DOUGLAS IN THE SECOND HALF DREW NOISES FROM THE PRESS BOX THAT SHOULD ONLY BE HEARD AFTER THE WATERSHED. A SPECIAL PLAYER.

TABLE

	TEAM	P	GD	PTS
1	WOLVES	24	26	55
2	BRISTOL CITY	24	15	47
3	CARDIFF	24	13	47
4	DERBY	24	17	45
5	LEEDS	24	10	42
6	SHEFF UTD	24	10	41

BRISTOL CITY   1
(REID 53)

WOLVES   2
(DOUGLAS 66, BENNETT 90+4)

CHAMPIONSHIP: 30/12/17   ATTENDANCE: 25,540

"THE SHEER JOY AND EMOTIONS – IT FEELS EXTRA SPECIAL IN THE LAST MINUTE. IT'S A BIG STATEMENT"
BARRY DOUGLAS

Almost everything that could go wrong, did – and Wolves still won. Their captain and head coach were sent off, they'd seen a brilliant free-kick hit the post and they'd gone 1-0 down to a fired-up Bristol City in front of a baying home crowd. What followed was one of the most remarkable turnarounds produced by a Wolves team in recent years. Nuno Espírito Santo's team, as they have done on so many occasions this season, defied the odds and somehow managed to find a way to win. Yet again. For all their fantastic football in the past five months, this was their most impressive victory under Nuno to date – and their most wonderfully dramatic. Given the circumstances, given how the football gods seemed to be conspiring against them, this was a quite stunning win. And the celebrations, both after Ryan Bennett's winner and at full-time, told you exactly how important this was in the context of the season.

When Bristol City were leading, they were five points behind Wolves in the live league table and, if they could have seen it through, would have a chance to cut the gap to just two points on January 1, with Wolves not playing until a day later. Instead Wolves increased their oh-so-handsome lead to 10 at the end of the second anarchic encounter between these two teams in four months. They'd have probably settled for a point at the start of the night – and certainly would have done after 18 minutes, by which point Danny Batth had been harshly sent off and Nuno sent to the stands for the second time in two months. Somehow they won all three in what was an astoundingly thrilling finish.

Top scorer Leo Bonatini and captain Batth were brought into the side at the expense of Ivan Cavaleiro and Bennett, who dropped to the bench. At a packed Ashton Gate, there was a spine-tingling atmosphere as the game kicked off between arguably the division's two form sides and the hosts pegged Wolves back early on – John Ruddy was forced into two saves, the first an excellent fingertip to deny a Jamie Paterson header. Wolves were having problems containing City from the flanks, with a number of whipped deliveries from both wings testing their defensive rearguard. And their task was suddenly made a good deal harder when skipper Batth saw red after just 14 minutes. After skilfully skipping past a challenge, a heavy touch saw him crash into Hordur Magnusson, initially leading with his studs up. Batth won the ball but referee Bankes had no hesitation in showing a red card.

That was the start of a five-minute period in which it felt like Wolves were unravelling. Nuno appeared to be angry with how counterpart Lee Johnson demanded a red for Batth and then when Diogo Jota was fouled inches outside the box the head coach's temper boiled over and he was duly sent to the stands for a second time in two months. To finish off the bedlam, Barry Douglas was only inches from giving Wolves the lead from the resulting free-kick, with his excellent effort smacking off the upright.

The rest of the half was a game of cat and mouse as defensive-minded Wolves looked to protect their clean sheet while only sporadically breaking through Helder Costa and Jota, who were pretty lonely up front, Leo Bonatini having been the sacrificial lamb when replaced by Ryan Bennett after Batth's red. There was an inevitability about Bristol City's goal in the 53rd minute, scored by the in-form Bobby Reid who, with Willy Boly out of position, wasn't tracked as a he played a one-two and lashed past Ruddy.
Nuno, who was sat in the director's box but still communicating with his staff, sent on Cavaleiro and the Portuguese forward responded by changing the game. It was his wonderful pass that sent Doherty, on a rare overlap, in on goal – keeper Frank Fielding charged off his line and wiped out the Irishman, who had shown great determination to reach the ball first. If Batth's red card was contentious, this certainly wasn't, and all of a sudden it was 10 v 10 and game on. Within two minutes Wolves were level. Douglas dug out his inner whip yet again with this free-kick beating Steele, whose first touch was to retrieve the ball from his net.

Cavaleiro was on fire. He sent a wicked 25-yard effort just wide and then picked out Romain Saiss with a quite gorgeous pass, with Steele out quickly to block the Moroccan's shot. With time running out it looked for all the world it would finish 1-1 but then with just seconds left Douglas' magical left boot picked out the unlikeliest of heroes in Bennett, whose header sparked bedlam in the away end and on the bench.

That they came away from such a demanding test at Ashton Gate with their lead at the top of the table not just intact but increased was due to the same battling characteristics that have defined their opening half of the season. Lesser teams would have buckled under the pressure of an in-form home team whose confidence was sky-high and whose fanbase whipped up a cracking atmosphere in this top-of-the-table clash. But Wolves, despite a couple of wobbles, got their basics right, kept it tight and kept it simple.

This is a Wolves team that doesn't do 'lying down'. They just don't know when they're beaten – and if that trend continues they will be celebrating next May or perhaps even earlier. This club began 2017 with little idea of where it was heading. They will begin 2018 with their Premier League destiny in their own hands –

NUNO

It means a lot. I have to congratulate the boys, our fans for the way they were celebrating with us, it means a lot for the boys. I'm happy with the game, not all the circumstances of the game, people didn't do their jobs properly. Besides that, we dug in well, the sending off changes everything but we reacted really well in how we stayed organised in the game. Bristol didn't create anything. The reaction was fantastic, the boys did really well and it was incredible the character they showed. What supports the talent is the strength and the power and the humility. This referee, it's the second time he's had our game and the second sending off (after Conor Coady at Sheffield United). I think it's unfair. I'm sorry for my sending off. I was sent off because he said "you go inside of the pitch" – it's true I put one step, one foot inside the pitch and the rules said I should be sent off. But I was not rude, I didn't have abusive or bad words for the referee.

and then some. No team can stop this Wolves juggernaut. The only thing that can deny them is themselves. Maybe the only thing that's been lacking in this wonderful campaign so far is an 'I was there' moment – not anymore.

LINE UP

BRISTOL CITY (4-4-1-1):
FIELDING; WRIGHT (C), FLINT, BAKER, MAGNUSSON (TAYLOR, 78);
BROWNHILL (ELIASSON, 79), PACK, SMITH, BRYAN; PATERSON
(STEELE, 65); REID.

SUBS NOT USED: WOODROW, KELLY, VYNER, LEKO.

WOLVES (3-4-3):
RUDDY; BATTH (C), COADY, BOLY; DOHERTY, SAISS, NEVES, DOUGLAS;
COSTA (CAVALEIRO, 62), BONATINI (BENNETT, 17), JOTA (ENOBAKHARE 87).

SUBS NOT USED: NORRIS, HAUSE, N'DIAYE, GIBBS-WHITE.

STAR MAN

BARRY DOUGLAS

THE GUY'S LEFT FOOT IS SO ACCURATE IT COULD LOCATE NEW
SPECIES ON MARS. PUT ONE FREE-KICK AGAINST THE POST,
ANOTHER IN THE NET (VIA A DEFLECTION) AND ANOTHER ON RYAN
BENNETT'S HEAD FOR A FAMOUS WINNER. IN OPEN PLAY, HIS
EVENING WAS LARGELY RESTRICTED TO DEFENDING, WHAT WITH
WOLVES BEING A MAN LIGHT FOR A LARGE CHUNK OF THE GAME.
BUT, AS SO OFTEN THIS SEASON, HE CAME UP WITH THE GOODS
FROM DEAD-BALL SITUATIONS. HIS EXPERTISE HAS BECOME A
PROLIFIC WEAPON IN WOLVES' ARMOURY AND DOUGLAS, AT £1M,
MUST BE ONE OF THE BARGAINS OF THE YEAR.

TABLE

	TEAM	P	GD	PTS
1	WOLVES	25	27	58
2	DERBY	25	18	48
3	BRISTOL CITY	25	14	47
4	CARDIFF	25	12	47
5	LEEDS	25	9	42
6	SHEFF UTD	25	9	41

FAN VERDICT

RUSS COCKBURN

What a season they are giving us. Everything that could go against us did, yet we were able to show tremendous spirit, good defensive shape and quality in the final third to turn the game on its head. This was as good a comeback as Dirty Den. The league table now reads 11 points clear of third place but, more importantly, the manner of the victory dealt a psychological blow to the rest of the league. It wasn't a vintage performance – that was pretty much taken away from us when the ref harshly decided to send Danny Batth off for winning the ball. Despite losing Batth and Nuno, the players somehow dug in and managed to make life difficult for Bristol City, restricting them to few clear cut opportunities. When their goal came it was the result of us losing possession and Conor Coady being dragged over to cover, a rare mistake from our Liverpudlian captain. I'd pretty much settled for our first loss in 11 games, but thankfully our team hadn't. Sparked by the arrival of Ivan Cavaleiro, the game changed in a second. Matt Doherty, who was surging more than an Uber ride on New Year's Eve, drew a foul from Frank Fielding and gave Barry Douglas the opportunity to use his wand of a left foot. 1-1! We looked the mostly likely scorers for the last 24 minutes and, right on cue, Ryan Bennett steered home a header in the last minute to send the away end ballistic. If you could bottle the feeling when the ball hit the net you would be a millionaire. In half a season, Nuno has transformed us from a boring mid-table team into one that is bossing a very competitive Championship. His celebrations show how much he has invested in this project – and long may it continue.

NATALIE WOOD

Many people say they think we are mad for travelling up and down the country following Wolves but that last minute is why we do it! Such a special moment for the team and fans. It was always going to be a tight contest and the first 10 minutes were quite even – an entertaining start. I couldn't really see the Danny Batth red card, from our angle it looked like Danny had just got himself in a silly situation. The mindset changed after that and we played more conservatively but I wouldn't say Bristol City were on top. We held our own for the rest of the half and the conversations in the stand at half-time were that we could just nick it on the counter. Second half, it became more obvious a City goal was almost a certainty. After that came it all changed, once the we had the introduction of a certain Mr Cavaleiro. Almost instantly he changed the game, he added the speed and intensity that had dropped off. After a matter of minutes he had put Matt Doherty through on goal which would have been a certain equaliser and brought the most blatant red card you will ever see! Thankfully Barry Douglas converted the free-kick otherwise that sending-off wouldn't have felt so sweet. After that I think we would have been disappointed with a draw, but it could have also gone Bristol's way. The fight Wolves showed right up to the last minute was so great to see. As Douglas lined up the free-kick there was an air of excitement – the guy has such a talent for these dead-ball kicks that any free-kick turns into a goalscoring opportunity. He is becoming probably the most important player for us. Ryan Bennett finished very well after getting himself into the right place at the right time. After that it was just pure bedlam in the away end and, it appears, on the pitch. I think the celebrations showed what that goal meant to everyone at the club. I think it will become a defining moment in our season, the moment we showed who we really are.

"I HAVE TO CONGRATULATE THE BOYS...
IT WAS INCREDIBLE CHARACTER THEY SHOWED"
NUNO

WOLVES
(NEVES 57, DOUGLAS 59, JOTA 80)

BRENTFORD

"I'M VERY HAPPY AT WOLVES. I HAVE TO TAKE RISKS AND SHOOT FROM LONG RANGE AND HOPEFULLY I SCORE"
RUBEN NEVES

With their rivals falling by the wayside – and as Nuno Espírito's team just keep on winning – it seems the only team that can stop Wolves is – well, Wolves. Their lead is now 12 points to Derby and 14 to third-placed Cardiff. That's a daunting gap for their rivals, whom you imagine are giving up hope of being able to catch Nuno's seemingly unstoppable juggernaut. Wolves have emerged from a tricky-looking festive period – Ipswich, Millwall, Bristol City and now Brentford – with an almost perfect 10 points out of 12, while those around them have tripped up. Any doubts about fatigue, their foreign youngsters coping with the relentless fixture schedule or of other teams sussing Wolves out have proved completely unfounded and they are steamrolling the league.

They're unbeaten since October, score goals for fun (they have 50, with the next best being Derby on 41), have the league's most miserly defence, possess no obvious deficiencies and even have the luxury of strength in depth – and new signings to come (Spanish forward Rafa Mir looks to be the first this month). They now have 61 points – that's three more than last season's final total. And with the average points total of the Championship's second-placed team in the

past 10 years being 87, they likely have to win only 10 of their final 20 matches to get over the finish line. Only a very brave man or a fool would bet against them now. The rate Wolves are going, this could be very comfortable indeed and with Nuno's penchant for devastating efficiency and clinicalness, that looks the most likely outcome.

Nuno made just one change from the team that had dramatically beaten Bristol City 2-1 on Saturday, with Ryan Bennett replacing the suspended Danny Batth. Helder Costa got the nod over Ivan Cavaleiro, who remained on the bench. Brentford arrived at Molineux in great form having rocketed up the table since the teams last met, earning 33 points from 17 matches. But Wolves are in even better form and it was Nuno's team who took the game by the scruff of the neck in the first half. To be honest they could have been 5-0 up by half-time. They certainly should have scored at least twice, but a combination of bad luck, dodgy finishing and a brilliant performance from ex-Southend keeper Daniel Bentley meant it somehow stayed goalless.

Costa, anonymous at Bristol City on Saturday, looked a different player from the off as he teed up Leo Bonatini, whose second-minute shot struck the post. At a well-stocked but fairly quiet Molineux, both teams were playing some nice football. Brentford weren't shy in getting forward in good numbers but they lacked the quality in the final third to really test Wolves, aside from a Yoann Barbet header which dropped inches past the post. Otherwise it was all Wolves. Diogo Jota headed a corner goalwards, but it was cleared off the line and Matt Doherty was played into the box by a gorgeous Willy Boly chip, but Bentley got a hand to his left-footed shot. Costa then latched on to a low through-ball, but Bentley raced out to block his chip. And then just before half-time Barry Douglas directed a cross-field

ball across goal to Jota, whose bullet shot from 15 yards was superbly tipped past the post by Bentley, who was proving unbeatable.

The second half started in the same fashion. Bonatini showed great feet and strength to hold off a couple of challenges, but Bentley proved equal to his shot. Cavaleiro changed the game at Bristol and Nuno called for him on 53 minutes, taking off an improved and clearly-disappointed Costa. The 23-year-old made an immediate impact, creating half-chances for Bonatini and Doherty – and, within six minutes of his introduction, Wolves were 2-0 up. First Ruben Neves sent a gorgeous 20-yard free-kick into the corner, finally beating Bentley for his first Molineux goal (and a third wonderful goal for the club after long-range strikes at Hull and Sheffield Wednesday). And rampant Wolves carved Brentford open to double their lead just seconds later, with Cavaleiro playing across the box where a handful of team-mates were queueing up and Douglas unleashed a phenomenal right-footed shot which nearly broke the net.

Molineux certainly wasn't quiet now – in fact the atmosphere went through the roof as the bench celebrated wildly. Wolves' persistence had paid off. With Brentford having given up hope, the final minutes were just about a matter of how many Wolves could score. Cavaleiro had a stinging effort saved, Jota's effort was blocked and then Jota scored perhaps Wolves' scrappiest goal of the season, turning home after Brentford failed to clear a corner. The final minutes were a walk in the park with Bright Enobakhare and then Kortney Hause coming on, the latter for his first league appearance of the season. Wolves could have put a few sozzled lads from the South Bank in defence and they'd have still won. It was that easy.

NUNO

We had to change our attitude (at half-time) and we changed it. It was about getting the energy and the spirit of the team back, support each other and go and win the game. Keeping the shape was very important and then in the second half our talent came and we were able to get a good and deserved victory. What I saw in the first half was a team that controlled the game but we needed more energy. We must go for the game, we cannot have any attitude that wasn't a desire to win and go for it. It was a very important game for us, after this period of time, after what we did in Bristol, coming here and not closing the cycle of recent games well – we couldn't do that.

FAN VERDICT - RUSS EVERS

A class free-kick from a class player Ruben Neves opened the floodgates with Barry Douglas smashing in a right footer two minutes later. Diogo was lying on the floor as he completed the scoring to the delight of an expectant rather than boisterous Molineux. Fair play to the Steve Bull stand who got the ground rocking in the first half whilst Cavaleiro's introduction for a much-improved Costa proved to be the key to unlocking the Brentford defence. And to cap it all, Nuno dedicated the win to Mr Wolves, Foz Hendley. Class.

"THEY NOW HAVE 61 POINTS – THAT'S THREE MORE THAN LAST YEAR"

LINE UP

WOLVES (3-4-3):
RUDDY; BENNETT, COADY (C), BOLY (HAUSE, 83); DOHERTY, SAISS, NEVES, DOUGLAS; COSTA (CAVALEIRO, 53), BONATINI, JOTA (ENOBAKHARE, 81).

SUBS NOT USED: NORRIS, VINAGRE, N'DIAYE, GIBBS-WHITE.

BRENTFORD (4-2-3-1):
BENTLEY; YENNARIS, MEPHAM, BJELLAND, BARBET (CLARKE, 78); WOODS, MOKOTJO; WATKINS, SAWYERS, CANOS (JOZEFZOON, 64); VIBE (MAUPAY, 71).

SUBS NOT USED: DANIELS, MACLEOD, MCEACHRAN, MARCONDES.

STAR MAN

CONOR COADY
FOR ALL WOLVES' ATTACKING BRILLIANCE, IT'S THEIR ROCK-SOLID DEFENCE WHICH IS THE FOUNDATION ON WHICH THIS SEASON IS BEING BUILT AND COADY HAS BECOME MR DEPENDABLE. LOOKS INCREDIBLY ASSURED AND AT HOME IN THE CENTRAL CENTRE-HALF ROLE. SNIFFS DANGER OUT, IS ENDLESSLY COVERING AND INTERCEPTING. BEGINNING TO MAKE IT LOOK EASY AND HE VERY, VERY RARELY LOSES POSSESSION. ANOTHER EXCELLENT DISPLAY.

TABLE

	TEAM	P	GD	PTS
1	WOLVES	26	30	61
2	DERBY	26	18	49
3	CARDIFF	26	11	47
4	BRISTOL CITY	26	9	47
5	ASTON VILLA	26	14	44
6	LEEDS	26	9	43

WOLVES

SWANSEA

"I WANT TO APOLOGISE FOR THE RED CARD AND SPECIFY IT WASN'T MY INTENTION TO HURT THE PLAYER"

RUBEN VINAGRE

FA CUP R3: 06/01/18   ATTENDANCE: 22,976

It wasn't the result Wolves wanted, but otherwise you suspect Nuno Espírito Santo got almost everything he wanted from this game. A team that played in the 'Nuno way' despite six changes? Check. A number of promising individual performances? Check. Matching Premier League opposition for the third time this season? Check. There were several positives to take from what was an entertaining goalless draw between the teams ranked 21st and 20th in the English football pyramid at a healthily-stocked Molineux, which housed Wolves' second biggest FA Cup home attendance in the past 10 years (after the sell-out versus Chelsea last season).

And what this game did was prove, again, just how far Wolves have come in such a short space of time. Would their 'reserve' players in the past five or six years have essentially outclassed a Premier League side for long spells? They certainly edged this encounter against a Swansea side which featured several seasoned Premier League names including Wilfried Bony, Leroy Fer and wily wingers Nathan Dyer and Wayne Routledge. Wolves fielded a 17-year-old making his first appearance of the season, a 19-year-old who hadn't started a match since October and a central defender who'd played only 127 minutes in 2017/18.

There were six alterations from the team that had beaten Brentford 3-0 on Tuesday. In came Will Norris, Kortney Hause, Alfred N'Diaye, Morgan Gibbs-White, Ruben Vinagre and Bright Enobakhare. Hause was making his first league start of the season, while under-17 World Cup winner Gibbs-White made his first appearance of any kind in the campaign. There was no Jack Price in the squad, but new signing Rafa Mir was named on the bench.

It was Championship leaders Wolves who made by far the better start, taking the game to their Premier League opponents in the opening stages. The wing-backs were overloading down the flanks, Helder Costa and Enobakhare looked lively and Leo Bonatini was linking the play nicely. Chiefly though Gibbs-White was seriously impressing in the 'Neves' role. Confident and assured, the youngster was constantly demanding the ball, getting his head up and moving play on. He did so with a gorgeous chip in the opening minutes to find Costa, who drove dangerously across goal. The teenager was then presented with a glorious opportunity to score his first senior goal when Bonatini played him in, but, on his left foot, Gibbs-White shot too close to the keeper. Wolves were well on top with N'Diaye regularly winning the ball back in midfield. They were full of confidence while Swansea looked like a struggling team short on ideas.

Portuguese star Renato Sanches fired a dreadful effort into the stands, much to the joy of the South Bank who labelled him a "rubbish" Ruben Neves. Sanches actually injured himself in the process and had to be replaced. Wolves continued to press – Enobakhare had a great chance to break the deadlock but crashed wide from 10 yards after N'Diaye's header was blocked. And then the Swans began to get a foothold in the game, chiefly through set pieces. Norris remained untested but then, seven minutes before half-time, produced a quite stunning save to tip Martin Olsson's free-kick on to the bar, although bizarrely the referee gave a goal-kick.

Anthony Taylor was the man in the middle and two minutes later he made what most of Molineux thought was another bizarre decision which changed the game. Wing-back Vinagre went in hard on Nathan Dyer but there was shock when Taylor whipped out a red card.

The youngster was undoubtedly over-zealous but there seemed to be no malice involved – although replays showed it to be the correct call. Nuno and the home fans voiced their displeasure. Barry Douglas was called for, replacing the desperately unfortunate Gibbs-White, and that was half-time.

Wolves' formation was now quite fluid but essentially a 3-3-3, with N'Diaye on his own in central midfield and Enobakhare and Costa a little deeper in support of Bonatini. With Nuno's team doing anything but sit back despite their man disadvantage the game began to open up. Enobakhare shot wide from range, ignoring Costa's run, and Douglas fired a free-kick into the wall.

Then came two pivotal moments in the space of a minute. First Bony mis-kicked a free shot from 10 yards with arguably the chance of the game. Then referee Taylor was at it again with his strangest decision of the match. Leroy Fer tripped Costa as Wolves tried to break – it looked a yellow card all day long but Fer was oddly sent off with Taylor surely looking to even things up. The final stages were all about the new boy Mir, who after coming off the bench sent a deflected shot just wide, headed dangerously towards the top corner and then sent another header inches past the post although he was flagged offside. Swansea were the ones pressing in stoppage time but Carroll shot too close to Norris with the final chance of the game.

The only downsides were Vinagre's red card, which will mean a three-match suspension, and the fact Wolves now have to play another game – and not exactly one that's close to home. However their fringe players are proving more than capable of thriving in the Nunolution.

NUNO

We were the better team, but we are not frustrated – we are pleased with the performance. First of all, of the individual players that came in, of the first moments of the season for some players, young players who were dominant in the game, controlling the game, creating chances, being better than the opponent – you have to be pleased and proud. The creating part, the production of the team, the way we controlled the game, the way we break the opponent and totally dominate the game – this is what we should look at. I think we would naturally win the game (with 11 men) because we were better than them.

FAN VERDICT – RUSS EVERS

I love the FA Cup and probably my biggest football wish would be to see us lift the trophy at Wembley. Luckily, we are still in the hat for the fourth round, having been held by a Premier League side to a goalless draw meaning Will Norris still has not been beaten by a top flight player – or any player – this season. We should have won, having had several good chances to do so, but had to settle for a replay in the deep south of Wales. Bright Enobakhare should be kicking himself as he had the best opportunities but unfortunately failed – however, the dream is still alive. If the first team had started it could have been a rout. Let's hope we get a good draw and the incentive is there for the replay. Abide with me.

LINE UP

WOLVES (3-4-3):
NORRIS; BENNETT, COADY (C), HAUSE; DOHERTY, N'DIAYE, GIBBS-WHITE (DOUGLAS, 45), VINAGRE; COSTA, BONATINI (MIR, 77), ENOBAKHARE (CAVALEIRO, 64).

SUBS NOT USED: BURGOYNE, MIRANDA, RASMUSSEN, GONCALVES.

SWANSEA (5-4-1):
NORDFELDT; ROBERTS, BARTLEY, FERNANDEZ (C) (AYEW, 56), VAN DER HOORN, OLSSON; DYER, SANCHES (CARROLL, 34), FER, ROUTLEDGE; BONY (MESA, 74).

SUBS NOT USED: MULDER, FULTON, NARSINGH, MCBURNIE.

STAR MAN

MORGAN GIBBS-WHITE

GIBBS-WHITE SHOWED GLIMPSES OF HIS TALENT LAST SEASON BUT THIS WAS HIS FIRST COMPLETE PERFORMANCE. LOOKS TO HAVE GROWN IN CONFIDENCE AND STATURE AND THE CENTRAL MIDFIELD ROLE SUITED HIM. CONSTANTLY DEMANDED THE BALL AND GOT HIS HEAD UP TO EITHER SPRAY IT TO THE FLANKS, PLAY IT SHORT OR CHIP IT OVER THE TOP, AS HE BRILLIANTLY DID TO PICK OUT COSTA. SHOULD HAVE SCORED BUT ON HIS WEAKER FOOT HE SHOT TOO CLOSE TO THE KEEPER. MADE A COUPLE OF PIERCING RUNS INTO THE BOX. HIS FINEST OUTING IN A WOLVES SHIRT – IT WAS JUST A SHAME IT DIDN'T LAST LONGER.

BARNSLEY 0

WOLVES 0

CHAMPIONSHIP: 13/01/18   ATTENDANCE: 16,050

"IT'S GOING TO BE A RECURRING THEME NOW WHERE TEAMS ARE GOING TO TRY AND FRUSTRATE US"

JOHN RUDDY

How you viewed this one probably depends on your general disposition. Glass half-empty? You're most likely frustrated with a below-par Wolves performance and only a point against struggling opposition. Glass half-full? It's one point closer to the Premier League, Wolves kept yet another clean sheet and extended their unbeaten run – can't win 'em all, eh? In assessing the game itself the truth, as ever, lies somewhere in between. Yes, Wolves were nowhere near their best here and, yes, they should have seen off a limited if resolute Barnsley team. By their very high standards, Wolves had an off-day and uncharacteristically failed to muster a shot on target for the first time this season.

However, it should certainly be noted that the Tykes made life difficult for them. Paul Heckingbottom's team defended deep and defended hard. They restricted Wolves' space, particularly for Ruben Neves, whose influence was minimal. Rugged challenges were commonplace, the referee let a few go and the game quickly descended into a scrap. Indeed, the first half was a turgid, dreary, instantly-forgettable affair reminiscent of some of those truly dire 0-0 draws Wolves produced under Kenny Jackett a couple of seasons ago. When the fourth official signalled six minutes of stoppage time, 16,000 people wanted to throttle him – it was that bad. The second half continued in the same manner until a few substitutions and some tiring legs finally opened things up and we had a belated football match on our hands. For the third time in four matches, Ivan Cavaleiro came off the bench and was a big positive influence on Wolves' attacking play. Surely he starts against Nottingham Forest next weekend. New boy Rafa Mir also played his part with a committed, all-action cameo reminiscent of his debut

against Swansea. This was in complete contrast to the almost anonymous Leo Bonatini, who surely needs a break to recharge the batteries.

Nuno reverted to the team that had beaten Brentford 3-0, meaning six changes were made from last weekend's 0-0 FA Cup draw with Swansea. Almost 5,000 travelling fans roared Wolves on to the field and it was all set up for an entertaining encounter at Oakwell – however, the first half was as dreary as anything witnessed at a Wolves match this season. The visitors started well but the game soon became an ugly, scrappy affair with ponderous Wolves lacking imagination, tempo and ideas. Sure, Barnsley were organised, resolute and certainly not shy in putting a tackle in. But Wolves just weren't on it. Neves sent a dipping 20-yarder just over the bar in what was their best moment of the half as they failed to muster a shot on target. The newly-blond Romain Saiss stood out in midfield, not just for his new appearance but also for holding things together and producing a couple of excellent passes. But that was about it from Nuno's team.

Wolves were crying out for an increased tempo and the introduction of Cavaleiro, with the two going hand-in-hand of late. Nuno though waited until the 64th minute to send for him, with Helder Costa the man to depart. Things had improved at the start of the second half with an increased sense of purpose about Wolves' play but keeper Adam Davies remained untested. Wolves did have the ball in the net again via Diogo Jota but again he was flagged offside, while a teasing inswinging Barry Douglas corner just evaded Saiss and Ryan Bennett.

Bonatini horribly misjudged a close-range shot from the left, lofting it miles over, and that was his last action with recent signing Mir called for with 18 minutes to go. With the game opening

up there was then a real scare when Adam Hammill prodded inches wide from 10 yards before Jota, from nowhere, unleashed a 20-yard thunderbolt that almost broke the crossbar, but bounced to safety. It was the quality Wolves had been lacking and after this and two offside goals, despite a below par performances, Wolves were beginning to count themselves unfortunate. Cavaleiro had, again, made a difference from the bench and it was his ball across goal that created Wolves' chance of the match, where inexplicably the off-balance Jota diverted the ball over from about a yard out – and despite knocking at the Barnsley door for the last 10 minutes, it ended goalless.

With another 10 minutes they would most likely have won it – they certainly should have done through the again off-colour Jota whose miss summed up his recent struggles. With Mir and Cavaleiro pushing for starts, it may be that we see a shake-up of Nuno's tried and tested XI, particularly if further splurges are to be made in the transfer market before the month is over. In front of the watching Jorge Mendes (you hope he's a fan of pies and mushy peas) and Fosun boss Guo Guangchang, Wolves huffed and puffed – there was no lack of effort or application, but they couldn't blow the Barnsley door down. While the draw wasn't what Wolves came for and Nuno's team were below their best, there remain no signs or signals that any wheels are about to wobble. A few of their star players, particularly Jota and Bonatini, are perhaps fatigued but Wolves can still grind out a result, still keep a clean sheet and still remain unbeaten since the clocks went back. If they can come through the next six weeks unscathed, then the Premier League will be within touching distance.

NUNO

There is disappointment not because of the game but because of the result – that's the first sign of a team that wants to grow. Winning is a tough, tough thing to achieve and every game is very hard. Football will give you things as long as you work hard. Growing is that – being disappointed at not getting three points, disappointment of not celebrating with our fans the way we want to. We did a good game, it was a tough pitch to play, it's difficult to break Barnsley down they are well-organised. Let's go for the next one, well done boys. Neves came off because he couldn't run! It shows how much he left on the pitch with cramps, it's a sign he gave everything he had.

FAN VERDICT – HEATHER LARGE

It was a pretty average performance with not a lot to excite the huge crowd of travelling fans. While on paper we looked like the favourites to take three points, it just wasn't Wolves' day. We looked tired and a little lethargic in the first half, maybe it was a delayed side effect of the busy Christmas and New Year match schedule? We certainly lacked the pace and creativity going forward that we've come to expect from this side. We did at least improve after the break. It's another point in the right direction and a clean sheet away from home so certainly nothing to worry about. The top of the table is still looking pretty good!

STAR MAN

IVAN CAVALEIRO
THREE EXCELLENT CONTRIBUTIONS FROM THE BENCH IN HIS PAST FOUR SUB APPEARANCES. SEEMS THAT HE'S STILL NOT QUITE OVER A HEAVY KNOCK HE TOOK AT MILLWALL AWAY ON BOXING DAY, OTHERWISE THERE'S NO REASON NOT TO START THIS GUY. A PIERCING RUN DOWN THE BARNSLEY RIGHT WHEN HE SHOWED PACE AND STRENGTH BEFORE CROSSING FOR JOTA DESERVED AN ASSIST.

TABLE

	TEAM	P	GD	PTS
1	WOLVES	27	30	62
2	DERBY	27	21	52
3	CARDIFF	27	15	50
4	ASTON VILLA	27	15	47
5	BRISTOL CITY	27	8	47
6	SHEFF UTD	27	9	43

SWANSEA **2**
(AYEW 11, BONY 69)

WOLVES **1**
(JOTA 66)

"IF WE DON'T WIN FOR THREE MATCHES IN A ROW SOMETHING IS WRONG AND WE HAVE TO FIX IT"
DIOGO JOTA

Well, it had to happen sooner or later. Wolves were unbeaten since October, a run stretching to 14 matches in all competitions, but on a foul night in Swansea they finally came unstuck. They paid for a dreadfully poor start and, after an all-too brief rally following the introduction of Diogo Jota, were undone by something as rare as hen's teeth this season – a poor defensive error. Kortney Hause was the culprit, but he was by no means the only guilty party on a night when Wolves weren't, well, Wolves.

They certainly gave it their best shot (Matt Doherty, Barry Douglas, Romain Saiss, Diogo Jota and Leo Bonatini were all on the field at full-time) but circumstances combined to dump them out of the Cup. With a massive lead at the top of the Championship, a huge squad to choose from and an appetising tie at Notts County in round four, a Cup run was within Wolves' capabilities. It's a shame for the likes of Will Norris (finally beaten here after five successive clean sheets), Morgan Gibbs-White and Bright Enobakhare, as you wonder how often they'll feature in the coming months. However, Wolves can now, as

"WOLVES CAN NOW, AS THEY SAY, EXCLUSIVELY CONCENTRATE ON THE MAIN PRIZE"

they say, exclusively concentrate on the main prize. And that's what this season is all about.

Nuno handed a full debut to new signing Rafa Mir up front, while Danny Batth returned after suspension and Roderick Miranda made his first start since October 28 – the day of Wolves' last defeat in all competitions – at QPR. The head coach named a strong bench that included Jota, Ruben Neves and Bonatini. Swansea boss Carlos Carvalhal named a stronger XI than in the first game, with Alfie Mawson and Jordan Ayew brought into the side. And it paid early dividends for the Premier League side, with Ayew the scourge of Wolves in the early stages.

He twice went closing in the opening minutes, with Roderick Miranda superbly denying him on nine minutes. But two minutes later, not a single Wolves player – and a few had an opportunity – could stop Ayew as he danced past several challenges before beating Norris. It was a superb goal, but Nuno would chastise sluggish defending – and not for the last time in the half.

Wolves just couldn't get their foot on the ball, with a boggy, soaked pitch after two hours of teeming rain before kick-off not helping. Swansea matching their formation and pressing Wolves at every opportunity were other factors, but there were too many individual errors in what was a poor 45 minutes. None of the back three covered themselves in glory. Alfred N'Diaye regularly gifted possession away and Helder Costa – Wolves' only real outlet when they did finally get into the Swansea third – couldn't produce any magic.

Mir was left feeding off scraps, although Wolves did fashion a couple of good chances with N'Diaye and Enobakhare both seeing well-struck efforts blocked at point-blank range. Barry

Douglas's set-pieces were another weapon to use, but in general it was a half to forget for Nuno's side who would have been further behind were it not for the quick-thinking Norris, who dived at Connor Roberts' feet when he was played in by Bony. No doubt on the back of some stern half-time words, there was a renewed energy and drive about Wolves' play at the start of the second half. Within a couple of minutes, Mir held it up well for Costa, whose curler on the turn flashed over.

Talking of holding it up, the sodden pitch was making free-flowing football almost impossible as the rain continued to lash down in south Wales. Nuno called for both Jota and Bonatini, which drew a huge roar from the away end. Mir and Enobakhare were withdrawn and all of a sudden Wolves had some momentum about them. Within just two minutes, they were level. Miranda's gorgeous chip found Jota, who sent a sliding defender to Cardiff and then coolly beat the keeper with a sublime goal.

Suddenly it was all Wolves – they had the bit between their teeth and there only looked like one winner. Jota curled inches wide from 20 yards and there was a spring in everyone's step. This should have been their moment to take charge – but instead Wolves undid their own hard work. A regulation cross bounced off Hause who couldn't react in time to prevent Bony from sliding it home from six yards. The balloon had popped and Wolves were deflated. Hause in particular was struggling, with misplaced passes commonplace. Via the lively Jota, they had hope – he embarked on a superb run and his low shot was blocked, with Bonatini's rebound too close to the keeper. However, there was to be no equaliser or extra-time. Swansea – who were keeping the ball in the corner in the 87th minute – closed the game out and dumped Wolves out of the Cup. There haven't

been many nights to forget this season but were there to be one, Wolves and their supporters would rather it was in this competition. Their eyes are now exclusively focused on one thing only.

LINE UP

SWANSEA (3-4-3):
NORDFELDT; NAUGHTON, FERNANDEZ (C), MAWSON; ROBERTS, FER, MESA (SUNG-YUENG, 73), CARROLL; AYEW (DYER, 73), BONY (CLUCAS, 79), NARSINGH.

SUBS NOT USED: MULDER, BRITTON, BARTLEY, MCBURNIE.

WOLVES (3-4-3):
NORRIS; BATTH (C), MIRANDA, HAUSE; DOHERTY, N'DIAYE, GIBBS-WHITE, DOUGLAS; COSTA (SAISS, 73), MIR (BONATINI, 64), ENOBAKHARE (JOTA, 64).

SUBS NOT USED: BURGOYNE, BENNETT, COADY, NEVES.

STAR MAN

DIOGO JOTA
COMPLETELY CHANGED THE GAME WITH HIS POSITIVITY, HIS SKILL, HIS ENERGY AND HIS DIRECT APPROACH, MUCH AS CAVALEIRO HAS FROM THE BENCH IN RECENT WEEKS. IT'S BEEN A WHILE SINCE WE'VE SEEN JOTA IN FULL FLOW BUT HE WAS SPELLBINDING HERE WITH HIS SUPERBLY TAKEN GOAL AND ANOTHER COUPLE OF DAZZLING RUNS FROM DEEP. MORE OF THIS, PLEASE.

WOLVES ⓪

NOTTINGHAM FOREST ②
(DOWELL 40, OSBORN 43)

CHAMPIONSHIP: 20/01/18 ATTENDANCE: 29,050

"IT'S AN UNCHARACTERISTIC PERFORMANCE, WE WERE JUST SLOPPY WHICH ISN'T LIKE US"
CONOR COADY

Jordan Smith would have been expecting a busy afternoon. The Nottingham Forest keeper had let in 43 goals so far this season – only four teams have conceded more – and when faced with a trip to face the top-scoring league leaders, the 23-year-old probably thought he'd need to enjoy a stellar 90 minutes between the sticks if his team were to produce a shock result. Instead he had absolutely nothing to do.

That was just one of the surprising elements of this peculiar day at Molineux. An error-prone, off-colour performance which produced only five shots and resulted in a deserved 2-0 loss – this isn't the Wolves we know. Nuno Espírito Santo's all-conquering side have been excellent at bouncing back from defeats this season but the reaction the head coach requested after the FA Cup reverse to Swansea just wasn't forthcoming. His team were flawed all over the park. Creativity was lacking, imagination was in short supply, even basic passes were beyond them at times in what was a disconcertingly mediocre display.

Throwing attackers at the problem didn't produce a solution. In fact, even Nuno had an off day here, withdrawing his wing-backs at half-time when the formation didn't seem to be the problem. The 'all out attack' approach changed little.

Ivan Cavaleiro got the nod over Helder Costa for his first start since the 2-2 draw at Millwall on Boxing Day, while Leo Bonatini was preferred to Rafa Mir up front. Diogo Jota, who was lively from the bench at Swansea in midweek, took Bonatini's smart pass and cut inside before curling a beautiful effort inches past the post with nine minutes on the clock. It should have set the tone for the rest of the half, but instead Wolves were sluggish and sloppy in possession and barely offered a goal threat. Ruben Neves

seemed to be the only one playing, particularly with some searching passes which found Matt Doherty with pinpoint accuracy. Elsewhere Wolves were pretty anonymous.

Forest certainly weren't shy in letting Wolves know they were in a game, earning two very deserved bookings for crunching fouls on Cavaleiro and Jota as they became the latest team to target Wolves' flair players. It seemed to work because Wolves went into their shells and the visitors gradually got a foothold in the game. By the time they took the lead they had already twice gone close, with Doherty heading inches wide of his own post and then Osborn flicked up a free-kick and volley marginally off target via a deflection.

That led to a corner and, from that, Forest broke the deadlock on 40 minutes with Dowell's effort taking a wicked deflection and wrong-footing Ruddy. Three minutes later it was 2-0. There was no fortune about this strike though – a 15-yard curler into the top corner from Osborn which sent the visiting fans into raptures and the rest of Molineux into shellshock. It was only the second time Wolves had fallen behind at home all season, with the first occasion being during their only home defeat, to Cardiff.

Something needed to change at half-time but no-one was expecting to see both Barry Douglas and Doherty withdrawn. Costa and Morgan Gibbs-White were introduced as Nuno, in what could moderately be described as a bold move, went for the hitherto unseen 3-2-3-2 formation with Cavaleiro and the two subs playing behind Jota and Bonatini. With 15 minutes to go Wolves still hadn't meaningfully tested keeper Jordan Smith in the entire game.

Mental or physical fatigue? Are teams working them out? Just an off day? You can't call it the

latter as two poor performances had preceded this. In fact Wolves haven't really looked themselves since the late November thrashings of Bolton and Leeds.

In December, a granite-like defence and some occasional magic at the other end saw them grind out results when not at their best, like all promotion-winning teams do. The past seven games have seen a drop in standards. Two wins, three draws and two defeats is their worst run of the campaign by a distance, so an excursion to sunny Spain for a week of training, rest, recuperation and a few rays (current Marbella temperature, 20C) feels like good timing.

Mick McCarthy enlisted a similar tactic in Wolves' 2008/09 season and, while a few days of sunshine won't exactly get them acclimatised for a muck and nettles trip to face McCarthy's Ipswich at cold Portman Road next Saturday, Nuno will hope it presses the reset button for a few of his underperforming players, chiefly his forwards.

Wolves have scored one goal in their past four matches – or 11 in the last 11. Leo Bonatini hasn't netted since December 4 (10 appearances and counting), Jota isn't hitting the (very high) heights of the first four months of the season, Cavaleiro has been their best outlet of late but was poor here, Mir is still adjusting to his new life in England and Costa's end product was, again, sorely lacking against Forest.

Nuno's charges have set extremely high standards this season and, while their lead is a very healthy nine points, they do need to return to something resembling those levels in the next couple of weeks if they're not to become a realistic target for Derby, Cardiff, Villa and Co to catch. There are issues to address but, as he has done all season, you'd back Nuno to promptly find them.

NUNO

I'm responsible, maybe for not telling the boys that there's still a long way to go and nobody can relax here. So it's me first – it was my responsibility first of all, because the way the team plays is the way I want them to play. We must improve and we have to bounce back from this immediately. There's still a long way to go, Ipswich are the next opponent. Teams are trying to adapt themselves (to play Wolves), sometimes they succeed and sometimes they don't. Congratulations to Nottingham but they achieved two goals when we were the better side. This is football, sometimes it happens to you and sometimes the other team.

FAN VERDICT – HEATHER LARGE

It was disappointing that we failed to take advantage of the opportunity to extend our lead but hardly a disaster when you consider it was our first league loss since October. Every side goes through a rough patch in form at some point and it seems we've reached that stage of the season. Hopefully it's just a blip and Nuno has a plan to help us bounce back from the last few lacklustre performances. And at least there is still time to do something about it and bring in new blood to give us other options going forward which is where we've been lacking a bit of spark in recent matches. Nuno, over to you!

LINE UP

WOLVES (3-4-3):
RUDDY; BENNETT, COADY (C), BOLY; DOHERTY
(GIBBS-WHITE, 45), SAISS, NEVES (MIR, 79), DOUGLAS (COSTA, 45);
CAVALEIRO, BONATINI, JOTA.

SUBS NOT USED: NORRIS, BATTH, MIRANDA, N'DIAYE.

NOTTINGHAM FOREST (4-1-4-1):
SMITH; LICHAJ, WORRALL, MANCIENNE, FOX; BOUCHALAKIS;
CASH, BRIDCUTT (CLOUGH, 69), OSBORN, DOWELL (DARIKWA, 83);
BRERETON.

SUBS NOT USED: HENDERSON, MILLS, TRAORE, CARAYOL, VELLIOS.

STAR MAN

MORGAN GIBBS-WHITE
INJECTED POSITIVITY AND SOME INITIATIVE, LOOKING TO BURST
FORWARD FROM MIDFIELD. GIBBS-WHITE HAS GUMPTION AND
A FANTASTIC ATTITUDE TO PLAYING THE GAME. HIS STYLE ISN'T
A NATURAL FIT IN NUNO'S TEAM BUT HE OFFERS SOMETHING
DIFFERENT FROM THE BENCH AND COULD SEE PLENTY OF GAME
TIME IN THE COMING WEEKS ON THIS DISPLAY.

TABLE

	TEAM	P	GD	PTS
1	WOLVES	28	28	62
2	DERBY	28	21	53
3	CARDIFF	28	15	51
4	ASTON VILLA	28	17	50
5	BRISTOL CITY	28	8	48
6	SHEFF UTD	28	10	46

IPSWICH — 0

WOLVES — 1
(DOHERTY 15)

CHAMPIONSHIP: 27/01/18   ATTENDANCE: 15,971

It's amazing what a bit of vitamin D can do for you. If ever you're stuck in a rut at work, a week in Marbella should be your doctor's prescription. And what a difference a week makes. Against Nottingham Forest, Wolves couldn't pass water – six days in the sun later, they produced one of their best performances of the campaign at what felt like a very opportune moment.

The scoreline seriously flattered Ipswich. Nuno Espírito Santo's team could have run out three or four-goal winners and not even Mr Blunderbuss himself Mick McCarthy, who'd quibble over what time the sun should rise every morning, couldn't have complained. Wolves jetted off to Marbella with their tail between their legs and duly returned refreshed, reformed and looking like their old selves. They should fly to Spain every week. With their passing crisp, their movement dynamic and their creative juices flowing, this was much more like the Wolves who've had their fans calling this the best team they've seen for decades.

It was reminiscent of another dominant display not so far away in Norwich. Then, as here, Wolves faced a tough week away on the back of a defeat. And then, as here, Alfred N'Diaye was a dominant force in central midfield, breaking up play and setting Wolves on the attack with

"THEY CARVED THE TRACTOR BOYS OPEN"

impressive regularity. After their Carrow Road win, Wolves embarked on a 13-game unbeaten streak. If they do that again now – well, put simply, promotion will be theirs.

They were organised at the back and devastating on the break – in all but the finishing touch, which was the only thing lacking here with Diogo Jota, Helder Costa and Leo Bonatini all spurning opportunities or finding man-of-the-match Bartosz Bialkowski in inspired form between the Ipswich posts. On a number of occasions they carved the Tractor Boys open, only for either the killer final pass or clinical finishing to let them down. Ipswich threatened sporadically at the other end, but really this should have ended as a comfortable victory. All that ultimately mattered though, after their worst run of the season, was getting back to winning ways.

Nuno made two changes from the team that lost 2-0 to Nottingham Forest last week. Bonatini dropped to the bench and Romain Saiss wasn't involved in the squad due to a slight hamstring strain, with Costa and N'Diaye coming into the XI. Conditions weren't ideal at Portman Road – torrential rain was making an already soft pitch difficult to play on and, after a poor showing in similar circumstances at Swansea, you wondered how they'd cope, but Wolves soon adapted and made the better start.

Ipswich tested John Ruddy with a couple of half-decent efforts but it was confident Wolves who took an early lead in the 15th minute. N'Diaye made a bursting run into the box and cutely passed to the overlapping Barry Douglas, whose lifted cross was headed down and into the net by Matt Doherty. After two defeats, it was just what Wolves needed and they looked likely to add to their lead. Douglas's 20-yard free-kick was well saved low to his left by

Bialkowski before the keeper made another solid stop to keep out a well-struck Jota shot.

Cavaleiro set up Costa but he couldn't dink over the onrushing keeper from a tight angle on the right as Wolves pushed for a killer goal in the second half. Martyn Waghorn then fired into the side netting as Ipswich again reminded Wolves that the game was far from won. Nuno called for Bonatini and he almost made an instant impact when crashing a first-time volley goalwards from a Douglas cross, but it was blocked.

The impressive Bialkowski then superbly saved from the Brazilian striker, pushing away his powerful shot from the right of the box. Bialkowski saved Ipswich again a minute later, palming substitute Bright Enobakhare's 18-yard volley to safety as the spurned Wolves opportunities piled up. They should have been out of sight and had to endure a nervy final few minutes with Grant Ward shanking a volley from close range, but Nuno's team saw it through and their fans defiantly sang "we shall not be moved" as the full-time celebrations ensued,

Credit to Nuno for switching them back on after what appears to have been a thoroughly productive distraction-free week away. While there were plenty of pictures or videos posted on social media of the players lounging poolside, playing golf, paintballing or even having a selfie with Tyson Fury, this was no jolly in the Spanish sun. By all accounts, their training sessions were every bit as intense and focused as their usual ones at Compton Park, with a strong focus on shape and organisation. The reset button was hit – they returned to playing to their strengths.

They lead by 12 and who would bet against them finishing the job from here? Just what the Doc ordered. Crisis? What crisis?

NUNO

It wasn't comfortable. We had organisation, shape, hard work and focus. That's what is important for us. The Ipswich goalkeeper was one of the best players on the pitch – that says a lot. We created a lot and it could have been a different score. Keep building, keep creating and naturally things will come. It was a good week (in Marbella) and it was planned long ago. We have a plan and we stick with our plan. We said to ourselves it was a good moment to go and a good moment to work. We worked really hard – it was not about going there and just sitting in the sun. A word for our fantastic fans, they came a long way to support us and in the end they celebrated with us.

FAN VERDICT – CHRIS HUGHES

Don't let the 1-0 scoreline fool you, this was a game we probably should, have won much more comfortably. The pace and movement of Diogo Jota, Helder Costa and Ivan Cavaleiro in attack caused Ipswich all sorts of problems as they created space for themselves and others throughout the game while also applying pressure in a high-pressing game that forced Ipswich into making errors. There was more energy and a higher tempo than against Forest last Saturday and it made Nuno's decision to take the squad to Marbella for a week look like a masterstroke.

LINE UP

IPSWICH TOWN (4-2-3-1):
BIALKOWSKI; SPENCE, CHAMBERS (C), CARTER-VICKERS, KNUDSEN; GLEESON (HYAM, 83), CONNOLLY; CELINA, WAGHORN, MCGOLDRICK (SEARS, 83); GARNER (WARD, 83).

SUBS NOT USED: CROWE, WEBSTER, BRU, KENLOCK.

WOLVES (3-4-3):
RUDDY; BENNETT, COADY (C), BOLY; DOHERTY, NEVES, N'DIAYE, DOUGLAS; COSTA (ENOBAKHARE, 78), CAVALEIRO (BONATINI, 71), JOTA.

SUBS NOT USED: NORRIS, BATTH, MIRANDA, VINAGRE, GIBBS-WHITE.

STAR MAN

ALFRED N'DIAYE

THE FACT N'DIAYE WAS ONLY MAKING HIS FIFTH CHAMPIONSHIP START OF THE SEASON IS THE BEST EXAMPLE YOU'LL FIND FOR JUST HOW GOOD WOLVES' STRENGTH IN DEPTH IS. WOULD SURELY WALK INTO MOST, IF NOT ALL, OTHER TEAMS IN THE LEAGUE. IT'S BEEN DIFFICULT FOR HIM TO MAKE AN IMPRESSION OFF THE BENCH, ONLY GETTING FIVE OR 10 MINUTES HERE AND THERE, BUT HE TOOK FULL ADVANTAGE OF ROMAIN SAISS'S HAMSTRING STRAIN WITH AN EXCELLENT PERFORMANCE FULL OF PHYSICALITY, DRIVING RUNS FROM MIDFIELD (ONE OF WHICH LED TO THE GOAL) AND A DECENT PASSING RANGE, WHICH HASN'T ALWAYS BEEN THE CASE WITH N'DIAYE. HAS DONE ENOUGH TO START AGAINST SHEFFIELD UNITED NEXT WEEKEND.

TABLE

	TEAM	P	GD	PTS
1	WOLVES	29	29	65
2	DERBY	28	21	53
3	CARDIFF	28	15	51
4	BRISTOL CITY	29	10	51
5	ASTON VILLA	28	17	50
6	FULHAM	29	14	48

WOLVES
(NEVES 5, JOTA 30, CAVALEIRO 76)

SHEFFIELD UNITED

CHAMPIONSHIP: 03/02/18   ATTENDANCE: 29,311

"WE HAVE TO KEEP AT IT FOR 16 GAMES AND PLAY EVERY ONE LIKE IT'S A FINAL"
ALFRED N'DIAYE

In years to come, people will be able to say 'I watched Wolves in 2017/18'. Yes, we're at that stage now. No more pussyfooting around the subject, no more downplaying how good this team is, or questioning whether there's the slightest chance they won't go up. In terms of technical ability, style and panache, this is one of the greatest football teams ever produced by Wolverhampton Wanderers. And they will be playing in the Premier League next year. With 16 games to go, they need to win just half of those to reach 92 points. No team has ever failed to win automatic promotion with such a total (Sunderland finished third in 1998 with 90) and it's unthinkable to imagine Wolves won't win eight more matches from here.

It's not just the exquisite football they play and their ability to rip a team apart piece by piece. It's not just the fact they're incredibly hard to play against and have kept 17 clean sheets in 30 matches. It's not just the fact they have in their midst a gifted head coach whose attention to detail, man-management and tactical prowess is second to none. It's all those things and so much more. Wolves are just too good for this league. And after a ropey few weeks – by their high standards – they've returned to top form. It's an ominous sign for the chasing pack, who will soon give up hope of catching Wolves if they haven't already.

This was a demolition job of the highest order in which Nuno Espírito Santo's team found fifth gear and looked unstoppable. When they're in this mood there's probably only a fairly small number of teams in the country who are better to watch – Wolves are that good. Their desire, their will to win, their lust for goals – it's all relentless. And my how Molineux lapped up this victory. A packed house was treated to a show of high quality passing, movement, pace, creativity and skill from a team at the top of its game – and the fans duly responded with incessant noise.

The loudest cheer of the game was reserved for a player who is a window into Wolves' past, Benik Afobe, when he replaced Ivan Cavaleiro with 13 minutes left. Afobe, who almost scored to put the icing on this delicious cake, may or may not be part of Wolves' future long-term, but if the likes of Ruben Neves, Diogo Jota and Ivan Cavaleiro are, it's almost scary to think where Wolves could end up. It must be stated again just how important the week-long trip to Marbella has already proved to be; Wolves left for Spain jaded and returned refreshed and revitalised, producing two of the best performances of the season in successive weeks.

Nuno kept faith with the team that had won 1-0 at Ipswich a week earlier meaning 'new boy' Afobe had to settle for a place on the bench. Sheffield United had three ex-Wolves players in their team – Richard Stearman, Lee Evans and captain Leon Clarke, who scored both goals when the Blades beat Wolves 2-0 back in September. They are one of only four teams to have beaten Wolves in the league this season – but there was to be no repeat here. Instead, Wolves demolished Chris Wilder's team in a first-half display as good as anything they've produced this season – which is saying plenty. Nuno's team simply oozed class, confidence and skill. Some of the football they played looked out of place in a Championship encounter – it belonged at a much higher level. The trickery, the pace, the touches, the movement and the sheer audacity of some of the ridiculous skill they put on show was almost beyond belief. You almost felt sorry for Sheffield United.

The fun started just five minutes in when Neves picked his spot from 25 yards – and that spot was the very top corner, with the ball kissing the post on the way in. The noise Molineux produced was one you only normally hear after the watershed. The half-time scoreline of 2-0 was flattering to the Blades – Wolves toyed with them at times. If Neves's goal was a magnificent individual effort, the second strike was the product of a wonderful team move involving Helder Costa, Jota, Cavaleiro and Matt Doherty who sliced through the Blades before Jota played a one-two with Cavaleiro and beat the keeper.

Costa volleyed wide, Willy Boly headed over and a three-on-one break ended in controversy when Costa was bundled over but the referee was unmoved. There was no change in personnel at half-time but the tempo and urgency wasn't quite there at the start of the second half as Wolves took it down a notch and the visitors began to enjoy more of the ball although they weren't troubling Wolves where it mattered.

Leo Bonatini, currently enduring a goal drought that stretches back to December 4, fired just wide shortly after replacing Costa as Wolves threatened to extend their lead and kill the game. They did so with 14 minutes on the clock after the Blades gave them a helping hand – keeper Moore was sent off for clattering Jota outside the box with a dangerously high challenge and from the 20-yard free-kick Cavaleiro's effort deflected off the wall and wrong-footed sub keeper Jake Eastwood, whose first action was to pick the ball out of the net.

That was Cavaleiro's last action as he was withdrawn for Afobe, who received a hero's ovation as he made his second Wolves debut. He so very nearly crowned it with a goal, heading Doherty's perfect cross just inches past the post. That was that for the goalmouth action, with the final few minutes played out with ease.

NUNO

The early Neves goal changes everything. It was a fantastic goal, and the second one was really good as well. Our fans are happy because they've seen really good football and really good goals from a team that fights and works hard. It was a very good performance from the boys, in all aspects of the game – defensively, offensively, with and without the ball. We knew it would be a tough challenge against a team that beat us in the reverse fixture, but we prepared well and were well organised and played some good football.

FAN VERDICT – ADAM VIRGO

Back to our best for sure. Last week at Ipswich we played well but this was a notch up and definitely one of our best performances this season. Sheffield United couldn't get close to us all evening, we were miles better in every department and it shows the class we have throughout. The first two goals were brilliant in their own way, we can score all types of goals and that's what you need to win games. To think it felt like a chore in the last two seasons to watch us at home but now it's the complete opposite and you can't wait for the next game. I think I'm running out of adjectives to describe Ruben Neves' ability.

It's a privilege to watch this Wolves side and at this rate the final three months of the season will be a procession. Wolves have answered all the questions put to them this season. The only one left is how soon will promotion be confirmed?

LINE UP

WOLVES (3-4-3):
RUDDY; BENNETT, COADY (C), BOLY; DOHERTY, NEVES, N'DIAYE, DOUGLAS; COSTA (BONATINI, 65), JOTA (GIBBS-WHITE, 81), CAVALEIRO (AFOBE, 77).

SUBS NOT USED: NORRIS, BATTH, HAUSE, ENOBAKHARE.

SHEFFIELD UNITED (4-3-3):
MOORE; BALDOCK, O'CONNELL, STEARMAN, STEVENS; BASHAM (LEONARD, 71), EVANS, FLECK; WILSON (EASTWOOD, 75), CLARKE, HOLMES (DONALDSON, 71).

SUBS NOT USED: LUNDSTRAM, SHARP, DUFFY, LAFFERTY.

STAR MAN

RUBEN NEVES

THE YEAR IS 2068. A WIDE-EYED YOUNG SCAMP IS OBSESSED WITH 10-TIME CHAMPIONS LEAGUE WINNERS WOLVES AND KEEN TO LEARN MORE ABOUT THEIR RICH HISTORY FROM HIS GRANDAD, ESPECIALLY WHICH PLAYERS LAUNCHED THEM INTO FOOTBALL FOLKLORE. "GRANDAD, GRANDAD," HE EXCITEDLY ASKS, "DID YOU ACTUALLY SEE RUBEN NEVES PLAY?!". "SIT DOWN LAD, HAVE I GOT SOME STORIES FOR YOU," THE PROUD OLD MAN BEGINS. "I'LL NEVER FORGET WHEN WE BEAT SHEFFIELD UNITED 3-0 AND HE STUCK ONE IN THE TOP CORNER FROM 25 YARDS, OH HE WAS BRILLIANT THAT DAY, THEY COULDN'T GET ANYWHERE NEAR HIM – THE THINGS THAT MAN COULD DO WITH A FOOTBALL, HE WAS AN ARTIST".

TABLE

	TEAM	P	GD	PTS
1	**WOLVES**	30	32	68
2	DERBY	30	24	57
3	ASTON VILLA	30	19	56
4	CARDIFF	29	18	54
5	FULHAM	30	16	51
6	BRISTOL CITY	30	9	51

WOLVES **2**
(N'DIAYE 12, COSTA 21)

QUEENS PARK RANGERS **1**
(WASHINGTON 51)

CHAMPIONSHIP: 10/02/18   ATTENDANCE: 30,168

"WE WERE OUTSTANDING IN THE FIRST HALF – WE MOVED THE BALL AND SCORED TWO FANTASTIC GOALS"
CONOR COADY

Wolves have come up against some excellent players in the Championship this season; the likes of Bobby Reid, Britt Assombalonga, Matej Vydra and Albert Adomah have run many opposition defences ragged. Yet it's an unfashionable 28-year-old Brummie who used to turn out for Droylsden and Solihull Moors who's arguably caused Wolves more problems than any other player. Matt Smith, a 6ft 6in journeyman striker who's netted 61 goals in his 243-game professional career, hasn't even started the two games he's played against Wolves this season. Yet on both occasions he's come off the bench to change the game in QPR's favour.

Back in October, he earned them three points when heading a late winner after giving Roderick Miranda a torrid time, to the extent that Miranda hasn't been seen in the league for Wolves ever since. Here, he entered the fray at half-time with the visitors 2-0 down and immediately set about unsettling all three of Wolves' centre-halves. It worked. Willy Boly's a man mountain of a defender who is too good for the Championship but he, in football's equivalent of suave sophisticated Cat in Red Dwarf transforming into jabbering geek Dwayne Dibley, lost all his composure in what became a frantic second half. It was all far more nervy than it needed to be.

Yet ultimately, as so often this season, all that mattered was that Wolves won. Again. They have

accrued the most important of habits – winning football matches and that seems almost second nature to them now. And despite the second half wobbles it shouldn't be forgotten that Wolves' attacking play was magnificent for spells of this open, entertaining clash.

Nuno's team had an air of unbridled confidence in a first-half display that threatened to blow QPR away. Despite being the league's top scorers, Wolves have hardly dished out any thrashings this season, yet at 2-0 with 21 minutes on the clock and with Wolves producing some devastatingly devilish football a massacre looked on the cards. The stunning, delicious, intricate passing and moving that characterised last week's win over Sheffield United was back, with the dynamic Portuguese triumvirate of Diogo Jota, Helder Costa and Ivan Cavaleiro having a metaphorical party.

It was the same XI who had beaten Sheffield United with Alfred N'Diaye playing in the continued absence of Romain Saiss – and the first 12 minutes were all about the Senegal international. The midfielder made a sloppy start to the game, conceding possession carelessly including one slack pass which let Conor Washington in for one of two good early chances for the striker. Wolves hadn't really got out of the blocks – but then thanks to N'Diaye they soon took control. Cavaleiro crossed from the left and N'Diaye, making a late dart into the box, turned home from close range.

On 21 minutes they doubled their advantage when one of many free-flowing moves saw Cavaleiro play a one-two with Jota and then played in Costa, who couldn't miss his open goal, to score his first from open play since returning from injury last September. The fearsome Portuguese trio up front were purring, ably supported by a team at the top of its game.

All was well in Wolves' world. It seemed only a matter of how many goals they would score, or how much fun the 30,000 crowd would have. Cue beanpole striker Smith. As at Loftus Road, his introduction caused Wolves no end of problems and they began to look, for one of just a few occasions this season, vulnerable. A two-goal lead was halved when Ruddy saved the striker's header from a corner but could do nothing to block the follow-up – a spectacular overhead kick from Washington which flew into the roof of the net. Ruddy was forced to make important saves and Ryan Bennett made one of the tackles of the season to deny that man Smith from a low cross.

With 10 minutes to go the contest was finely poised. Two subs combined nicely when Benik Afobe headed Morgan Gibbs-White's cross not far wide. And then came Afobe's big moment – a superb opportunity from six yards out from Jota's cross – but he turned it wide. Wolves looked to be back in the ascendancy but they had to endure a late wobble. Ruddy saved from Washington, who was through on goal, and Eberechi Eze's follow-up was cleared off the line by Conor Coady, doing what he does best. Cue a big sigh of relief at full-time. Not every week will be the same – Wolves have won games in all manner of ways this season – but a 12-point lead is all that matters. It was another three points on their way to what will surely be the Premier League – where Nuno will pray they don't have to face Matt Smith again.

"WINNING SEEMS ALMOST SECOND NATURE TO THEM NOW"

NUNO

It was a tough win but a good win, a good result. I think we deserved it – we created a lot of chances and it was good work from the boys. We battled. Sometimes you have to attack, sometimes you have to defend and we defended well. They're a tough team to defend against, long balls, big guys, so I'm happy for the win. The support of our fans was fantastic through the game, thanks to them for that. They were direct, second balls, the goal came early. We should take time to settle down and be more compact. It was Coady this time, before it was another one and it will be another one (again). It's a team effort.

FAN VERDICT – NATALIE WOOD

We made it more difficult than it needed to be but not every game is going to be a walkover. QPR played some great stuff at times and really gave us a good game. First half we produced some of our best football of the season. Ruben Neves, Helder Costa and Ivan Cavaleiro just looked a class above, running rings around QPR for fun. I spent most of the first half wondering how many we would score and really we should have been 3-0 or even 4-0 up. We looked unstoppable. Second half saw the arrival of Matt Smith and the chaos ensued! We were suddenly on edge making silly mistakes and unable to deal with the QPR onslaught. A couple of great saves from John Ruddy and heroic off the line blocks from Ryan Bennett and Conor Coady saved our blushes.

LINE UP

WOLVES (3-4-3):
RUDDY; BENNETT, COADY (C), BOLY; DOHERTY, N'DIAYE, SAISS, DOUGLAS; COSTA (GIBBS-WHITE, 77), JOTA, CAVALEIRO (AFOBE, 64).

SUBS NOT USED: NORRIS, BATTH, MIRANDA, VINAGRE, MIR.

QPR (5-3-2):
SMITHIES; ROBINSON, PERCH (EZE, 42), ONUOHA, LYNCH, BIDWELL; WSZOLEK, FREEMAN, COUSINS (SMITH, 45); SCOWEN, WASHINGTON.

SUBS NOT USED: INGRAM, BAPTISTE, CHAIR, OSAYI-SAMUEL, OTEH.

STAR MAN

CONOR COADY
YOU'D WANT THIS GUY ON THE BATTLEFIELD WITH YOU. REVELS IN THE BACKS-TO-THE-WALL SITUATION THAT WOLVES FOUND THEMSELVES IN AT TIMES DURING THE SECOND HALF. A SUCCESSION OF IMPORTANT INTERCEPTIONS AND CLEARANCES AND THEN HE SAVED WOLVES TWO POINTS WHEN CLEARING OFF THE LINE IN THE LAST MINUTE. NOT THE FIRST TIME HE'S DONE THAT EITHER.

TABLE

	TEAM	P	GD	PTS
1	WOLVES	31	33	71
2	DERBY	31	24	58
3	ASTON VILLA	30	19	56
4	CARDIFF	30	18	55
5	FULHAM	31	16	52
6	BRISTOL CITY	31	9	52

PRESTON NORTH END ①
(BROWNE 52)

WOLVES ①
(COSTA 61)

CHAMPIONSHIP: 17/02/18   ATTENDANCE: 18,570

If Wolves are to reach the promised land this season, they won't miss games like this. Blood and thunder, muck and nettles, call it what you like – this was about as typical a Championship encounter as you could imagine. Tough tackling? Yep. No quarter given? Of course. Partisan home crowd? Absolutely. Dodgy pitch? Well, yes. In fact this was reminiscent of a recent Wolves visit to Deepdale. In 2015, they launched wave after wave of attacks at the Preston goal in the second half after the hosts had been reduced to 10 men (and then nine men) but all they had to show for their efforts was a 1-1 draw. On this occasion it wasn't quite The Alamo, but it was certainly one-way traffic after John Welsh had been sent off on the hour mark.

When Helder Costa equalised just two minutes later, that should have been the signal for an avalanche of attacks. Instead, Wolves looked strangely subdued. Benik Afobe replaced Alfred N'Diaye as Nuno Espírito Santo went for the kill, but instead of overloading Preston with attacking talent, Wolves were a little disjointed and, with Preston slowing proceedings down at every opportunity, couldn't garner any momentum. That little bit of magic, or that piercing final ball, or that perfect long-range shot (Ruben Neves attempted plenty) was lacking. So on what was a really tough afternoon, a point was a fair result. Nuno named the same team for the fourth game in a row, meaning the fit-again Romain Saiss and Leo Bonatini had to settle for places on a strong bench that also included Benik Afobe. Wolves

were given a game-and-a-half by Preston back in October when they edged a feisty encounter 3-2 and there was again little to separate the sides during a full-blooded first half at Deepdale. A bobbly pitch didn't help Wolves in terms of their free-flowing passing game but other than a few half chances they rarely threatened to exert their authority. Diogo Jota and Ivan Cavaleiro looked the most likely to conjure some magic in and around the box but often found an organised and resolute defence in their way.

Neves went closest with what would have been a bona fide goal of the season contender – he unleashed a 25-yard thunderbolt on the half-volley that would have broken the crossbar had it been a yard lower. At the other end, John Ruddy's work was restricted to pawing away deep crosses with a mini Preston aerial bombardment finding Wolves at their most uncomfortable. Defences were on top and there was no quarter given in midfield with a number of tasty challenges in what could be termed a typical half of Championship football.

In the first 10 minutes of the second half, Preston hit a post through Alan Browne, whistled one just over the bar through Darnell Fisher – and then took the lead through Browne, who got on the end of Robinson's floated corner to the back stick where he sent a free header past Ruddy. It was a deserved lead and the game was Preston's for the taking – they were 1-0 up with the wind in their sails. Defeat for Wolves looked likely at this juncture but after a bugbear of an inability

to defend set-pieces cost them, they had a hand from an old favour in the form of an opposition red card. John Welsh, who had crunched through Jota shortly before half-time with a late and crude challenge, pegged back Cavaleiro as the forward tried to break and was duly handed a deserved second booking. Ten players have been sent off against Wolves this season and Welsh could have no complaints.

Immediately the pendulum swung Wolves' way and, only two minutes later, they took advantage through the in-form Costa who, after taking 24 appearances to notch his first goal from open play this season, netted another in his 25th. He was teed up by the imperious Cavaleiro for his third assist in two matches. There were legitimate doubts raised over Cavaleiro's attitude last season and his £7million fee (a club record at the time) certainly wasn't justified. That's all changed now. The 24-year-old is, on his day, arguably Wolves' most potent and creative attacking force. Cavaleiro's problem has always been consistency but 'his day' now happens more often than not and he now tops the Championship assist table with 10 (one ahead of Barry Douglas). With some tough love at the start of the season (remember when he was held back in favour of Bright Enobakhare in the opening weeks?) Nuno has got the forward in the right mindset. Cavaleiro has thrived and looks to be loving his football.

After that equaliser, Benik Afobe was immediately sent into the fray for N'Diaye as Nuno went for the kill. However, little changed in an almost incident-free ending. In fact they only created one meaningful chance of note – Doherty fed Afobe, who was in a great position, but keeper Declan Rudd came out to block his shot. So Wolves had to settle for a point, but it felt like a point closer to promotion rather than

NUNO

Everybody knew Preston, their form (one defeat in 16) says a lot. We have to give credit to them. After the red card they dropped and defended well. The boys, everybody thought we were closest to winning the game. Playing against one man less requires a different approach. I'm not happy with the result, we prepare every game to win. I'm very proud of the attitude of the team and the work of the boys. We were relentless – this is the word, relentless. This is how we have to be every game. A word for the fans, they were incredible. We came to win but for the boys seeing them was very important.

FAN VERDICT – ROB CARTWRIGHT

This was your typical Championship 'blood and guts' style match. Plenty of hard and late challenges, but nothing to get too upset about. I wouldn't have changed formation, as we were so on top. Afobe didn't really make an impact in his half-hour. A little frustrating, though I feel this will turn out to be a big point gained. Ivan Cavaleiro is having his best run in the team and deserves his starting place. Helder Costa is looking better with every game he plays.

two dropped. Tough tests lie ahead in the form of away matches at Fulham, Villa and Cardiff. If Wolves are unbeaten through those, they will be within touching distance of their ultimate goal.

"SO ON WHAT WAS A REALLY TOUGH AFTERNOON, A POINT WAS A FAIR RESULT"

LINE UP

PRESTON (4-2-3-1):
RUDD; FISHER, DAVIES, HUNTINGTON (C), EARL; WELSH, JOHNSON (HARROP, 88); BODIN, BROWNE, BARKHUIZEN (MOULT, 88); ROBINSON (HORGAN, 70).

SUBS NOT USED: MAXWELL, WOODS, SPURR, O'REILLY.

WOLVES (3-4-3):
RUDDY; BENNETT, COADY (C), BOLY; DOHERTY, NEVES, N'DIAYE (AFOBE, 62), DOUGLAS; COSTA (SAISS, 81), JOTA, CAVALEIRO (BONATINI, 88).

SUBS NOT USED: NORRIS, BATTH, MIRANDA, GIBBS-WHITE.

STAR MAN

CONOR COADY

ANOTHER COMMANDING DISPLAY FROM THE CENTRE-HALF WHO READ THE GAME SUPERBLY AND SWEPT UP A HOST OF LOOSE BALLS BEFORE GETTING WOLVES ON THE ATTACK. A COUPLE OF INCH-PERFECT 50-YARD RAKES LOOKED JUST MARVELLOUS. CAPTAIN COADY IS A NATURAL IN THIS POSITION AND HIS LEVEL OF CONSISTENCY IS REMARKABLE. THE GLUE THAT BINDS WOLVES TOGETHER.

TABLE

	TEAM	P	GD	PTS
1	WOLVES	32	33	72
2	CARDIFF	32	21	61
3	ASTON VILLA	32	19	59
4	DERBY	32	22	58
5	FULHAM	32	18	55
6	BRISTOL CITY	31	9	52

WOLVES (2)

(LEWIS OG 12, N'DIAYE 25)

NORWICH (2)

(ZIMMERMANN 27, OLIVEIRA 90+3)

CHAMPIONSHIP: 21/02/18   ATTENDANCE: 29,100

"SOMETIMES IN FOOTBALL THIS HAPPENS. WE DIDN'T PLAY THE SECOND HALF HOW WE WANTED"

ALFRED N'DIAYE

At this stage of the season all that matters is points, not performances, but unfortunately Wolves ticked neither box on a disappointing evening. They were far from their best at an edgy Molineux against impressive, probing opposition who put up far more of a fight than they did at Carrow Road, as their boss Daniel Farke predicted they would. As against QPR in their last Molineux outing, Wolves contributed to this uneasy 90 minutes with some questionable defending, yet again conceding from a set-piece but also by being nervous, haphazard and, more importantly, defending too deep. As against QPR, it looked as though they'd got away with it. At 2-1 up and with the three added minutes having been completed it was all-but over, but one last swing of the boot from Nelson Oliveira saw Norwich nick the latest of late points.

They certainly deserved it. Wolves never looked comfortable during a tetchy second half. Nuno produced a couple of tweaks to his trusty formation and Wolves were disjointed, with Ivan Cavaleiro rather puzzlingly withdrawn before the hour was up. Morgan Gibbs-White injected incessant positivity during a fantastic cameo but, after Cavaleiro and also Alfred N'Diaye left the field, Wolves lacked dominance and composure and perhaps it was only a matter of time before Norwich scored their deserved equaliser. Wolves throwing away a two-goal lead is about as rare as Nuno shouting "chuck it in the mixer, lads" but that's what they contrived to do here.

For the fifth match in a row, Nuno selected an unchanged XI, meaning there was no recall for Romain Saiss, who remained on an unchanged bench. Norwich had 10-goal Wolves target James Maddison in their line-up and showed three changes from the side that dramatically claimed a derby point against Ipswich in the

94th minute on Sunday. Wolves may have been hoping those derby exertions would have had Norwich flagging. But, after a tepid start to the match, the Canaries were presented with a golden chance to take the lead when Harrison Reed got in behind Willy Boly, but he sent his lob over the crossbar.

Ruthless Wolves punished Daniel Farke's team within seconds. Ruben Neves found Diogo Jota who beat his man, raced into the box and fired towards the corner – keeper Angus Gunn made a great save but inadvertently pushed the ball on to Jamal Lewis whose touch took the ball over the line for an own goal. After that early opening Wolves grew in confidence – Neves beautifully dinked the ball over two defenders, a Cavaleiro cross caused havoc and Barry Douglas sent a wicked 25-yarder just wide of the post. The hosts were in control and on 25 minutes it looked like game over at 2-0. Douglas provided his 10th assist of the season, taking him level at the top of the Championship charts alongside his teammate Cavaleiro, with a now trademark whipped inswinging corner which N'Diaye met at the near post to send a bullet header past Gunn for his second goal in three games.

Despite there not being half-an-hour on the clock, it looked like a cakewalk would ensue. Not so. Within two minutes Norwich had halved the deficit when Christoph Zimmermann replicated N'Diaye's run and header, this time from a Maddison free-kick to the left of the area, and beat John Ruddy. That was a warning sign for Wolves who were functional at best in what was a tepid first-half performance despite their two goals. There were flashes of brilliance, mostly from Helder Costa who took every opportunity to try and dance past the purple-shirted Norwich defenders down Wolves' right flank, but otherwise there was little in terms of the electrifying

creativity Wolves have displayed in recent weeks. A Maddison shot troubled Ruddy just before the break and that was that for the half.

Nuno changed things up at half-time, replacing Costa with Saiss and tweaking the system slightly with the Moroccan and N'Diaye forming a trio ahead of the deeper Neves and Cavaleiro and Costa both playing more centrally up front. It was a switch that didn't have the desired impact. Norwich wrestled back the momentum, playing some decent football in and around the Wolves box and creating a good chance which Marley Watkins spurned when he fired straight at Ruddy.

Nuno reacted again by taking off the impressive but tiring N'Diaye, sending on the exuberant Morgan Gibbs-White with 20 minutes to go and the youngster was arguably the standout performer of the closing stages. With Wolves sitting too deep and lacking their usual zest in what was by now a disjointed formation, the academy graduate was a relentlessly energetic presence breaking from midfield. He should have sealed the win too with seven minutes left, racing in on goal after a mistake by Zimmermann but he couldn't get a shot away and also refused to go down when appearing to be tripped by the desperate defender. At the other end Wolves looked far from comfortable, particularly when Maddison was running at them, and were often sat too deep inviting pressure.

But with the clock showing 93 minutes, three having been added on, Nelson Oliveira let fly from range and the bouncing ball beat Ruddy at his near post to stun Molineux into silence. It was the penultimate kick of the game and a cruel way to drop two points – but Norwich had earned it. Despite that setback, Wolves' lead remains oh-so handsome thanks to Derby slipping up again, with 13 points the gap to third-placed Villa. Not

NUNO

It's a moment of sadness, it feels like a punch and then the final whistle tells you that you don't have time left and you lost something you almost had. Until the end you have to maintain focus. Let's keep on doing better. I think the first half was good and we were in control, creating chances and goals. We were totally upset because a set-piece puts Norwich back in the game. We are growing, the result is not the most important thing.

FAN VERDICT – HEATHER LARGE

A late equaliser in the dying seconds of a game is always going to hurt and this was no exception. It can almost certainly be seen as two points dropped – at 2-0 up we should have been looking to kill the game. We had spells of being in control of the game but nervy and sloppy passing was our downfall and we made it easy for Norwich to attack. Fair play to the visitors, they seemed to have the confidence and control that we were sadly lacking for large parts of the game. A look at the table puts it all in perspective though, it's still another point closer to promotion. There is a lot of work to do so we will need to bounce back quickly for Saturday.

even a South African cricketer called Devon Loch would choke from here, surely? After Saturday's very testing trip to in-form Fulham, which Wolves will undertake without the suspended Neves, the picture may be even clearer.

LINE UP

WOLVES (3-4-3):
RUDDY; BENNETT, COADY (C), BOLY; DOHERTY, N'DIAYE (GIBBS-WHITE, 69), NEVES, DOUGLAS; COSTA (SAISS, 45), JOTA, CAVALEIRO (AFOBE, 59).

SUBS NOT USED: NORRIS, BATTH, MIRANDA, BONATINI.

NORWICH (3-4-1-2):
GUNN; HANLEY, ZIMMERMANN, KLOSE; REED, VRANCIC (HERNANDEZ, 83), LEITNER, LEWIS; MADDISON; WATKINS (MURPHY, 83), SRBENY (OLIVEIRA, 68).

SUBS NOT USED: MCGOVERN, HUSBAND, RAGGETT, TETTEY.

STAR MAN

ALFRED N'DIAYE
AFTER A COUPLE OF FLAT PERFORMANCES HE WAS INFLUENTIAL HERE. IF NEVES WAS THE STEERING WHEEL OF THIS METAPHORICAL WOLVES CAR THEN N'DIAYE WAS THE ENGINE. BOMBED AROUND COVERING BOTH BOXES, REGULARLY BROKE UP PLAY AND GOT WOLVES ON THE FRONT FOOT WITH SOME GOOD PASSES IN THE FINAL THIRD, PLUS HE POPPED UP WITH HIS SECOND GOAL IN THREE GAMES. RAN HIMSELF INTO THE GROUND AND HAD TO BE SUBBED.

TABLE

	TEAM	P	GD	PTS
1	WOLVES	33	33	73
2	CARDIFF	33	22	64
3	ASTON VILLA	33	19	60
4	DERBY	33	22	59
5	FULHAM	33	18	56
6	BRISTOL CITY	33	9	54

FULHAM
(SESSEGNON 38, MITROVIC 71)

 2

WOLVES
0

"WE'VE GOT 12 CUP FINALS LEFT AND THE BOYS NEED TO STEP UP AND SHOW THEIR CHARACTER"
BARRY DOUGLAS

CHAMPIONSHIP: 24/02/18 ATTENDANCE: 23,510

If Wednesday was a minor blip, then this latest Wolves setback felt far more meaningful. It wasn't so much the result – only Wolves' fifth defeat of the season – that raised a few concerns. After all, Fulham are the division's form team and currently enjoying the kind of momentum that managers dream of, with nine wins and four draws from 13 matches. No, it was the limp performance Wolves offered up that will raise a few alarm bells among their supporters. They were well beaten and outfought, they committed sloppy defensive errors, they won desperately few second balls and created next to no clear-cut chances. It was arguably their most subdued performance of the season and came at an important – if not necessarily pivotal – moment, with the business end rapidly approaching.

Nuno will have demanded a reaction from his players after the late setback against Norwich but he just didn't get it. It needed to be Wolves that set the tone early on – instead it was Fulham. It needed to be Wolves that made a statement with a big win against a promotion contender – instead it was Fulham. The Cottagers got in Wolves' faces from the get-go

"THERE WAS AN ALMOST FRANTIC URGENCY ABOUT FULHAM THAT WOLVES JUST DIDN'T MATCH"

at a boisterous Craven Cottage, where the clapper-clad home supporters cheered every sliding tackle as if it were a goal. There was an almost frantic urgency about Fulham that Wolves just didn't match. The physical battle was theirs. Indeed, Wolves looked lightweight in midfield and Helder Costa was consistently pushed off the ball by Tim Ream. There was little imaginative about Wolves' play and, while Leo Bonatini held the ball up well on occasions, he endured an anonymous 90 minutes and very much looks like an out-of-form striker who hasn't scored since December 4. The control and composure of Ruben Neves was sorely missed and play was often end-to-end and haphazard in nature – the kind of game Nuno hates.

There were two changes to Nuno's XI – he surprisingly dropped Diogo Jota for the first time this season, with Bonatini coming into the team. As expected, Romain Saiss replaced the suspended Neves. Fulham, who came into the game on the back of winning eight and drawing three of their previous 11 matches, had former Wolves man Kevin McDonald in their midfield, while dangerman Ryan Sessegnon started on the left wing. The Cottagers' form has been even better than Wolves' of late and it soon showed. The confident hosts took the game to Nuno's team, making life uncomfortable for them from the off with a high tempo, intense pressing and plenty of tough tackles. Fulham were soon on top with Conor Coady making a number of important blocks and interceptions, particularly when clearing off the line after Aleksandar Mitrovic had lifted the ball over John Ruddy.

It was no shock that the hosts went in 1-0 up at the break – but the manner of the goal was certainly surprising from a Wolves point of view, as it was arguably the sloppiest they've conceded all season. A poor Ryan Bennett

clearance saw Fulham work the ball to Mitrovic, who span Coady and fired low – Ruddy parried the ball but it went straight to Sessegnon who fired in from close range. It was by no means one-way traffic in the first half. Wolves created a few half-chances such as an Alfred N'Diaye piledriver which whistled over, a decent effort from Ivan Cavaleiro which Marcus Bettinelli had to save and a couple of promising moments involving Costa which petered out.

But, in general, they were second-best and sorely lacking the composure of Neves in midfield. Nuno made his move on 63 minutes, with Jota and Morgan Gibbs-White replacing Costa and N'Diaye, however the changes made little impact and Wolves rarely threatened the Fulham goal. In the meantime, the rampant Cottagers, smelling blood, doubled their lead when Mitrovic went past Coady again and drove low and true from 20 yards, beating Ruddy at his near post.

Benik Afobe replaced Saiss as Nuno went four at the back with Coady moving into midfield for the first time this season. And it was Coady whose pass helped create the golden chance that Wolves were looking for – but they somehow spurned it. Coady released Afobe whose shot was blocked – it came back to him and he teed up Jota, who ballooned his shot over the bar when it was easier to score. That summed up Wolves' day and there was to be no late comeback.

The time to panic is not now. In fact this is a time for cool heads, for remembering what Wolves have done so, so well during the course of the season and, also, a time for looking at the league table, which shows that their lead to third place is 10 points. They have more than enough in their locker to address this form immediately. But address it they must.

NUNO

It was a tough afternoon but we don't lose anything, we keep going, we do exactly the same. We created options in attack in the second half but we couldn't finish those options, the pass, the cross. That gives you control of the game and we struggled. We must improve on that. Fulham worked well, organised defence, very tight. The team needs to improve in every aspect, not only the offensive part but the defensive part. We are conceding goals, so let's look at everything like we always do. Wednesday didn't affect us but what did affect us was the tough cycle that we had, three games in a short period of time. There's evidence of that, it's human nature. But in terms of psychological impact, nothing.

FAN VERDICT - RUSS EVERS

Life without Ruben Neves – and the near 5,000 travelling supporters had an inkling of what was coming when Diogo Jota's name was also missing from the team sheet. Add in lacklustre performances throughout – none more so than from Leo Bonatini and Helder Costa – and an utterly freezing early evening and the scene was set for a performance that was as flat as anything I can recall from Nuno's men this season. But now is not the time to panic. Calm heads and home victories should see us over the line – we just need to do what we have done since August and believe.

LINE UP

FULHAM (4-3-3):
BETTINELLI; FREDERICKS, KALAS, REAM, TARGETT; JOHANSEN, MCDONALD, CAIRNEY (C) (ODOI, 90+2); AYITE (OJO, 64), MITROVIC, SESSEGNON.

SUBS NOT USED: BUTTON, FONTE, NORWOOD, CHRISTIE, KAMARA.

WOLVES (3-4-3):
RUDDY; BENNETT, COADY (C), BOLY; DOHERTY, N'DIAYE (GIBBS-WHITE, 63), SAISS (AFOBE, 76), DOUGLAS; COSTA (JOTA, 63), BONATINI, CAVALEIRO.

SUBS NOT USED: NORRIS, BATTH, MIRANDA, HAUSE.

STAR MAN

IVAN CAVALEIRO
WOLVES' STANDOUT PLAYER, ESPECIALLY IN TERMS OF EFFORT AND IMAGINATION. TRIED TO TAKE THE GAME BY THE SCRUFF OF THE NECK AND RUN AT FULHAM, BUT HE OFTEN HAD NO HELP FROM HIS TEAM-MATES. FIRED OFF A COUPLE OF DECENT SHOTS AND, FOR ONCE, HE LASTED THE WHOLE 90 MINUTES. IS ARGUABLY WOLVES' MOST IMPORTANT MAN RIGHT NOW.

TABLE

	TEAM	P	GD	PTS
1	WOLVES	34	31	73
2	CARDIFF	33	22	64
3	ASTON VILLA	34	21	63
4	DERBY	34	22	60
5	FULHAM	34	20	59
6	BRISTOL CITY	33	9	54

LEEDS **0**

WOLVES **3**
(SAISS 28, BOLY 45, AFOBE 74)

CHAMPIONSHIP: 07/03/18 ATTENDANCE: 26,434

"IT'S THE BEST FEELING TO SCORE. THE WIN WAS A GREAT MESSAGE TO OUR RIVALS"
BENIK AFOBE

Welcome back Wolves, you've been missed. It's only been a couple of weeks since they played like one of the best teams this league has seen in recent years, but those two weeks had caused some minor alarm for their nervy fanbase. Just a pair of below-par results against Norwich and Fulham and, all of a sudden, Cardiff had closed the gap to second from 13 points to just three. Not to worry, this Wolves team always seems to pick up a win when they really could do with one (a la Ipswich away) and they duly returned to form in scintillating style with one of their most dominant displays of the season.

They played with flair, with precision and with freedom. Diogo Jota and Ivan Cavaleiro glided around the Leeds third like a pair of elegant swans, Barry Douglas and Matt Doherty rampaged and grunted down the flanks like Harley Davidsons in a motorway fast lane and in defence a new back three of Danny Batth, Conor Coady and Willy Boly repelled everything Leeds could muster like burly bouncers on a nightclub door. Wolves were electric. They should have been 4-0 or 5-0 up at the break and were more than good value for their eventual 3-0 victory. Nuno had spoken of his team getting back to the levels of earlier in the season. On his signal they unleashed hell and were simply a class apart from a befuddled Leeds side who could do little but try and keep the score down. With the wing-backs given licence to bomb forward Wolves

looked like the Red Arrows again. It suits them. Saturday's trip to Villa now looks far less daunting, with a 10-point lead. It won't take many more performances like this for Wolves to get exactly where they want to be.

Nuno made two changes from the team that lost 2-0 at Fulham 11 days ago, restoring captain Batth to the XI for his first start since December. He came in at the expense of Ryan Bennett, while Jota replaced Helder Costa in a front three alongside Ivan Cavaleiro and Leo Bonatini. Wolves came into the game on the back of their worst run of the season and having seen the gap to second and third cut to just three and seven points respectively on Tuesday evening. However if they had any nerves, they didn't show them. On the contrary, Nuno's team came out showing intent and positivity, closing Leeds down and racing forward in big numbers on the counter in the stylish manner we have seen so often this season.

Jota was vibrant and buzzing around the Leeds third, Cavaleiro could be seen chasing back and winning sliding tackles, while Bonatini's link-up play was back up to standard and the wing-backs were overlapping with gusto. It was Wolves at their best and it was no exaggeration to say they should have been 4-0 up at the break. An unmarked Bonatini sent a Douglas free-kick bobbling past the post with his knee, before impressive keeper Peacock-Farrell rushed

out to block Jota. This was all within the opening 25 minutes. Wolves were rampant and, while they lacked composure perhaps due to being low on confidence, they were slicing through Leeds with breathtaking regularity. The pressure finally told on 28 minutes and it was the precise left boot of Douglas that created the goal, with his 11th assist of the season being a whipped inswinging corner that Romain Saiss expertly guided home from six yards.

Bonatini managed to spurn another golden opportunity after being played in by N'Diaye, with his dink not beating the keeper, but on the stroke of half-time rampant Wolves deservedly doubled their lead – and it again came from a Douglas set piece. This time Batth met the corner and crashed his header against the bar but the freshly shaven-headed Boly took advantage of more atrocious Leeds defending to nod the rebound home. They were proving too hot for Leeds to handle in what was one of their best 45-minute performances of the campaign.

The open nature of the game continued at the start of the second half. Douglas saw a shot deflected wide and Bonatini glanced a corner from, yes, Douglas, goalwards but it was cleared off the line. Stuart Dallas was almost presented with a great opportunity at the other end when Batth misjudged a cross, but Ruddy claimed.

Wolves didn't have to wait long to seal the points – and they found the perfect manner to do so. Benik Afobe, who had replaced Bonatini, latched on to a Jota through and brilliantly beat the onrushing keeper with a sumptuous long-range lob that nestled in the corner. After five goalless appearances since his return on loan it was a timely strike for the front man and the proverbial icing on Wolves' cake. Hold your nerve, Wolves – just a few games to go now.

"JOTA WAS VIBRANT AND BUZZING AROUND THE LEEDS THIRD"

NUNO

I think we improved a lot from the last performance. Our approach was very good, we recognised we had to get better and that requires character. The team showed character, they were solid, talented, made chances, set pieces, goals, all these things. It's very good for Benik and for the team first because it totally closed the game. It's important for him because he can help the team. He's improving, like everybody. What we see on the pitch is a group of very hard-working people, our only focus is on the game. We're humble enough to recognise when people are better than us but we don't go sending messages into the air (like Leeds owner Andrea Radrizzani), we're very straight on what we say.

FAN VERDICT – ADAM VIRGO

From start to finish we controlled the game magnificently, maybe the mini break we've had helped as the players looked fresh. The scoreline flattered Leeds, we could have easily scored six especially with some of the chances we created in the first half. Thankfully we got a 2-0 cushion and the missed chances didn't come back to bite us. Any nerves beforehand have surely been settled now after that performance. It's great to see Benik Afobe back on the scoresheet for us again. The finish was fantastic and he showed terrific pace to beat the defender. It's easy to panic when the keeper comes rushing out but he stayed calm and to finish it how he did took some serious skill.

LINE UP

LEEDS (4-2-3-1):
PEACOCK-FARRELL; ANITA, JANSSON, COOPER (C) (PENNINGTON, 36), BERARDI; PHILLIPS, FORSHAW; SACKO (HERNANDEZ, 45), SAIZ, DALLAS; LASOGGA (EKUBAN, 73).

SUBS NOT USED: WIEDWALD, O'KANE, VIEIRA, ALIOSKI.

WOLVES (3-4-3):
RUDDY; BATTH (C), COADY, BOLY; DOHERTY, N'DIAYE, SAISS, DOUGLAS; CAVALEIRO (GIBBS-WHITE, 86), BONATINI (AFOBE, 70), JOTA (COSTA, 75).

SUBS NOT USED: NORRIS, BENNETT, HAUSE, MIRANDA.

STAR MAN

WILLY BOLY
THE DICTIONARY WILL TELL YOU THAT SOMEONE WHO IS IMPERIOUS 'EXPECTS TO BE OBEYED' – THAT'S BOLY IN A NUTSHELL. POSSIBLY HIS BEST GAME IN A WOLVES SHIRT. COMMANDING, DOMINEERING AND PLAYED SOME OUTRAGEOUSLY GOOD PASSES THAT SEASONED CREATIVE MIDFIELDERS WOULD BE PROUD OF. GOT ON THE SCORESHEET TOO WITH HIS THIRD OF THE SEASON. JUST A CLASS ACT ALL ROUND.

TABLE

	TEAM	P	GD	PTS
1	WOLVES	35	34	76
2	CARDIFF	35	24	70
3	ASTON VILLA	35	24	66
4	FULHAM	36	24	65
5	DERBY	36	21	61
6	MIDDLESBROUGH	36	16	58

ASTON VILLA 4
(ADOMAH 8, CHESTER 57, GRABBAN 62, BJARNASON 85)

WOLVES 1
(JOTA 20)

CHAMPIONSHIP: 10/03/18 ATTENDANCE: 37,836

"WE'RE VERY DISAPPOINTED BUT WE HAVE TO BOUNCE BACK LIKE WE HAVE ALL SEASON"
CONOR COADY

Of Wolves' six league defeats over the course of the season it was this one – despite the standard of opposition – that was the most surprising. After Wednesday's huge win at Leeds, when Wolves were totally dominant, you'd have put good money on the league leaders exerting their authority at Villa Park. Instead they produced an alarming second half capitulation. While Villa were excellent, this chastening defeat was all of Wolves' own making. At half-time they had Villa exactly where they wanted them, having recovered from an early Albert Adomah goal to control the majority of the first half. You expected them to take it on another level after the break – instead they folded like a pack of cards in a limp and lifeless display. Defensive errors contributed to each of Villa's four goals. Not one individual could say they did themselves justice and for Danny Batth in particular it was a torrid afternoon, with the skipper humiliatingly hauled off by his head coach in favour of Romain Saiss who filled in at centre-half.

Not only did Wolves not match Villa for quality in that second half (they produced just one shot of note in the entire 45 minutes and that came in stoppage time) but they also failed to match them for desire, which will irk Nuno more than anything. The manner in which Birkir Bjarnason ghosted past non-existent challenges from Saiss and Matt Doherty to score the fourth was fairly pathetic. And Nuno is certainly not above criticism here. His

substitutions were, not for the first time this season, odd to say the least. How Leo Bonatini lasted the 90 minutes and Diogo Jota and Ivan Cavaleiro didn't is a mystery. All credit to Villa who clinically punished Wolves on what was an afternoon to forget. It makes Wednesday's win at Leeds even more important, ahead of home games against Reading and Burton that Nuno will certainly want six points from. If Wolves manage that, their position will still be comfortable.

The Wolves team featured just one change from that which won at Leeds in midweek, Ruben Neves making his expected return to the line-up following suspension, with Saiss dropping to the bench. Villa brought Mile Jedinak into their XI and the Australian would play a key role in the opener as Villa got off to a dream start inside eight minutes. His header from Robert Snodgrass's corner set in motion a scramble which ended with Adomah firing home his 14th league goal of the season from inside the six-yard box.

On 20 minutes the visitors were level, thanks to a goal even scrappier than Villa's opener – Doherty breezed past Neil Taylor down Villa's left and delivered a low cross into the box with neither John Terry, James Chester or goalkeeper Sam Johnstone could deal with before Jota forced the ball home a yard out. It was also a feisty affair at times, with referee David Coote reaching for his yellow card on no fewer than eight occasions. It was from a free-kick Villa would re-take the lead 12 minutes into the second half. Neves

brought down Snodgrass 30 yards from goal and the latter whipped in a sumptuous cross which Chester, having stolen a march on the Wolves defence, redirected into the bottom corner. Five minutes later and Villa Park was well and truly rocking as the hosts produced the move of the match to further extend the lead. Jack Grealish moved down the left and played in Adomah, whose cross was finished first-time at the near post by a leaping Lewis Grabban. The hosts were lucky to escape when a Neves free-kick appeared to strike an arm but with five minutes to go, Bjarnason sealed the victory with a sensational solo effort, breezing past Wolves' limp defence before beating John Ruddy.

If a week seems like a long time in football then a month is an eternity. On February 10, after beating Queens Park Rangers 2-1 at Molineux, Wolves sat oh-so-prettily at the top of the table with a lead of 13 points to second place and 15 points to third. Five games – and just five points – later, their lead has been reduced to a mere three to Cardiff and seven to Villa.

Wolves contrived to produce their worst half of the season and their heaviest defeat on such a big and important occasion. But it remains more unlikely than likely that Villa will overhaul that seven-point deficit. Cardiff, whose run of form, like that of Villa and Fulham, is freakish and surely cannot go without bumps in the road before long, travel to Brentford and Derby in the next six days. Meanwhile, Wolves have two home games that probably couldn't have been more appetising had they been hand picked. Reading (one win in 16) and Burton (five points in nine matches) visit Molineux and six points are the very obvious target. If Wolves manage that, their position will still be very much comfortable. But after such a humbling and humiliating defeat, that's a big if.

"THIS CHASTENING DEFEAT WAS ALL OF WOLVES' OWN MAKING"

NUNO

Lots of things went wrong. With a result like this we have to admit we didn't do a good game, a lot of things went wrong. For example, set-pieces, poor defending I think for the first and second goals. Set-pieces are something we've been working on – we have to defend better and take a look at the game. They'll be upset of course, it's a tough moment for me, the boys, for our fans, everyone at Wolves. We have to stick together and bounce back. Even when you win, you do mistakes that you try to sort for the next time. We don't have time to stay in sorrow. The mental strength, this is when we have to show it.

FAN VERDICT - CHRIS HUGHES

As much as a 4-1 scoreline would indicate a hammering, this was far from it – it was more a tale of clinical finishing. Villa had four shots on target and scored four goals. We dominated possession, but did nowhere near enough with it. For the first two goals our nasty habit of not defending set pieces effectively resurfaced and the other two goals were a result of some generally poor defending on our part too. The overall performance wasn't particularly bad. We controlled the game and used the ball well, but didn't create enough in front of goal. There will be nerves creeping in again with the gap to second and third place shrinking, but we still have enough winnable games (particularly at home) to see promotion through.

WOLVES 3
(DOHERTY 40, 73, AFOBE 58)

READING 0

"THERE'S BEEN NO PANIC FROM US. I LAST SCORED TWICE WHEN I WAS ABOUT NINE YEARS OLD!"
MATT DOHERTY

A few months ago Wolves tried to abandon the 'rollercoaster' tag that has stuck to them like glue for about 20 years. Managing director Laurie Dalrymple called for the club to ditch the label at last season's end-of-year awards, but a week like this does nothing to disprove the theory that life at Molineux, even when they're top of the league, has plenty of ups and downs. On Saturday, Wolves reached their lowest ebb (admittedly there's not much competition for that title) of the season when being humbled 4-1 at Villa Park – fast forward to Tuesday night and just about the most comfortable victory of the campaign has seen – combined with Villa's shock defeat at home to QPR – the gap between the pair instantly restored to 10 points. If Carlsberg did Tuesday nights...

Wolves' unlikely hero as they re-established their authority was Matt Doherty, whose double salvo either side of another Benik Afobe goal – on the striker's first start for the club since rejoining from Bournemouth – ensured they coasted to victory against meek opposition. An almost perfect night for Nuno's men was soured slightly when influential wide-man Diogo Jota was helped off midway through the first period with what looked like a bad ankle injury.

Nuno isn't one for making wholesale changes but he made four from the Villa Park XI, with Afobe in for Leo Bonatini and Ryan Bennett, Romain Saiss and Helder Costa recalled for Danny Batth, Alfred N'Diaye and Ivan Cavaleiro. The inclusion of Dave Edwards was one of two changes for visitors Reading, with the Welsh international starting on

his first Molineux return after ending a nine-year association with Wolves last summer. Also in from the off for Jaap Stam's Royals was former Molineux front-man Jon Dadi Bodvarsson. Ahead of last weekend's chastening Villa defeat, Nuno's men had responding to rare setbacks in style this season – winning four and drawing one after a league reversal – and that trend continued here. Reading began the evening with just one victory in 16 Championship outings and would prove to be the ideal opponents from the very off. Indeed, the Royals would muster only one shot on target.

The hosts dictated the tempo and showed an imaginative range of passing without testing Anssi Jaakkola in the Reading goal inside 15 minutes. Early signs of frustration from the crowd at Jaakkola's leisurely goal-kicks looked like being a running theme and then the hosts carved out an opening as the returning Costa turned on the style, darting from right to left and letting fly from 25 yards – the stinging drive was parried loosely by Jaakkola into the path of Jota, who was unable to sort his feet out for a simple tap-in.

As Nuno waved Wolves forward the hosts came closest yet through Afobe's header, with the striker latching on to Bennett's flick on from a Barry Douglas corner and forcing a smart parry from Jaakkola. It was a positive first half from Wolves – and any lingering doubts started to be banished four minutes before the break. A delicious right-sided delivery from Costa was headed back across goal by Douglas for his opposite wing-back Doherty to convert a bullet header, for his third goal of the season.

As Reading trudged out after the break, Wolves fashioned a glorious chance when Doherty picked out his good friend Afobe, who had been left totally unmarked near the penalty spot, with an inch-perfect low cross, but after taking a first touch and spinning Afobe could only drag his effort wide. Wolves had upped the ante and Douglas's fierce 22-yard free-kick was deflected narrowly wide of the angle. The Royals, who have more than one nervous eye glanced over their shoulder at the Championship trapdoor, appeared to have weathered an early second-half storm. But their hopes were quickly dented as Afobe this time made no mistake – a magnificent driven cross-field pass from Neves released Costa down the right, he beat Reading's hapless Tyler Blackett before squaring for Afobe to pounce from 10 yards and ease any tension among the Molineux hordes.

Wolves exuded confidence as Cavaleiro and Costa toyed with Reading's beleaguered players. Doherty then notched an improbable second goal – and doubled his goal tally for the season – with 18 minutes remaining as he swept home from the edge of the box after being found by Cavaleiro, as Wolves delightfully worked the ball from a tight spot in their own right-back position. All in all then a thoroughly professional display from Nuno's men who showed their class at just the right time. While Villa floundered they've held their nerve – and this, rather than last Saturday, could end up being one of the defining moments of the 46-game season.

NUNO

It was a good game of football, a good performance and a good result. I think our fans enjoyed the game and we were in control of the game. We controlled the game, defended well and organised the situations. We gave nothing to Reading. Reading is a good team that always scores in every game but we were able to control that. Of course we are happy but we are looking at consistency, we need consistency. We looked in charge, yes. It was a deserved win and a well-played game

FAN VERDICT - ADAM VIRGO

That was arguably the easiest game we've had so far this season. Granted, it wasn't our biggest win but it looked as if Reading hadn't even got off the team bus. Nuno made the correct changes, the main one being Ryan Bennett who brought added calmness to our back line. Ruben Neves once again proved to the rest of the Championship that he's the best player in the league. The pass to Helder Costa for Benik Afobe's goal was outstanding, all game he was pinging long balls about for fun and he just oozes class. Afobe has to be our main striker for the remainder of our games. He can link up play, run in behind and finish even though he missed a big chance at 1-0, he snatched at it but he had more time than he thought. Villa losing makes Saturday's defeat pointless, four or five more wins should definitely be enough to secure promotion.

"IF CARLSBERG DID TUESDAY NIGHTS..."

LINE UP

WOLVES (3-4-3):
RUDDY; BENNETT, COADY (C), BOLY; DOHERTY, SAISS (N'DIAYE, 78), NEVES, DOUGLAS; COSTA, AFOBE (BONATINI, 72), JOTA (CAVALEIRO, 25).

SUBS NOT USED: NORRIS, BATTH, MIRANDA, GIBBS-WHITE.

READING (4-3-3):
JAAKKOLA; GUNTER (C), ILORI, MOORE, BLACKETT; EDWARDS, EVANS (BACUNA, 63), CLEMENT; ALUKO, BARROW, BODVARSSON (SMITH, 83).

SUBS NOT USED: MANNONE, KERMORGANT, RINOMHOTA, LOADER, HOLMES.

STAR MAN

MATT DOHERTY
NEVES, JOTA, COSTA, BONATINI, AFOBE, CAVALEIRO ET AL RIGHTLY HOG THE HEADLINES FOR THEIR EYE-CATCHING PLAY IN FRONT OF GOAL BUT MATTHEW JAMES DOHERTY HAS PERFORMED WEEK IN, WEEK OUT ALL SEASON LONG – AND HERE HE ENJOYED HIS MOMENT IN THE SUN. TWO WELL-TAKEN GOALS TO DOUBLE HIS TALLY FOR THE SEASON AND INVOLVED IN AN ENDLESS SUCCESSION OF WOLVES ATTACKS. NOT BAD FOR A £75,000 SIGNING FROM BOHEMIANS.

TABLE

	TEAM	P	GD	PTS
1	WOLVES	37	34	79
2	CARDIFF	37	27	76
3	ASTON VILLA	37	25	69
4	FULHAM	37	25	68
5	DERBY	37	21	62
6	MIDDLESBROUGH	37	18	61

WOLVES 3
(COSTA 15, AFOBE 41, 56)

BURTON 1
(DYER 44)

CHAMPIONSHIP: 17/03/18 ATTENDANCE: 29,977

"IT WAS VERY COLD BUT THE WEATHER DOESN'T MATTER, IT WAS A GOOD WIN FOR US"
RUBEN NEVES

Twelve points, four wins, perhaps only even four goals – that's how close Wolves are now. In fact, they may not even need that. As Villa and Fulham proved on a near-perfect weekend for Nuno Espírito Santo's men, there are some odd results knocking around at this time of year. And complacency, or taking their eye off the ball – as Villa appear to have done this week – is surely all that stands between Wolves and a return to the Premier League for the first time since 2012. A cliché may be a phrase that is overused but there are two that are particularly pertinent for Wolves right now. 'Actions speak louder than words', so they say, and that's certainly the case in the past few days for Messrs Keith Wyness and Steve Bruce, who both perplexed and riled Wolves something rotten with their peculiar tweets and quotes (as of course has Leeds owner Andrea Radrizzani). All the various comments, barbs and criticisms seem to have done is generate a siege mentality among a young and hungry squad fiercely determined to finish what they've started.

Cliché number two – a week is a long time in football. After that 4-1 humbling at Villa, the visits of Reading and Burton to Molineux looked the

"BURTON WERE PUPPETS AND NEVES WAS THEIR MASTER"

most appetising of fixtures – and so it's proved to be. Just seven days ago, Nuno Espírito Santo's team saw their lead to third cut to seven points, but here it was restored to 13 points with just eight games to go. The opposition have been meek and obliging – offering just one shot on target between them. Reading rolled over and begged for their bellies to be tickled and, while Burton proved a slighty tougher nut to crack, they were simply no match for Wolves' superior quality. Wolves' character had been called into question following two potentially crippling defeats in three games to promotion rivals. Instead of wilting, instead of changing their style, instead of going into their shells, Wolves have expressed themselves in two games of breathtaking comfort.

As expected, Nuno made just one alteration from the team that beat Reading with Ivan Cavaleiro coming in for the injured Diogo Jota. It didn't take long for Wolves to break the deadlock and it was no surprise to see the lively Helder Costa score it. Conor Coady stepped out of defence and sprayed a perfect pass to the Portuguese winger who beat the offside trap and slotted past keeper Stephen Bywater. Nuno's team were gradually prising apart the Burton defence as they searched for a second goal – Cavaleiro forced Bywater into a diving save with a curling effort and then Romain Saiss won the ball 20 yards from goal and fired inches wide with the keeper motionless. It seemed only a matter of time before they doubled their lead and on 42 minutes they did, with Benik Afobe this time beating the offside trap to latch on to a gorgeous Ruben Neves pass and beat the keeper with ease. It was so comfortable for Wolves – but perhaps a little too comfortable. At a quiet Molineux the visitors surprisingly pulled one back against the run of play just before half-time, with Lloyd Dyer's deflected shot wrong-footing John Ruddy and flying into the net.

That was a minor setback though and just after half-time Wolves made short work of killing the game off. Shortly after Cavaleiro had crashed wide from a great position, the same player teed up Afobe who coolly side-footed home from 12 yards for his fourth goal in four games. He nearly reached his hat-trick soon after, only to be denied almost right on the line after superb work from Cavaleiro and Matt Doherty. With Molineux having found its voice the final 30 minutes were a stroll, with Burton not offering a single shot in the second half as Wolves extended their lead in comfortable fashion.

Neves in particular was deeply impressive. The midfield maestro does things that few other players in the country can do, let alone the Championship. His vision, his composure, his touch, his technique, his quite remarkable passing range – it all belongs at a much higher level. Burton were puppets and Neves was their master. The three points set Wolves up perfectly for the international break, during which they can rest, recuperate and recharge themselves for the final eight-game run in. And it's at Molineux where promotion could be signed, sealed and delivered. Hull City, Derby County, Birmingham City and Sheffield Wednesday visit WV1 – four victories and a place in the top flight is surely theirs. That will certainly be the case if Afobe (four goals in four games) continues the goalscoring run everyone hoped he would go on, while behind him Costa, Cavaleiro and Neves are playing as well as they have all season, making a mockery of any fatigue suggestions. On this form you wouldn't bet against Wolves wrapping it up with time to spare. What a difference a week makes.

NUNO

Everything I asked for I got and that's the most important part. It was a good performance and a performance that showed control and character and knowing that playing well is what is needed to get victories. The crowd enjoyed it and the boys enjoyed playing their football. The talent comes when you're organised, intense, in shape, reacting to the loss of the ball. Some of the players will be busy in the international break. I'm very proud because we have players playing for their countries. But the best way to prepare (for the break) is when you compete like this. Benik is getting to his best now – like the team. Today it was him, before it was Diogo Jota, Helder Costa, Ivan Cavaleiro, Morgan Gibbs-White – all these players are important. All the things we're doing with them is focused on building a team.

FAN VERDICT – NATALIE WOOD

This game had all the hints of a typical banana skin for but instead we got an excellent team performance and three superb goals. Helder Costa is really starting to grow in confidence and become the player he was before his injury. Overall an excellent team performance and a great end to a pivotal week. After Aston Villa I was fearing the worst, we looked like we had run out of steam but the past two games we have seen the old Wolves clambering their way back. Promotion is within touching distance now – and if this performance is anything to go by it is becoming a matter of when rather than if.

LINE UP

WOLVES (3-4-3):
RUDDY; BENNETT, COADY (C), BOLY; DOHERTY, SAISS, NEVES (N'DIAYE, 90), DOUGLAS; COSTA, AFOBE (BONATINI, 81), CAVALEIRO (GIBBS-WHITE, 75).

SUBS NOT USED: NORRIS, BATTH, MIRANDA, MIR.

BURTON (5-4-1):
BYWATER; FLANAGAN, NAYLOR, BUXTON, MCFADZEAN (VARNEY, 45), MCCRORY; SORDELL (SBARRA, 45), DAVENPORT, AKPAN, DYER; BOYCE (EGERT, 82).

SUBS NOT USED: MURPHY, BENT, CAMPBELL, BARKER.

STAR MAN

RUBEN NEVES
HE DIDN'T JUST DOMINATE THE MIDFIELD, HE WAS THE MIDFIELD. STANDING UP AND APPLAUDING ISN'T REALLY THE DONE THING IN THE PRESS BOX BUT IT WAS INCREDIBLY HARD TO REMAIN SEATED WHEN NEVES PRODUCED ONE OF THE PASSES OF THE SEASON – IN THIS OR ANY OTHER LEAGUE – TO SOMEHOW PICK OUT HELDER COSTA WITH A PERFECTLY-WEIGHTED BALL THAT ALMOST DEFIED BELIEF. THIS GUY COULD FIND SHERGAR, HE'S THAT GOOD. DRIPPING WITH CLASS, POISE, QUALITY AND COMPOSURE. BETTER VISION THAN THE HUBBLE TELESCOPE. IT IS A PLEASURE AND PRIVILEGE TO WATCH RUBEN NEVES AT WORK.

TABLE

	TEAM	P	GD	PTS
1	WOLVES	38	36	82
2	CARDIFF	37	27	76
3	FULHAM	38	25	69
4	ASTON VILLA	38	24	69
5	DERBY	37	21	62
6	MIDDLESBROUGH	38	18	62

MIDDLESBROUGH
(BAMFORD 90+4)

 1

WOLVES
(COSTA 32, CAVALEIRO 37)

2

CHAMPIONSHIP: 30/03/18 ATTENDANCE: 27,658

"IT WAS AN UNBELIEVABLE GAME, ABSOLUTELY EVERYONE DUG IN AND IT'S A HUGE RESULT"
CONOR COADY

There are predominantly three reasons why anyone of a Wolves persuasion who attended will never forget this game. Firstly, they watched a crazy, frantic football match unfold which descended into The Battle of Boro™ in a ludicrous second half where Wolves lost their heads and were reduced to nine men. Secondly, they saw their team move a big step closer to realising their promotion dream, on a day when Cardiff and Fulham also won. Thirdly, they witnessed history in what was Wolves' first win away at Middlesbrough since 1951, ending a remarkable run of 25 matches in 67 years without victory.

King George VI was on the throne when Wolves last tasted success here, mankind wouldn't put a human on the moon for another 18 years and Stan Cullis was Wolves manager. Their disbelieving supporters hope and pray that their beloved Nuno becomes even half as successful as the great Cullis. Well, this win took the Portuguese head coach some way to achieving the first of Wolves' big goals – promotion. This barmy encounter saw them at their best – clinically dispatching two first-half goals which put them in charge at half-time – and also at their worst when bizarrely losing all semblance of discipline in a madcap second half. But at the end of it all, Wolves won. Again. That's what they do, almost whatever the circumstances. And the foundations put in place as far back as the start of pre-season – defensive organisation and a never-say-die attitude, stood them in good stead during this most stringent of examinations.

As expected Nuno named the same XI that beat Burton before the international break. Tony Pulis's Boro came into the game in good form, earning 10 points from four games, and after an even opening few minutes it was the home side who looked the more likely scorers. Pacey winger Adama Traore was the obvious danger-man and he soon went through the gears, literally running a ring around Barry Douglas at one point and later taking on three players at once, showcasing phenomenal ability. John Ruddy had a couple of iffy moments in goal and the Wolves back line looked occasionally suspect, with Willy Boly not his usual commanding self. Meanwhile, in midfield Pulis seemed to have instructed his players to kick Wolves repeatedly in the shins. Ivan Cavaleiro was on the end of a filthy challenge from Grant Leadbitter and then Douglas was kicked off the ball by Ryan Shotton. But this was nothing new for Nuno's team and they rode the storm before gradually eking out opportunities.

Two of those came from the piercing right boot of Ruben Neves who clearly fancied scoring one of his wondergoals, testing Darren Randolph in the extreme with two swerving 25-yard thunderbolts which both required top-drawer saves. Wolves were also getting plenty of joy down the flanks – and that's where their opening goal came from. Matt Doherty played inside to Helder Costa who showed quick feet before firing at Randolph – Cavaleiro kept it alive and Douglas chipped right-footed to the unmarked Costa whose firm volley flew into the net. While Boro had enjoyed the better of the clash, Wolves showed

the confidence and clinicalness in front of goal that their opponents lacked. Soon it was 2-0. Douglas again had a hand with an inswinging corner, Boly's header was saved and Cavaleiro couldn't miss from a yard out. It was devastating efficiency from Nuno's team, who went into the dressing room in complete control.

What happened at the start of the second half, then, was completely unnecessary. Wolves looked content soaking up pressure and trying to hit Boro on the counter attack. They almost did just that when the superb Neves sent Costa clean through on goal – he was clear of the last man but suddenly went down, however referee Stuart Attwell gave neither a foul nor a dive. With the Wolves bench raging, the players lost their heads too in what was a shocking display of indiscipline for the next 20 minutes. Neves picked up two yellows in the space of a minute, one for trying to foul Traore and then another for very much fouling George Friend.

Ryan Bennett and Romain Saiss both earned deserved bookings as the game was reduced to a scrap – exactly what Boro wanted. And then Doherty also saw red, leading with an arm with an aerial challenge and giving Attwell no choice. The referee was struggling to keep control but Wolves weren't helping themselves. They'd been in charge just 20 minutes earlier and were now forced to defend for their lives in their own box. Douglas crucially got a toe on to the ball with Patrick Bamford about to shoot and then Ruddy brilliantly saved low from Traore as the pressure mounted. It was all Boro but Wolves were defending resolutely.

Boro continued to press and then scored in the fourth minute of six added on through a Bamford strike. The nerve-ometer ramped up to 11 and the hosts sensed blood and threw bodies forward.

NUNO

"Everything went crazy but we won! It's difficult to control emotions when you see injustices being made – that's why we celebrated like that, it was important for our fans too. The situation of Helder, it was a bad decision of the referee, then the players lost control of their emotions. The players lost the focus, started worrying about the referee and approached the game in a different way. I think it's the job of the referee to try and talk to them and calm them and explain to them. We're not an aggressive team with so many cards, we're not that kind of team (but) we should be more in control of our emotions, it's important. When we had the same men on the pitch we were better. The mentality has been growing game by game and it began at the beginning of July. When a team cannot play football it has to defend – and we are ready to do that."

It was carnage – and they almost grabbed a last-gasp equaliser, but Conor Coady bravely blocked a goal-bound shot with his chest – akin to Gandalf standing his ground screaming 'you shall not pass' – and then Stewart Downing fired the rebound wide with the goal gaping. Drama worthy of a Hollywood blockbuster and a furious end to a breathless encounter. The rabid full-time celebrations, with Nuno sprinting on to the pitch and going bananas in front of an emotionally-drained 2,000 or so fans, while Saiss collapsed to the ground having given everything to the cause, told you everything you need to know about how much this meant. "The Wolves are going up," they sang back at Nuno. It's impossible to argue with that now. What a win!

"KING GEORGE VI WAS ON THE THRONE WHEN WOLVES LAST TASTED SUCCESS HERE"

LINE UP

MIDDLESBROUGH (4-3-3):
RANDOLPH; SHOTTON (CRANIE, 70), AYALA, GIBSON, FRIEND; CLAYTON (ASSOMBALONGA, 70), LEADBITTER (HOWSON, 63), BESIC; TRAORE, BAMFORD, DOWNING.

SUBS NOT USED: DIMI, FRY, BAKER, HARRISON.

WOLVES (3-4-3):
RUDDY; BENNETT, COADY, BOLY; DOHERTY, SAISS, NEVES, DOUGLAS; COSTA (GIBBS-WHITE, 84), AFOBE (BONATINI, 62), CAVALEIRO (N'DIAYE, 58).

SUBS NOT USED: NORRIS, BATTH, HAUSE, VINAGRE.

STAR MAN

CONOR COADY

THE HEARTBEAT OF THIS WOLVES TEAM. THE EPITOME OF COURAGE. AGAIN HE LED BY EXAMPLE WITH A HERCULEAN EFFORT, TYPIFIED WHEN HE TOOK A GOAL-BOUND SHOT FULL IN THE CHEST IN THE 96TH MINUTE TO SEAL THIS MOST FRANTIC OF VICTORIES. HIS CELEBRATIONS AT FULL-TIME SHOWED YOU EXACTLY WHAT IT MEANT TO HIM, AS IT DOES WEEK AFTER WEEK. COADY IS LIVING AND BREATHING THIS PROMOTION RACE AND LEADING WOLVES OVER THE LINE AS IF HIS NAME WAS MAXIMUS DECIMUS MERIDIUS, COMMANDER OF NUNO'S ARMY. HE WILL HAVE HIS VENGEANCE FOR BEING SOLD BY LIVERPOOL, IN THIS LIFE OR THE NEXT.

TABLE

	TEAM	P	GD	PTS
1	WOLVES	39	37	85
2	CARDIFF	38	29	79
3	FULHAM	39	27	72
4	ASTON VILLA	38	24	69
5	DERBY	38	18	62
6	MIDDLESBROUGH	39	17	62

FAN VERDICT

RUSS COCKBURN

And that, ladies and gentlemen, is why we follow Wolves! Never do it easy do we? I can remember saying at half-time 'let's see the game out now, nothing silly' – that went well. What a performance. Guile, class and skill for 55 minutes then commitment, shape, defensive excellence and heart. Forget playing football on the beaches of Vilamoura and Praia da Rocha, these boys have got the guts and attitude that comes from being brought up in Gornal, Bilston and Sedgley. The attitude that if the world doesn't like you, who cares – we've bottled that spirit. Conor Coady's smile tells you everything you need to know. Lost our soul? Sold out? No way, this is a team that believes and connects with the fans and I can't remember the last time it felt this good to follow Wolverhampton Wanderers. In terms of the actual game, we bossed the first half after an even first 15 minutes, with Ruben Neves again pulling the strings and Ivan Cavaleiro looking dangerous. The first goal was a joy to watch with the rejuvenated Helder Costa turning the full-back inside out and then having enough composure to arrow the ball into the top of the net. It was no surprise when the second went in after Willy Boly's header led to a simple nod-in for Ivan. Second half started pretty much the same way and if Attwell had done what he's paid to do then we would have been 2-0 up and coasting against 10 men. In typical fashion, the ref chose to ignore the blatant trip and then decided to become the centre of attention by sending off two of our players. What followed was a masterclass in defensive shape. So that's one win down, three to go and we get the (P) by our name. Come on boys, we can do it!

CLIVE SMITH

Fifty-odd minutes gone, looking comfortable at 2-0 and Helder Costa is fouled when in on goal. What happens next? A red card, a Barry Douglas free-kick, 3-0 perhaps. Or pandemonium. That was how part two of the game started. Part one had been ok. John Ruddy was well-protected by the organised defensive shield and Neves had time and space to play some trademark diagonals. There was no real sting from Boro unless you count a few long throw-ins that Rory Delap used to deploy under the same manager. Throw in a couple of robust challenges and we could easily have been playing Stoke. I made a mental note that Costa looked off the pace while Willy Boly went through a few careless moments. Thankfully these thoughts could soon be deleted. A Ruben Neves diagonal, controlled by Matt Doherty, ends up with a Douglas assist and a crisp Costa finish. We have seen all those jigsaw pieces before. Add a Boly header from a corner, finished off by Cavaleiro and history beckoned. Dare I say it, but part one was fairly routine. Back to part two and the game-changer moment. Did I imagine it? With the ref looking from behind and the linesman at 90 degrees they saw no foul. Over 30 minutes listening to Radio Tees after, and it did not get mentioned once! As an aside, the locals were not happy, they said lots of nasty things about our team on the radio. We lost our composure after that incident, however. The feeling of injustice crept into our play in a rush. In a game where we made 13 fouls, we collected seven yellow cards. Even taking into account John Ruddy's card for time-wasting, that seems a little heavy-handed. Eleven became 10, and very soon after, nine. It was a brilliant display of protecting our goal. Costa put in a shift like never before – even Mick McCarthy would have praised him. Countless headers were won in the box and bodies put on the line regardless of the cost. It made you feel quite proud. They deserved a clean sheet, but they deserved the victory even more. The chant 'you're fit to wear the shirt' never gets sung, but it would be appropriate here. Around 1,800 of us can now update our CV and tick the box, we won at Boro. And it was emotional too! Extraordinary. A privilege to be there.

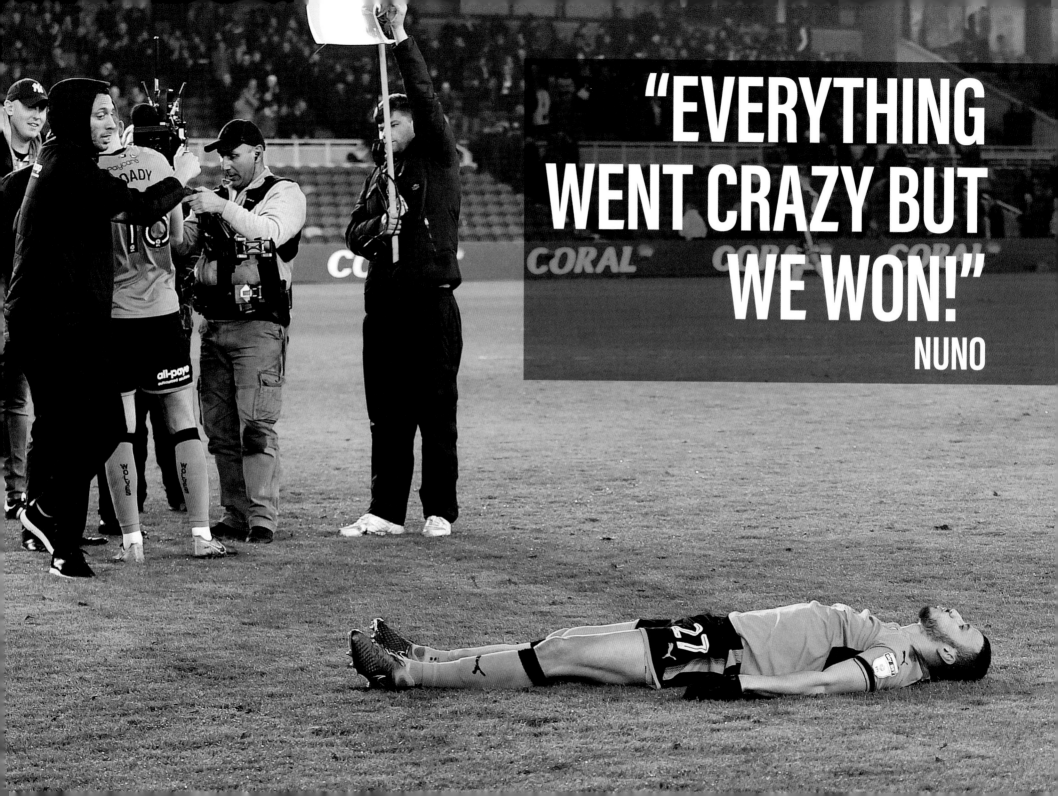

"EVERYTHING WENT CRAZY BUT WE WON!"
NUNO

WOLVES **2**
(JOTA PEN 18, RASMUSSEN 83)

HULL **2**
(MEYLER PEN 37, BENNETT OG 78)

CHAMPIONSHIP: 03/04/18   ATTENDANCE: 29,718

Sentences you never thought you'd read this season: Oskar Buur Rasmussen has salvaged a point for Wolves. It's a good job the 20-year-old Danish youngster has a Wikipedia page, otherwise 29,000 inside Molineux may not have had any way of finding out who this kid is. Called upon as a late substitute with Wolves' disjointed system flattering to deceive, the hitherto relatively unknown Rasmussen (he played in the Carabao Cup tie against Bristol Rovers but otherwise had been a regular in the under-23s) emphatically sent a rocket header past helpless goalkeeper Allan McGregor in a manner Steve Bull would have been proud of.

It was his Federico Macheda moment, and while Wolves carelessly dropped two points here, it should still be one closer to promotion and the league title. The latter may rest on Friday's massive trip to face Cardiff City, but either way Nuno Espírito Santo's team could certainly do with avoiding defeat in Wales, first and foremost, after the Fulham juggernaut continued with yet another victory to close the gap to 11 points. This sluggish display could be attributed partly to fatigue after Friday's draining win at Middlesbrough, partly to a disjointed line-up and partly to a tactical change that didn't work when Ivan Cavaleiro switched to right wing-back (hence Rasmussen's introduction). If Wolves turn up in Cardiff it could be another night to remember. If not, there's the risk they could make this run-in far harder than they need to,

but overall they certainly would have taken four points from games at Middlesbrough away and Hull at home.

Head coach Nuno came up with four changes from the team that so dramatically beat Middlesbrough on Good Friday. Diogo Jota made an early return from an ankle injury to replace Benik Afobe up front, while Roderick Miranda and Alfred N'Diaye came in for the suspended Matt Doherty and Ruben Neves, with Ryan Bennett moving to right wing-back. It was Miranda's first start since October and a snub to Danny Batth, who was on the bench where he was joined by Danish youngster Rasmussen. There was a familiar name in the Hull line-up in the form of striker Nouha Dicko, who spent three-and-a-half years at Molineux before leaving earlier this season.

Wolves could have taken the lead in the second minute when an unmarked Romain Saiss headed too close to keeper McGregor from a typically whipped Barry Douglas free-kick. On 18 minutes, the hosts took charge and it was the returning Jota who edged them ahead. He was tripped in the box by Michael Hector and got up to stroke home the resulting spot-kick for his 15th goal of the campaign. Thereafter, Wolves went back into first gear, aside from when Saiss brilliantly sent Jota through on goal – the forward produced an awful touch and was brought down by McGregor. With the Wolves bench screaming for a penalty in vain, Helder Costa's follow-up shot

was well saved by the keeper.
Nuno's team were drifting towards half-time – and were clearly coasting a bit too much as they sloppily gifted Hull a shock equaliser. Costa's woeful pass into his own box put Miranda in trouble, but the defender still had no reason to drag down David Meyler for what was a clear penalty, which midfielder Meyler duly dispatched to make it 1-1 at the break. Nuno reacted by withdrawing Miranda for Afobe at half-time, moving Bennett to centre-half and Cavaleiro to right wing-back. It didn't make an immediate positive impact though, indeed Hull looked the more likely goalscorers.

Cavaleiro was promptly moved forward in a reshuffle, with 20-year-old Rasmussen replacing the tiring Jota. Wolves now had a more balanced look with players in their correct positions and they began to belatedly put pressure on the Hull defence. Costa flashed one across goal and they appeared to be in the ascendency...until Hull, who had earlier hit the post via a Hector header, stunned Molineux yet again when a superb low Kamil Grosicki cross into the box was put into his own net by Bennett, with a Hull player waiting for a tap-in. Wolves were heading for a shock defeat – and then the unlikeliest of sources drew them level with just seven minutes to go. If the identity of the man who set it up – Douglas with a left-wing cross – was very familiar, then the goalscorer wasn't, Rasmussen powering home an emphatic header from eight yards to earn a precious point. Wolves couldn't find a winner and were irked by Hull's time-wasting tactics – even a ball-boy took issue with it and grabbed the ball from the Hull bench, earning one of the loudest cheers of the night. An unsatisfactory result, then, but it's a point closer to the promised land.

"THIS SLUGGISH DISPLAY COULD BE ATTRIBUTED PARTLY TO FATIGUE"

NUNO

A draw shows we wanted to react and prove our character, but it wasn't a good performance. You just have to look what happened at Middlesbrough, that's a big aspect of today. Being with 10 men then nine men, of course today reflects on that. I don't say tiredness but some 'rush' on the decision-making that creates some of the mistakes. Mentally also, but physically of course because if you look at the space that divides the pitch and split that between nine, it's a lot of distance to run. Oskar does a lot of training sessions (with us) and played in the Carabao Cup. Tonight was his moment and he helped the team – good for him and good for us.

FAN VERDICT – CHRIS HUGHES

If you'd have offered me four points from the Easter games on Thursday I'd have gladly taken them but, having finally broken our Teesside hoodoo on Friday night, I was disappointed to only come away from this one with a point. It was obvious that we missed the metronomic magicking of the wonderkid from Porto in midfield but it was the absence of our Irish raider down the right flank that caused us a bigger headache. Hull tried to play for the draw at every opportunity. Even their dugout tried wasting time by holding on to the ball at a throw-in, only to see it wrestled away by an eager ball boy to get play going again. Overall it's another point closer but will ultimately mean we have to wait a bit longer before we can officially seal it.

LINE UP

WOLVES (3-4-3):
RUDDY; MIRANDA (AFOBE 45), COADY, BOLY; BENNETT, N'DIAYE (GIBBS-WHITE 77), SAISS, DOUGLAS; COSTA, CAVALEIRO, JOTA (RASMUSSEN 70).

SUBS NOT USED: NORRIS, BATTH, HAUSE, BONATINI.

HULL (4-4-1-1):
MCGREGOR; TOMORI, HECTOR, MACDONALD, CLARK; AINA, MEYLER, HENRIKSEN, KINGSLEY (CAMPBELL 70); TORAL (IRVINE 61); DICKO (GROSICKI 65).

SUBS NOT USED: MAZUCH, MARSHALL, BOWEN, STEWART.

STAR MAN

BARRY DOUGLAS
BETTER OFFENSIVELY THAN DEFENSIVELY AND PROVIDED HIS 14TH (FOURTEENTH) ASSIST OF THE SEASON, THE JOINT BEST IN THE LEAGUE WITH VILLA LOANEE ROBERT SNODGRASS, WITH A LOVELY LOFTED CROSS FOR OSKAR BUUR RASMUSSEN TO NOD HOME. YOU'D BACK DOUGLAS TO LOCATE THE CHINESE SATELLITE BEFORE IT CRASHED TO EARTH. UNERRING ACCURACY.

TABLE

	TEAM	P	GD	PTS
1	WOLVES	40	37	86
2	CARDIFF	39	29	80
3	FULHAM	40	29	75
4	ASTON VILLA	40	27	73
5	DERBY	39	19	65
6	MIDDLESBROUGH	40	17	63

CARDIFF CITY ⓿

WOLVES ❶
(NEVES 67)

CHAMPIONSHIP: 06/04/18 ATTENDANCE: 29,317

"I HAVE NEVER PLAYED IN A GAME THAT FINISHED LIKE THAT. IT WAS INCREDIBLE"
RUBEN NEVES

What a special team this is, what an incredible season they're having. Nuno Espírito Santo's boys feel pretty unique in a lot of ways and the way they won this utterly bonkers game was certainly that. Cardiff were awarded not one, but two penalties in stoppage time. Two golden opportunities to deny Wolves an all-but promotion-sealing victory – and they spurned them both. It sparked uninhibited celebrations of wild and unrestrained joy in the stands and on the pitch. Nuno couldn't hold back and Neil Warnock took such offence to him sprinting to join his players (not stopping to shake hands first) that he repeatedly told him to f*** off. It was theatre and pantomime rolled into one, but was ultimately a sideshow to the fact that Wolves as good as won promotion and the league title in just about the most astonishing end to a football match you could ever witness.

As the clocked reached 90 minutes at the Cardiff City Stadium, it had looked fitting that the best and most expensive player in the league had edged the biggest game of the season between its two top teams. Ruben Neves only scores worldies and this latest dream strike – his fifth from outside the box – was the most important of all. With 68 minutes on the clock Wolves would almost certainly have taken the 0-0 scoreline they were then presented with, but Neves had other ideas. Minutes after shanking a 25-yard free-kick, he found his range in typical Neves style, i.e. with the utmost class and elegance, to send a perfect shot into the corner past a helpless goalkeeper and spark scenes in the away end that will live long in the memory. However, those moments were to be topped by the mind-bogglingly implausible drama that unfolded in five minutes of added time. First Conor Coady fouled Anthony Pilkington and referee Mike Dean gave a spot-kick. Disaster.

Up stepped Gary Madine – but John Ruddy instantly made himself a hero with an excellent save. Enough drama for you? Well no. Two minutes later Ivan Cavaleiro brought down Aron Gunnarsson – another penalty said Dean. It was Junior Hoilett to take this time – but as the crowd collectively held its breath he smacked the ball against the bar. It was the most dramatic moment imaginable of an increasingly heart-stopping run-in for Wolves. Immediately the final whistle blew and the whole squad, staff and supporters celebrated like they'd won the league. They surely have. Wow!

This was a clash of styles and philosophies, with Cardiff lacking subtlety but asking questions of Wolves at regular intervals. Wolves stuck to their principles too and it looked as if the opposing ideologies would cancel each other out. Then Neves, as he has so often this season, took Wolves to another level and proved the difference with a helping hand from Ruddy and the bar. With a nine-point lead over the Bluebirds and 14 over third-placed Fulham, that's surely that for promotion? What a way to seal it if so. Absolutely unforgettable.

Nuno sprang a big surprise with his team selection, starting both Leo Bonatini and Benik Afobe with Helder Costa and Cavaleiro dropping to the bench. The suspension-free Neves and Matt Doherty also returned at the expense of Alfred N'Diaye and Roderick Miranda. Cardiff came into the game on an unbeaten run stretching back to New Year's Day and, in front of one of their biggest crowds in recent years, the atmosphere was rocking before kick-off. A helter-skelter first few minutes saw big chances for both teams. In opportunities that reflected the intentions for both teams, Sol Bamba got up well to head a corner just wide for Cardiff and then Neves sent an achingly-gorgeous 30-yarder

towards the top corner, with Neil Etheridge tipping wide.
Wolves had their tails up and the ball broke kindly for Diogo Jota 18 yards out, with his shot again forcing Etheridge into a good save. Wolves were enjoying a huge amount of possession and deep-lying Cardiff seemed content to let them have it. Wing-backs Doherty and Barry Douglas were being closely marked and the front three, perhaps predictably, looked like they'd never played together before with a lack of give-and-gos meaning Wolves struggled to get in behind the home back line. Up to the final third Wolves were fine but that creativity and spark just wasn't there. Not that the 0-0 half-time scoreline was a problem.

Within minutes of the restart, Wolves were inches away from taking the lead. Afobe slipped in Bonatini, the Brazilian rounded the keeper and, from an impossibly-tight angle on the right, side-footed against the upright. Cavaleiro came on for a tiring Jota as Nuno looked to inject some life into Wolves' attacking play, with the game becoming a bit stale. They won a central free-kick 25 yards out – perfect Neves territory – which the Portuguese maestro sent into row Z. However, just three minutes later from a slightly different angle to the left, if Cardiff were expecting a repeat they were sadly mistaken. Up stepped Neves to curl a beauty into the corner, past Etheridge at his near post, to send 3,000 Wolves fans into ecstasy. Cardiff reverted to Plan A with long throws and set-pieces, but Wolves held firm and N'Diaye replaced Afobe to try and see the game through.

They were doing so with largely minimal fuss despite the aerial bombardment and should have sealed it through Costa, who somehow shot wide when in on goal. It should have mattered

NUNO

I love the game ever since I remember – sometimes like this it gives to you, and sometimes it takes away. I won with two penalties missed in the last minute of the game. Football is like that. That's why we love it. I repeat myself (though), we should avoid that (finish). I apologise (to Neil Warnock for my celebrations) but at the same time I hope everybody understands it's very difficult to control your emotions after a finish like that. I wanted to give a big hug to big John (Ruddy) because he was unbelievable for us. Football requires us two different styles – it's not a question of judging what's best. It's your idea, the way you approach. We are a team that has a philosophy of controlling a game by possession but we have to defend. I admire the players of Cardiff, they are fighters who don't give up. Football is always innovating and it's a fantastic game. That's why we love it so much. It can give and take. I think we deserve it. If you look at the game, we had chances not to suffer in the end but that's why people voted for Ruddy in the Championship team of the season and he gave us victory. I was not even thinking about the first penalty (when second was awarded) but I think we should control the emotions better which is my job.

not but Cardiff, in one of football's great rarities, earned not one but two injury-time penalties... and wasted them both. It was an astonishing, logic-defying and scarcely believable end to a crucial match that could well be the highlight of a phenomenal few months. As Nuno so pertinently put, this is why we love the sport.

LINE UP

CARDIFF CITY (4-3-3):
ETHERIDGE; PELTIER, MORRISON (C), BAMBA, BENNETT; GUNNARSSON, BRYSON, PATERSON (MENDEZ-LAING, 51); HOILETT, ZOHORE (PILKINGTON, 84), WILDSCHUT (MADINE, 71).

SUBS NOT USED: MURPHY, MANGA, DAMOUR, TRAORE.

WOLVES (3-4-3):
RUDDY; BENNETT, COADY (C), BOLY; DOHERTY, SAISS, NEVES, DOUGLAS; AFOBE (N'DIAYE, 78), BONATINI (COSTA, 58), JOTA (CAVALEIRO, 66).

SUBS NOT USED: NORRIS, BATTH, HAUSE, GIBBS-WHITE.

STAR MAN

JOHN RUDDY

A NUMBER OF PLAYERS IN THIS SQUAD HAVE ENJOYED A DEFINING GAME OF THE SEASON – NEVES V SHEFFIELD UNITED, JOTA AT NOTTINGHAM FOREST OR DOHERTY AGAINST READING SPRING TO MIND AMONG MANY OTHERS – AND THIS WAS RUDDY'S. HE MADE A COUPLE OF EXCELLENT SAVES – ESPECIALLY FROM WILDSCHUT'S FREE-KICK – AND COMMANDED HIS BOX IN THE FACE OF AN AERIAL BOMBARDMENT FROM CARDIFF – AND THEN IN THE 92ND MINUTE HE PRODUCED A QUITE BRILLIANT PENALTY SAVE TO DENY GARY MADINE. A COLOSSUS. AND YOU COULD SEE EXACTLY WHAT THE PLAYERS AND STAFF THINK OF HIM AT FULL-TIME AND ON SOCIAL MEDIA AFTERWARDS. A HUGE CHARACTER ON AND OFF THE FIELD AND A KEY PART OF WOLVES' SUCCESS.

TABLE

	TEAM	P	GD	PTS
1	WOLVES	41	38	89
2	CARDIFF	40	28	80
3	FULHAM	40	29	75
4	ASTON VILLA	40	27	73
5	DERBY	39	19	65
6	MIDDLESBROUGH	40	17	63

FAN VERDICT

RUSS COCKBURN

I've been waiting some time for the footballing gods to shine down on my team. Wolves fans of a certain vintage (30s) have become accustomed to mediocrity, constant disappointment and Dean Saunders. The latter an affliction no football supporter should ever have to deal with. Well this was payback and what a stage to do it on. The style, elegance and pure footballing philosophy of the Portuguese maestro Nuno against the attrition, set-piece, percentage tactics of Mr Warnock. If there was any justice in the world then the good guys would win and win we did! I thought I'd seen everything football had to offer, but then last night came along. I mean to see one penalty saved in the last minute is off the scale, to see a second hit the underside of the bar was simply not even in the imagination of the most eccentric of scriptwriters. Celebrations were unbelievable and resulted in another pair of broken glasses, that's my hat-trick for the season and one of the reasons why Specsavers posted such impressive results recently. If Warnock likes handshakes that much he can join the Masons. Does he really think a manager is not going to celebrate when his side have nearly sealed the league title and survived two missed penalties? He must really hate Wolves, that's twice now we've spoilt his big day out in Cardiff. John Ruddy – what a performance, what a save, what a presence. I'll be the first to admit I've questioned some of his recent performances, but what a time to shove my criticisms where the sun doesn't shine. A real match-winning performance. Five more points to go until promotion is achieved and we can start to look forward to pitting our wits on the biggest of stages. Nuno has a dream and it might soon become a reality...

ROB CARTWRIGHT

It's the season that just keeps on giving. I've never seen a match like this before, ever. Step forward Nuno. Step forward Ruben Neves. Step forward John Ruddy; in fact, step forward the whole Wolves team and 3,000 fans who made this one special night. Warnock? You can sit down and take Greg Halford and Danny Gabbidon with you. We've seen some fantastic away games this season. Bristol City and Middlesbrough were right up there, but the drama at the end of this one tops them all. Nuno sprang a surprise with four changes. Not once did I think we would not win this game. Well, apart from when the second penalty was given in the 96th minute! We dominated this game until the 75th minute. The gulf in class between first and second was longer than the Severn Bridge. It was the tactical genius of Nuno and his impact substitutions, against the prehistoric lump-it-forward-and-hope tactics of Warnock. Cardiff threw everything at us, but it was Warnock who threw his dummy out at the final whistle. Like a talisman, as Ivan Cavaleiro entered play on 76 minutes, I along with everyone packed in the corner of the stadium knew a Wolves goal was coming. It was a premonition that Neves was going to score and he didn't let us down. The game management from that point was exceptional. Wolves had a genius in the dugout and 11 leaders all on the pitch. No problem with the first penalty. I knew Ruddy would save that. I do have issue with the second penalty. The challenge appeared to be outside the area. There was also no need to jump in there – I thought I was going to pass out. With 14 seconds left, Cardiff had a get out of jail card and they always score late in games, don't they? Cue the wild celebrations, the like we haven't seen since Reading away in 2003.

"THAT'S WHY WE LOVE FOOTBALL"
NUNO

WOLVES **2**
(JOTA 6, NEVES 51)

DERBY COUNTY **0**

CHAMPIONSHIP: 11/04/18   ATTENDANCE: 28,503

"I CAME TO ENGLAND TO PLAY IN THE PREMIER LEAGUE. WE ARE CLOSE"
RUBEN NEVES

There are some moments in football that simply take your breath away. Ruben Neves had already provided five this season, via his quintet of wonder-goals, but here he took his genius to another level and 27,000 Wolves fans will never forget it. Three quarters of the way through what was a regulation Wolves win – as they moved to within three points of promotion to the Premier League, by the way – Neves produced what many of the slack-jawed Molineux crowd will probably say is the best goal they've ever seen live. That's certainly the case for this correspondent. Neves collected a cleared corner, flicked the ball up and sent a dipping, swerving and perfectly-struck 35-yard volley into the top corner past a helpless goalkeeper. And they say there are only seven wonders of the world. It was his Mona Lisa, his Bohemian Rhapsody and his Casablanca rolled into one. Molineux gasped, cheered and then sang its delight towards its 21-year-old genius, who has been an absolute privilege to watch this season.

The goal was by far the highlight of what was otherwise a fairly forgettable but professionally executed victory from Nuno's team. It was

"NEVES PRODUCED WHAT MANY OF THE SLACK-JAWED MOLINEUX CROWD WILL PROBABLY SAY IS THE BEST GOAL THEY'VE EVER SEEN LIVE"

breathtakingly easy at times and also hard to believe this was first versus fifth, given the large gulf in class between the sides. It sets things up perfectly for Sunday's derby against Blues where another win will put Wolves where they've looked destined to finish all season. Their fans celebrated as such at full-time, but it was nothing compared to the party they'll have on Sunday should Wolves get the job done. The carnival has almost started.

Nuno recalled Ivan Cavaleiro at the expense of Leo Bonatini from the team that so dramatically beat Cardiff 1-0 on Friday. The visitors arrived in confident mood but Wolves looked focused and professional from the off with an air of intent on getting the job done. After a couple of Derby attacks were comfortably dealt with, Nuno's team took just eight minutes to open the scoring – and two of their star players this season combined to score it. Willy Boly looked up, spotted the run of Diogo Jota and sent a perfect 40-yard ball over the top where Jota escaped the loose shackles of the Derby defence, took a touch and, with all the coolness of the Fonz wearing sunglasses, dinked the ball past Scott Carson. It was Jota's 16th goal of a fabulous debut season in English football and Wolves duly took charge of the contest.

Neves stung the palms of Carson with a 25-yarder and then Wolves almost doubled their lead when Benik Afobe flicked on a Barry Douglas corner to the back stick and only a last-gasp clearance prevented Jota from tapping home. In fact, Douglas's precise, whipped, enticing set pieces were a feature of the first half with a succession of corners and free-kicks asking questions of the Derby backline. Neves also saw a close-range free-kick tipped over and Ryan Bennett headed another Douglas flag-kick north of the crossbar as Wolves gently

dominated the game in terms of both chances and possession. Derby sporadically threatened at the other end, but their half was summed up when defender Alex Pearce rather unfortunately kicked the ball into his own face and fell over.

You perhaps expected more from the Rams – who'd won successive matches and kept two clean sheets to boot – after the break, but instead Wolves exerted their authority. They almost sliced through when Jota picked out Neves on the counter-attack, but the midfielder was perhaps predictably tackled as he got inside the box. After all, Neves doesn't score from that kind of range. The 35-yard area is more his domain – and two minutes later he scored what could legitimately be described as one of the finest goals witnessed at Molineux in many a year. A corner was cleared as far as the midfield maestro, who flicked the ball up and sent a stunning, ferocious, perfect volley into the top corner of the net.

The whole stadium was stunned by what it had seen. Neves had scored five 'worldies' this season but this topped the lot and characterised the sheer brilliance of a wonderful football player. Nobody inside Molineux seemed to know what to do next, with everything thereafter seeming pretty futile. There was a constant buzz around the stadium, as if everyone was trying to comprehend what they'd seen. Jota almost made it 3-0 with a mere 10-yard shot that Carson saved and Nuno freshened up his forward line with Bonatini and Helder Costa sent on for Afobe and Jota. The final minutes were a walk in the park and the celebrations at full-time, with Nuno giddily playing to the crowd, reflected the fact Wolves are now within touching distance of the top flight. No one is more deserving of gracing it than Mr Neves.

NUNO

The goal is talent. We are fortunate to have these talents but what makes these opportunities are the rules and order of the team, the control, all these things that maybe people don't see allow us to enjoy and take advantage of these kind of moments. We still have a long way to go and Ruben knows he has a lot to improve. It was a good performance, the boys did well, balanced, organised, talent, possession, good goals, they did a very good job and I congratulate them. One of the things I mentioned we had to improve was our defensive organisation and today we did that. We didn't concede chances to a very good team. John Ruddy didn't do much and on Friday he was man of the match, so this says we are improving. We've been suffering goals at home so we avoided that and I'm very pleased with the reaction of the players.

FAN VERDICT - CHRIS HUGHES

There's nothing I can say that's not been said numerous times already this season. This is the best Wolves side I've ever seen, Ruben Neves is the best player I've seen pull on a Wolves shirt and he's just banged in the best goal I've ever seen live at a football match. We've played a team who will likely finish this season in a play-off position contesting for a place in the Premier League with us next season yet looked an absolute world apart. At times our players looked like they were having a leisurely kickabout in the park with their mates rather than competing in the second tier of English professional football.

LINE UP

WOLVES (3-4-3):
RUDDY; BENNETT, COADY (C), BOLY; DOHERTY, SAISS, NEVES, DOUGLAS; CAVALEIRO (GIBBS-WHITE, 82), AFOBE (COSTA, 66), JOTA (BONATINI, 74).

SUBS NOT USED: NORRIS, BATTH, HAUSE, N'DIAYE.

DERBY (4-2-3-1):
CARSON; WISDOM, PEARCE, DAVIES, BAIRD; LEDLEY (PALMER, 73), HUDDLESTONE; WEIMANN, VYDRA (HANSON, 85), LAWRENCE; NUGENT (JEROME, 82).

SUBS NOT USED: ROOS, FORSYTH, KEOGH, THOMAS.

STAR MAN

RUBEN NEVES
"THE DEFINITION OF GENIUS IS TAKING THE COMPLEX AND MAKING IT SIMPLE" – ALBERT EINSTEIN SAID THAT AND ERGO, BY HIS DEFINITION RUBEN NEVES IS A GENIUS. WE ALL DREAM OF CASUALLY FLICKING THE BALL INTO THE AIR AND PERFECTLY STRIKING IT ON THE VOLLEY INTO THE TOP CORNER FROM 35 YARDS – BUT A DESPERATELY SMALL NUMBER OF HUMAN MEN CAN ACTUALLY ENACT THIS DURING A FOOTBALL MATCH. RUBEN NEVES CAN – AND HE IS A GENIUS. IT IS NOT AN EXAGGERATION TO SAY HIS GOAL WAS ONE OF THE FINEST TO BE WITNESSED IN DECADES AT MOLINEUX AND IT IS NOT AN EXAGGERATION TO CALL NEVES ONE OF THE MOST SKILFUL, GRACEFUL AND TECHNICALLY GIFTED PLAYERS TO EVER DON A GOLD AND BLACK SHIRT IN ITS DEEPLY PROUD 141-YEAR HISTORY. IN 2017/18 WE HAVE WITNESSED GREATNESS – A STAR HAS BEEN BORN.

TABLE

	TEAM	P	GD	PTS
1	WOLVES	42	40	92
2	FULHAM	42	31	81
3	CARDIFF	41	27	80
4	ASTON VILLA	42	26	76
5	DERBY	41	20	68
6	MILLWALL	42	15	68

IT'S PROBABLY THE BEST I'VE SCORED. I KNOW I HAVE A GOOD SHOT SO WHEN THE BALL IS THERE I HAVE TO TAKE RISKS, BUT MY FIRST TOUCH WAS NOT GOOD! THE BALL WENT BEHIND ME. IF I LOSE THE BALL THERE IT'S DANGEROUS FOR MY TEAM SO I HAVE TO SHOOT.

IT WAS BAD CONTROL BUT I CAN'T LOSE THE BALL THERE SO I HAD TO SHOOT. LONG RANGE SHOTS IS ONE OF MY BEST POINTS. I HAVE TO TRAIN WELL DURING THE WEEK TO DO THESE KIND OF THINGS.

I HAVE TO TAKE RISKS AND I'M HAPPY TO HELP THE TEAM TO ACHIEVE THIS WIN.

RUBEN NEVES

 Tim Spiers✔
@tim_spiers_Star

OH MY GOD OH MY GOD OH MY GOD
OH MY GOD OH MY GOD

💬 🔁 ♡ ✉   8:53pm – 11 Apr 2018

 Tim Spiers✔
@tim_spiers_Star

RUBEN NEVES WHAT HAS HAPPENED

💬 🔁 ♡ ✉   8:54pm – 11 Apr 2018

 Tim Spiers✔
@tim_spiers_Star

How the hell to describe this. Corner
cleared to 35 yards out where RUBEN
NEVES flicks up the ball and unleashes
a stunning, sexy, perfect volley into
the TOP CORNER that is ABSOLUTELY
SENSATIONAL. Perfection. Look up
filth in the dictionary and there's a pic
of that goal.

💬 🔁 ♡ ✉   8:56pm – 11 Apr 2018

 Tim Spiers✔
@tim_spiers_Star

And they say there are only 7 wonders
of the world

💬 🔁 ♡ ✉   9.02pm – 11 Apr 2018

 Tim Spiers✔
@tim_spiers_Star

There's a bit of a stunned silence at
Molineux, like everyone's in awe of Neves
and privileged to be sat only 50 yards
from him. Is this what it's like when the
Pope's on tour. Or Robert Plant.

💬 🔁 ♡ ✉   9.15pm – 11 Apr 2018

PROMOTION TO THE PREMIER LEAGUE WAS CONFIRMED ON SATURDAY APRIL 14 AT 7.26PM, WHEN THIRD-PLACED FULHAM FAILED TO BEAT BRENTFORD AT CRAVEN COTTAGE. BRENTFORD STRIKER NEAL MAUPAY WAS THE MAN WHO SECURED WOLVES' PROMOTION, SCORING A DRAMATIC EQUALISER FOUR MINUTES INTO STOPPAGE TIME TO EARN A 1-1 DRAW. WOLVES' PLAYERS AND STAFF WATCHED THE GAME AT THEIR TEAM HOTEL AND THE CELEBRATIONS ACROSS THE CITY WENT ON LONG INTO THE NIGHT.

DANNY BATTH, CLUB CAPTAIN

It was an emotional moment. It's crazy actually the way it finished and obviously now having everything confirmed. I know there's been a few videos flying around of us jumping up and down cheering but it's hard to sum up what it feels like to be part of a squad that's achieved promotion out of this division. So many players, so much hard work, staff making sacrifices every day – all the things that go into a successful team have this season come together. Look back at the Cardiff and Middlesbrough games – if you're not going up those games go the other way. The lads have been outstanding all season and for those results to go our way have pushed us on and given us a bit of comfort knowing we're promoted. It's quite surreal, we've been jumping up and down, it's boiling hot in there everyone's been high-fiving and hugging. Credit to the manager and his staff for their superb season. Likewise we've got a big game tomorrow, full house and we want to put on a good performance for everyone. It's not over yet, there's still a competition to win and we want to focus on doing that. You can imagine the emotions – and now we're off to bed because the game's so early tomorrow. All the lads are going to be resting up and making sure we put a good display on. This is what we've worked towards. Those Tuesday nights you might have been driving up and down the motorway, hopefully it feels like it's all worth it now, seeing a team that's playing such great football and a club that's going in the right direction with so many good players. It's the first step in the journey. Off the back of all the mediocre seasons and to be promoted with four games to go is unbelievable. Thank you to every single person that's turned up this season – it's been like no other.

LAURIE DALRYMPLE, MANAGING DIRECTOR

This is the culmination of a huge amount of hard work from everyone within the club – from the players, the coaching team, the management team and the fans. I can't say enough about the fans this year, they've just been absolutely amazing. We're thrilled. Everyone's hugely elated. We're keeping a reasonable lid on it because we've got a game tomorrow but not in any way understating our excitement and satisfaction at what we've achieved this season. It was a little bit touch-and-go towards the end of the (Fulham) match, we were kind of resigned to the fact that game was going to finish 1-0 and we were going to go out and do it all ourselves tomorrow. We're extremely happy we've achieved it but it's one step in the long-term plan. When we finish the season, we'll start focusing on what the future looks like for this club. We've been in this game long enough that we don't take anything for granted. It's taken one game, one week at a time. What Nuno's brought in has been fantastic. He came in, he's changed the playing style, we've recruited well, he's galvanised the group in a very short space of time and very quickly he had us playing a different brand of football that was delivering results extremely quickly. He's a superb tactician, strategist and man-manager. He's extremely good with the players and staff. I don't want to single people out because it's been a unified club effort from start to finish but there's no doubting he's an incredibly important component in the whole thing. We want to finish the league as champions and in order to do that we've got to put all our focus into playing what will be a very difficult Birmingham side. It's all eyes down for a big game tomorrow.

"TO BE PROMOTED WITH FOUR GAMES TO GO IS UNBELIEVABLE"

DANNY BATTH

WOLVES 2
(JOTA 21, AFOBE 87)

BIRMINGHAM CITY 0

CHAMPIONSHIP: 15/04/18 ATTENDANCE: 29,536

"I'M ECSTATIC. THE FEELING – I'VE HAD TWO BOYS AND IT'S RIGHT UP THERE. IT'S FANTASTIC"

CONOR COADY

These are the days that everyone in the game – fans, players, managers, yes even media – live for. A sea of gold greeted their heroes and Molineux had one big party that the grand old place will cherish for years. It's the kind of day that, for most clubs, is a rare thing indeed. Some won't have had a day like this for a generation. But in Wolverhampton the sincere hope and the increasing belief among an exultant fanbase is that this is just the first of many – and with Fosun and Nuno Espírito Santo on board, who would bet against that being the case?

The day began early – too early for some who will have been nursing hangovers from Saturday night's immediate promotion party. But by midday, Molineux was rocking to the tune of Nuno's beat. Fans had earlier gathered outside the stadium entrance in their hundreds to welcome the players off the team bus. The excitement in the air was palpable, as was the adoring and unequivocal love those supporters have for this team.

Wolves could have taken their eye off the ball – they'd been celebrating on Saturday night, had a quick turnaround for the midday kick-off and there

"THE PLAYERS WERE GREETED ON TO THE FIELD LIKE HEROES"

was a party in the stands to distract them. But whatever the game, whatever the circumstances, Nuno's Wolves win and keep a clean sheet. That's just what they do. And while they were far from perfect, they kept their heads (despite plenty of provocation from a physical Blues team) and got the job done in a professional manner. Not only did they put on the show they wanted to in what was a big local derby at a packed house in front of the watching nation, but they earned the three points that meant they're effectively champions – and also moved closer to the 100-point mark that the players will crave. They have a 12-point lead over Cardiff and the Bluebirds have four games remaining plus an inferior goal difference. The title will have to wait for next weekend though when the party will continue into Bolton.

Helder Costa replaced Benik Afobe in the front three in the only swap from midweek. The atmosphere at Molineux was absolutely rocking and the players were greeted on to the field like heroes. There was a collector's item in the opening minutes when Ruben Neves hit a pass straight out of play – and when Blues almost scored soon after you wondered if it going to be an "after the Lord Mayor's show" sort of day. The reason they didn't score was John Ruddy, who produced an excellent double save. Maxime Colin was in on goal and the keeper saved low before keeping out the follow-up with an acrobatic reflex stop. Wolves then suffered a blow when Ivan Cavaleiro pulled up lame, feeling his hamstring. He had to be replaced by Leo Bonatini but Wolves soon perked up and began to produce the sort of free-flowing football we've all become accustomed to this season.

It was one such move that led to the opening goal – Romain Saiss picked out the overlapping Matt Doherty whose perfect low cross was tapped in by Diogo Jota for his 17th strike of

the campaign. The game was being played out in a carnival atmosphere. The fans asked for Mendes to wave at them (he didn't oblige) and Nuno too (he did), they sang "we're going to Man City, you're going to Shrewsbury" at the Blues fans and questioned if the teams would ever meet again. It was a joyous occasion and, in the second half, Wolves looked to fashion a scoreline to send them home even happier.

Their task was made easier on 52 minutes when Blues were reduced to 10 men. The visitors lost possession and suddenly Costa was haring through on goal – Harlee Dean tried to get to the loose ball but Costa got his toe on it first and Dean brought him down 30 yards out. As the last man he had to go. After substitutes Afobe and Bonatini both fired over from the edge of the box, Blues almost drew level when Ruddy fumbled a save before crucially blocking from Lukas Jutkiewicz. It proved to be a pivotal moment as just seconds later Afobe sealed the win. Alfred N'Diaye played him in and the striker netted his fifth goal of the past month-and-a-bit by delicately chipping over the keeper. It sparked joyous scenes at an adoring Molineux who watched their heroes put the icing on an unforgettable weekend for everyone associated with Wolverhampton Wanderers.

Molineux rose to acclaim their victorious soon-to-be champions, Nuno went wild and even the appeals for no pitch invasion worked (bar three idiots). We saw a different side to Nuno, certainly in the post-match press conference where he – after nine months of refusing to talk about points, or results, or promotion, or targets – finally spoke of his desire to reach 100 points – and, of course, lift the title. He even let his players have a beer in the dressing room – they're having the time of their lives too. The players danced, they sprayed champagne, they did a lap of the pitch, they played

NUNO

It's special. I'm very pleased, it's a big moment. First to our fans, why we work is for our fans. Through the season to the last moment it was a special feeling being with our fans always behind us. The club, the city, the support we've been having, it's special for the players. They've been fantastic since day one. The players have been the key, the way they started and they believed something wasn't changing. Every player enjoyed this moment. It was a very hard season, the players deserve it. Every one of them has made a contribution to this success. It's not the moment (to think about the Premier League) – we have 95 points, I say more! Let's achieve something special. This is the first time I've spoken about points – let's have more, let's achieve something special, some kind of glory. It's not the same as 101 or 104. Let's dream now and try to do it. It's time to celebrate. I never allowed beer in the dressing room, it's the first time. But it was the first time they asked for it! I will celebrate, we will celebrate together.

to the crowd, it was magical to witness. And then, with the fans having departed and the players and staff drifting away from the stadium to celebrate with their loved ones, the club captain produced the day's most emotional and pertinent moment of all, via a simple tweet. "Wish you could be with us," Danny Batth said. "The bravest, strongest, most inspirational man I have ever met." He was of course talking about Carl Ikeme, who is never far from anyone's thoughts. It was all for you, Carl.

122

LINE UP

WOLVES (3-4-3):
RUDDY; BENNETT, COADY (C), BOLY; DOHERTY, SAISS, NEVES (N'DIAYE, 70), DOUGLAS; COSTA, JOTA (AFOBE, 74), CAVALEIRO (BONATINI), 16).

SUBS NOT USED: NORRIS, BATTH, HAUSE, GIBBS-WHITE.

BIRMINGHAM (4-3-2-1):
STOCKDALE; HARDING, MORRISON (C), DEAN, GROUNDS (MAGHOMA, 62); COLIN, N'DOYE (GARDNER, 78), KIEFTENBELD (ROBERTS, 54); DAVIS, JOTA, JUTKIEWICZ.

SUBS NOT USED: KUSZCZAK, LOWE, DACRES-COGLEY, LUBULA.

STAR MAN

ROMAIN SAISS

PLAYED A BIG PART IN THE OPENER AS HIS SUBTLE TOE-POKE FOUND ITS WAY TO DOHERTY, TO SET UP JOTA. HE CAN SOMETIMES GO UNDER THE RADAR BUT WAS FRONT AND CENTRE FOR THIS ONE, HIS CRISP PASSING AND RELENTLESS PRESSING WAS A CUT ABOVE. ONE OF THE BEST DISPLAYS IN A WOLVES SHIRT FROM THE MOROCCAN MIDFIELDER.

TABLE

	TEAM	P	GD	PTS
1	WOLVES	43	42	95
2	CARDIFF	42	29	83
3	FULHAM	43	31	82
4	ASTON VILLA	43	27	79
5	MIDDLESBROUGH	43	19	69
6	MILLWALL	43	15	69

HEATHER LARGE

Normally you can't beat the feeling of a derby-day win but defeating a local rival when you know you're already promoted certainly tops it. After Saturday night's celebrations and knowing they had secured a spot in the Premier League, you could have forgiven the team for being below par. But this is Wolves – they knew they still had a job to do and fans to please so what we saw was their now trademark style of controlling the game so they could play the way they wanted to. There was a great atmosphere from a packed Molineux from the start and hearing 'Nuno had a dream' echoing around the ground uniting the fans was wonderful. All in all it turned out to be a fairly comfortable win, although if it hadn't been for some excellent saves from John Ruddy, it may have been more nervy. It wasn't the most exciting of games, especially in the second half, but it didn't need to be as moving three points closer to becoming champions was the goal. The scenes after the final whistle were brilliant, you could see exactly how much it meant to the players and to Nuno as well as the rest of the coaching staff. It's been a great season, one all of us will remember for a long time, and it's not over yet with more celebrations to come. Diogo Jota and Ruben Neves stood up well to the constant battering they got from the opposition. I thought Matt Doherty was excellent and his fantastic cross made it easy for Jota to net the opening goal. And it was a great second goal from Benik Afobe with the ball coming to him exactly how he likes it. But really every player contributed to a good team performance.

CLIVE SMITH

With promotion confirmed prior to kick-off there was nothing on the game. As if! Blues were fighting to remain in the league we are leaving at the other end. Their desperation showed in a string of challenges, many late, that might have received more punishment from other officials. Our passing game was in full flow and, like so often this season, it was pleasing to watch. It is the effort of the players without the ball that makes it work. Had we taken our foot off the gas there would not have been the movement and passing would have been harder. We did have a scare however and John Ruddy had more action in one minute than he has in some whole games. Two good saves preserved our clean sheet. Matt Doherty looked on a mission. Constantly he was in advanced positions, so much so that he got caught offside more than once. No surprise that he was involved in the first goal as, after five or six passes, he got inside the full-back to cross perfectly for a Diogo Jota tap in. Although we hardly pummelled their goal, there was an air of being in control of the game. Helder Costa was looking on his game and was our main dribbler. Ivan Cavaleiro had to leave early but Bonatini was an able sub. After the interval Costa raced on to a defence-splitting pass heading for a one-on-one with the keeper. A crude challenge brought him down. It was a replica of the situation at Boro two weeks ago. That time nothing happened, this time we saw a red card given. Funny old game eh? Ironically Blues played better with 10 men. They had a couple of chances that required some good defending from us. The game had opened up and we finally put it to bed when Benik Afobe beat the onrushing keeper. Another good day at the office for Wolves which was happily celebrated after the final whistle.

BOLTON ⓪

WOLVES ④
(DOUGLAS 16, AFOBE 45+1, JOTA 53, COADY PEN 66)

CHAMPIONSHIP: 21/04/18 ATTENDANCE: 19,092

This is why they're the best team in the league. Solid as you like in defence, probing and controlling in midfield, dynamic down the flanks and blistering in attack – it was all on show at the Macron as Wolves did what Wolves do and confirmed their title in some style. Any notion of them taking their eye off the ball after securing promotion last week was quickly dispelled as they mercilessly set about dismantling Bolton limb by limb and feasting on their helpless carcass, like the rabid pack of success-hungry Wolves they are. Far from clinching the Championship title by labouring over the line, they produced some of their most spellbinding football of the season here.

Bolton will be sick of the sight of Nuno Espírito Santo's team. The biggest margin of victory for Wolves this season has been four goals, which they've achieved three times – and twice against the Trotters. A 5-1 thrashing back in November was perhaps an unfair scoreline on Phil Parkinson's team, with Wolves scoring twice late on to add gloss to the victory margin. Here the scoreline was unfair on Nuno's team. Indeed, the perfection-seeking head coach was as grumpy as he's been all season in his post-match interviews (which is saying something), despite the fact he'd just secured one of the biggest achievements of his career, if not the biggest. The reasons for his somewhat indifferent mood weren't clear, but

"PROMOTION AND THE TITLE ARE IN THE BAG"

he did suggest on a couple of occasions that his team needed to improve and he thought the scoreline should have been greater. There was certainly no wiping the smile off the faces of 4,800 sun-kissed travelling fans who made the most of their party and sang non-stop all afternoon. The game could have been a banana skin, what with the home team badly in need of three points in their fight to avoid relegation. Instead, thanks to Wolves' performance, it had a carnival feel. They attacked with the flair, pace and creativity they've become renowned for, with the brilliant Helder Costa in particular proving far too good for Bolton to handle. Costa had the Trotters on toast and Diogo Jota was at his flying best too. After overcoming a few dangerous set pieces – which seemed Bolton's one and only route to goal – they soon exerted their authority, as they have time and again this season.

Wolves went straight on the attack, showing no signs of any post-celebration hangover as they set about getting the job done. Costa took Romain Saiss's pass and fired just wide via a deflection inside 60 seconds as Nuno's team set out their stall. They weren't at their best but you could sense they were one decent pass away from slicing Bolton open – and so it proved on 16 minutes. Jota came deep and fed Benik Afobe, he placed his shot which was well-saved by Ben Alnwick and there was the rampaging Barry

Douglas to drive home, low and true, for his fifth goal of the campaign.

Bolton threatened occasionally but Wolves were clearly the superior team with their pace and movement just too good for the hosts. Jota headed a Douglas corner at Ben Alnwick and then Costa's shot from a tight angle was well-saved by the keeper, with Afobe waiting for a cutback. However, Afobe didn't have to wait long for his moment, with the striker scoring on the stroke of half-time. One of the stars of the season, Conor Coady, sent a ball over the top which Afobe controlled and then he rounded the keeper to finish with ease for his second goal in two games and a sixth since rejoining the club on loan. It was party time in the away end as they soaked up the Lancashire sunshine in style.

Talking of which, Wolves won the title in style as they coasted clear after the break and sealed the points. Costa, who was having a fine game, cut inside and played to Jota, whose touch took him close to keeper Alnwick, so he cutely dinked it over him to send the travelling sun-kissed army potty again. It was now a matter of how many Wolves would score. They were hungry for more and when the fourth arrived it was a truly standout moment. The influential Costa helped create it with an excellent touch before teeing up Afobe, who saw a shot saved and was then brought down in the box. Afobe, or perhaps Costa or Jota, may have taken the spot-kick but instead up stepped the heartbeat of the team, Coady, who sent the away end wild merely by picking up the ball. The centre-half coolly dispatched the penalty for his first goal of the campaign in front of a delirious away end and ecstatic team-mates.

Wolves continued to rampage forward – Saiss curled one just over and the Moroccan also crossed inches ahead of the sliding Morgan

Gibbs-White for what would have been another special moment. There have been plenty of those this season – and there were more at full-time when the 5,000-strong army and their heroes celebrated becoming officially the best team in the Championship.

As they have shown time and again in 2017/18, they are simply too good for this division. The celebrations will continue for a while yet, with the trophy set to be lifted next weekend and then a huge party taking place across the city a week later. When the hangovers have ceased, attention will be firmly fixed on what lies in wait next season. If Wolves carry on this form, this confidence, this swagger and this indelible unification of a squad, a club and a city, then they will be a force to be reckoned with. Promotion and the title are in the bag. Everyone at Molineux hopes and believes this is just the beginning.

LINE UP

WOLVES (3-4-3):
RUDDY; BATTH (C), COADY, BOLY; DOHERTY, SAISS
(N'DIAYE, 81), NEVES, DOUGLAS; COSTA, AFOBE (GIBBS-WHITE, 68),
JOTA (BONATINI, 68).

SUBS NOT USED: NORRIS, BENNETT, HAUSE, MIRANDA.

BOLTON (4-5-1):
ALNWICK; FLANAGAN, BEEVERS, WHEATER, ROBINSON; AMEOBI,
MORAIS, PRATLEY (C) (VELA, 58), HENRY, BUCKLEY (NOONE, 65);
LE FONDRE (CLOUGH, 79).

SUBS NOT USED: HOWARD, TAYLOR, WILBRAHAM, BURKE.

STAR MAN

HELDER COSTA
THE WING WIZARD WAS AT HIS BEST HERE. A FABULOUS DISPLAY
OF TRICKERY, CREATIVITY AND PHENOMENAL PACE. HAD A HAND
IN TWO GOALS AND COULD HAVE SET UP MORE. HIS CONFIDENCE
HAS FULLY RETURNED AND HIS TOUCHES ARE JUST SUBLIME. HAS
BEEN IN JOTA AND CAVALEIRO'S SHADOW THIS SEASON BUT HE
TOO LOOKS READY FOR THE PREMIER LEAGUE.

TABLE

	TEAM	P	GD	PTS
1	WOLVES	44	46	98
2	CARDIFF	43	30	86
3	FULHAM	44	34	85
4	ASTON VILLA	44	31	82
5	MIDDLESBROUGH	44	20	72
6	MILLWALL	44	12	69

FAN VERDICT

CLIVE SMITH

As a football fan you have to take the rough with the smooth. More often than not the bad days outweigh the good so you really do have to make the best of the good days – well this day was just perfect. As good as it gets. Finding anyone in the away end at kick-off who didn't think we would clinch the Championship would have been difficult. Rarely have we all had this much confidence in our Wolves team. There was not a chance of being disappointed. Bolton, like Blues and Derby, had a reason to be a challenge, but failed to offer much resistance. Early on, they chased us down, tried to press high and fired a couple of free-kicks into our box. Once those moments had passed the Wolves bandwagon moved along and convincingly took over the game. Just like our first away goal of the season at Derby, it was Barry Douglas who was in the right place at the right time. This time it was a Benik Afobe shot, poorly parried by their keeper, that gave him the chance to score. From that moment the result was never in doubt. We dominated the ball, playing a mixture of long and short passes, with Romain Saiss and Ruben Neves constantly involved. We played fewer long diagonal balls, instead playing to the front three with passes up the channels. Just before the break an impressive box-to-box pass by Conor Coady saw Afobe have a good first touch, beaten only by his touch that put the ball into the net. A typical no-nonsense Afobe finish. In the away end it was happy times – 'some day we'll laugh with each other about these days, these days'. We will have all summer for that. Just when you thought things could hardly be any better, some Helder Costa trickery ended with a ball to Jota and a clever finish for 3-0. You could not have scripted the next bit. We all knew which player had not scored all season, and looked unlikely to. Only if a game was 'won' and we got a penalty might he get a chance. Our fairytale season granted us that wish and Coady had the honour of completing the scoring. Cue more ecstatic scenes in the away end. Total contentment all round. A rousing 10-minute love-in after the final whistle capped a wonderful day that will live in the memory a long time. I am really chuffed for Coady to get his goal. I would like to shake the hand of the person who decided he should play in that position. Take a bow son.

ROB CARTWRIGHT

This has been 23 years of hurt in the making: "Take that John McGinlay." Thank you Nuno, for yet another skeleton being laid to rest. I think a 9-1 aggregate score over Bolton means we can finally move on. The fans sang 'we'll never play you again' – well let's hope that is true. Good riddance I say. As good a day as this was, it was yet another comfortable victory. It was a familiar pattern. The opposition really gave it a good go for first 10 minutes; then realised they ain't scoring today, so we continued to keep the ball and picked them off at will. Three former players in their starting XI couldn't make an impact either. Something else that has changed under Nuno. The result was never in doubt – Bolton were never going to score. Wolves had 62 per cent possession and with 21 shots really should have had more to show for it, but who cares? Champions once more, only this time I have the feeling that this is only the beginning, not the end. Fosun mean business. Nuno has a dream. We scored a couple of nice goals in the first half, first with Barry Douglas being in the right place for a rebound from a Benik Afobe shot from outside the box. Then, a perfect full-pitch pass from Conor Coady to Afobe who rounded the keeper and slotted into the empty net. It was as though Nuno had told them they must be 2-0 up at the break, as nothing much was happening at that point. We controlled the second half. Helder Costa and Diogo Jota linked to get the third goal and then Afobe was fouled by Karl Henry for the penalty. It looked like Afobe fancied taking it, but encouraged by his team-mates, Coady stepped forward. He enjoyed that as much as we did. So, the last 20 minutes were played out in a celebratory mode. Personally, I'd have liked them to score more, maybe seven. There were a lot of chances to add a fifth. This didn't stop the joy at the end which in the usual fashion carried on outside the stadium for a long while too. This would be a great feature outside the Premier League stadiums next season. They won't know what's hit them!

WOLVES **0**
SHEFFIELD WEDNESDAY **0**

CHAMPIONSHIP: 28/04/18   ATTENDANCE: 29,974

"WHAT A DAY, WHAT A SEASON, WHAT A BUNCH OF LADS"
DANNY BATTH

Well, you can't win them all. There was a party before and after this match as Wolves and their supporters celebrated a truly magnificent season, but the game itself was a bit of a damp squib. Not that anyone seemed to mind. There was no lack of effort on Wolves' part and if they'd managed to break the deadlock they'd have been deserving winners, having created a few notable chances. But their usual vibrancy, class and pizazz just wasn't there. Indeed, it was left to the unlikely source of Romain Saiss to produce most of their creativity, with the Moroccan having a busy and productive game in midfield.

The best chances fell to Benik Afobe, Saiss and then substitute Bright Enobakhare but Wolves were either foiled by keeper Cameron Dawson or their finishing let them down, particularly the latter who skewed wide from a great position. They still kept yet another clean sheet though – a 24th of the season – with John Ruddy untroubled again. So in a stellar season Wolves couldn't quite produce the perfect Molineux finish. It means they can't break a club record points total – but they can still reach 100 with a point at Sunderland next weekend. With Sheffield

Wednesday having nothing to play for and Wolves having wrapped up the title already the game could have gone one of two ways – a flowing pressure-free classic or a drab encounter. Sadly it was the latter.

As expected Nuno named the same team that thrashed Bolton 4-0 last week. Enobakhare returned after a few months out with a quad injury and was among the substitutes. Afobe was a bright spark up front as he continued his quest to try to impress and earn a permanent move back to the club. He almost made it 1-0 when latching on to a slack back-pass and rounding Dawson, but the keeper pushed Afobe wide in the process and he couldn't find the net from an impossibly tight angle, with the ball trickling across goal and just wide. Saiss had an excellent half, both defensively and offensively, cutting out danger and frequently setting Wolves on the attack with some probing through-balls. He also went close to breaking the deadlock when getting his head on an inswinging Barry Douglas corner but keeper Dawson blocked at point blank range.

In contrast to Saiss, his midfield partner in crime Ruben Neves was unusually off-colour, playing

a few wayward passes, and this was indicative of a rather subdued Wolves performance. You certainly felt they had a few extra gears in them.

In fact, the highlight of the afternoon by far was the pre-match scenes with Sheffield Wednesday granting Wolves a guard of honour and the supporters each waving their flags – and creating a mosaic in the Steve Bull upper – as the players received a rapturous ovation. A video message from Carl Ikeme also brought the house down. As for the visitors, dangerman Fernando Forestieri caused a few problems but Ruddy was kept pretty quiet. The second half saw an instant improvement from Wolves who came out with renewed vigour. Within two minutes Diogo Jota twice went close, firing at the keeper and then shooting wide, before Danny Batth jumped highest to nod a cross just past the post.

Nuno called for Leo Bonatini after 55 minutes with Afobe withdrawn. Enobakhare came on for his first appearance since January, replacing Helder Costa with 16 minutes to go, and the youngster was soon involved as he helped start a decent move which ended with Saiss firing over the bar via a deflection. Enobakhare was then handed the chance of the match on a plate by fellow substitute Bonatini who played a great through-ball, but he dragged his shot across goal and wide from 10 yards.

All in all it was pretty dull – even the referee had enough and blew the whistle without adding any injury time – but the post-match celebrations made up for all that. The players, staff and their families all took to the pitch to take the acclaim of an adoring crowd – after captains Batth and Conor Coady had lifted the trophy, sparking the now usual spectacular firework display at a packed Molineux. The scenes were befitting of the season to end all seasons.

"THE SCENES WERE BEFITTING OF THE SEASON TO END ALL SEASONS"

NUNO

It was a fantastic day. When you get something material you can hold on to that's when you feel you're champions. I think we were the best team in the competition, more consistent, and it's deserved for the hard work of the boys. It's a day we'll always remember. The fans waited for us and celebrated with us, it was fantastic and will stay in our memories, fantastic. Teams perform better when they're in winning momentums. Let's proceed and try to engage this momentum into the next season. The result was important, I think we deserved to win. It wasn't possible but the work ethic was there, we are professionals until the end. We have to improve that final touch. Football is sometimes about being clinical and we missed that today, but the performance was good and we had good moments. I'm going to celebrate, I'll take a beer! We're going to celebrate because it's well deserved, then we'll rest and then play Sunderland and then we'll talk about the future. Against Sheffield Wednesday away was important because we had to find solutions. All season we've improved the team in certain moments. That moment we finished with a back five of six-foot players, then the next game we played at home with three fast players in front. These kind of things made us believe the team had enough resources and solutions to win the competition. But we thought game by game – we want to build a team that can find solutions for all games.

It's hard to quantify just how much these games and these moments mean to a deeply passionate fanbase starved of success.

LINE UP

WOLVES (3-4-3):
RUDDY; BATTH (C), COADY, BOLY; DOHERTY, SAISS, NEVES, DOUGLAS; COSTA (ENOBAKHARE, 74), AFOBE (BONATINI, 55), JOTA (GIBBS-WHITE, 87).

SUBS NOT USED: NORRIS, MIRANDA, HAUSE, N'DIAYE.

SHEFFIELD WEDNESDAY (5-2-3):
DAWSON; REACH, LEES (C), VENANCIO, PUDIL, THORNILEY; PELUPESSY, BANNAN; JOAO (MATIAS, 60), NUHIU, FORESTIERI.

SUBS NOT USED: WILDSMITH, JONES, RHODES, BOYD, BAKER, NIELSEN.

STAR MAN

ROMAIN SAISS
AN EXCELLENT AFTERNOON FOR THE MOROCCAN WHO DOMINATED MIDFIELD. DEFENSIVELY SAISS WAS ON THE MONEY, ESPECIALLY WHEN CUTTING OUT A PASS THAT WOULD HAVE GIVEN AN EASY CHANCE FOR FERNANDO FORESTIERI. PLAYED A NUMBER OF PROBING PASSES AND GOT FORWARD TO GOOD EFFECT IN WHAT WAS AN ALL-ACTION PERFORMANCE.

TABLE

	TEAM	P	GD	PTS
1	WOLVES	45	46	99
2	CARDIFF	45	30	89
3	FULHAM	45	35	88
4	ASTON VILLA	45	31	83
5	MIDDLESBROUGH	45	22	75
6	DERBY	45	19	72

FAN VERDICT

CLIVE SMITH

Not until the final whistle did everyone start enjoying the day. The game itself will not make the season's DVD highlights. The fireworks, flags and razzmatazz were in stark contrast to the thought-provoking pre-match video message from Carl Ikeme. Sheffield Wednesday were not going through the motions, they were here to play. Despite having plenty of the ball, it rarely got into our box and a John Ruddy clean sheet always looked a good bet. We started sluggishly and despite improving as the game wore on we were far from our best. That is not to say we did not create chances, with plenty of shots on goal, but too many were straight at the keeper or blocked. Benik Afobe did beat the keeper by going round him but from the angle he failed to put the ball in the open net. Just before the interval their keeper made a magnificent save when a far post corner found Romain Saiss heading from close range. Diogo Jota and Helder Costa looked lively throughout, but Jota's finishing let him down. The most surprising thing was seeing Neves give the ball away three times. The whole team passed poorly which is uncharacteristic as we gave away possession cheaply and over-played at times near goal. Hardly the end of the world though was it? After the final whistle, the celebrations began and the trophy was received. Smiles all round.

HEATHER LARGE

What a day. What a season. What a club. When we set off on this rollercoaster back in August, never did I think we would be celebrating being champions at the last home game of the season. It seemed like we were very much venturing into the unknown. But Nuno had a vision (or should we say dream) of the kind of team he wanted us to be and here we are – league winners with 99 points and one game still to go.
It's been a season we'll all remember for a very long time and we can look forward to starting our Premier League campaign in a strong position. Everything about the club seems so positive at the moment, so different to this time last year. The atmosphere in the ground was fantastic and it was such a touching moment to see the video from Carl Ikeme before kick-off. He's still very much in everyone's thoughts as the players proved with their tribute shirts after lifting the trophy. Carl, we're still with you. As for the match itself, it was watchable, certainly not among the most exciting we've seen and didn't live up to everyone's expectations but we really can't complain about a 0-0 draw given what we've already achieved. Hopefully we can go to Sunderland and make the 100-point target. Conor Coady was excellent, as he has been all season. He kept the side focused especially during spells when we were being sloppy with the ball. Helder Costa was another stand-out. His creativity gave us a bit of spark.

SUNDERLAND
(EJARIA 19, FLETCHER 45, MCNAIR 66)

3

WOLVES

0

CHAMPIONSHIP: 06/05/18 ATTENDANCE: 28,452

"WE NEED TO REST. I CANNOT TAKE ANYTHING AWAY FROM WHAT MY BOYS HAVE DONE THIS SEASON"

NUNO ESPÍRITO SANTO

So Wolves saved their worst for last. After 45 games of almost unequivocal joy in what's been a season to savour, they produced an uncharacteristically inept performance against a League One team in waiting. Before this game Sunderland had won only two home games of 22, both of them 1-0 (against Fulham and Hull). Wolves, meanwhile, possessed the best away record in the league by five points, losing only four times. Funny old game, as they say.

Their joint-heaviest league defeat of the campaign won't matter a jot in the grand scheme of things. But it will have rung a few alarm bells in the head of perfectionist Nuno Espírito Santo, who demands professionalism and work ethic from his players 100 per cent of the time, on or off the pitch. All the pre-match talk was of ending the season on a high, reaching 100 points and beating every team in the league. But remarkably rock-bottom and relegated Sunderland will be the only team that Wolves didn't beat in their 2017/18 title-winning campaign. From almost the first minute it looked like Wolves thought they'd been told the match was being played on Whitley Bay, with the primary attire being flip flops.

Their passing range was off, their creativity minimal and their defending slapdash. The fringe players didn't impress and neither did the regulars. For a second game in a row Ruben Neves lacked his usual poise and composure, while there was nothing from the flanks and Helder Costa and Diogo Jota couldn't produce any magic. Sunderland mustered 18 shots to Wolves' seven and the margin of victory could have been greater. Will Norris performed heroics in the Carabao Cup and FA Cup with an almost freakish run of five matches without conceding a goal in a Wolves jersey, but here he was at fault for two goals.

In fact, Norris conceded more goals than he had in his previous six Wolves appearances, in yet another bizarre twist on a barmy final day. Sunderland made a host of changes with temporary boss Robbie Stockdale looking to restore some belated pride after a shocker of a season. And the League One-bound Black Cats certainly did that by completely outplaying the Championship champions.

Nuno made three changes to the team that drew 0-0 against Sheffield Wednesday – handing two players their first league starts of the season. In came Norris and youngster Morgan Gibbs-White. Roderick Miranda was also handed a start with Benik Afobe dropping to the bench and John Ruddy and Willy Boly not involved in the squad.

Quicker to loose balls and playing with passion, pace and pride, Sunderland created a number of chances and scored from two of them to give the half-time scoreline a surreal look. Sadly for Norris he could be looked at for both goals, which came in the 19th and 45th minutes. The stand-in keeper blocked a regulation shot from a Paddy McNair cross and diverted it straight into the path of Ovie Ejaria who had the simple task of sidefooting home. For the second, the keeper rushed from his line and couldn't get near a bouncing through-ball, from which Ashley Fletcher got his foot ahead of Danny Batth to cutely lob into the empty net.

Sunderland were great value for their 2-0 lead in the first half. They had 16 shots to Wolves' measly two and had far more zip and creativity about their play. Wolves just didn't get going. Passes went astray, runs weren't made and the defending was sloppy. Batth and Barry Douglas had to make smart blocks from goal-bound shots, while Norris also tipped over the bar from a decent Ejaria effort.

Surprisingly there were no changes at the start of the second half. Wolves made a slight improvement with keeper Jason Steele having to push into the side netting from Jota's shot after good work from Douglas, but on 56 minutes Nuno called for Leo Bonatini and Bright Enobakhare with Costa and Gibbs-White making way. It made no difference – and on 66 minutes they fell further behind when McNair had the beating of three defenders and then drove past Norris.

Wolves were making absolutely no headway and the hosts remained the more likely goalscorers. The impressive Ejaria ran a ring around Enobakhare in the box but new keeper Harry Burgoyne – who had replaced Norris in a pre-planned change to make his first appearance of the campaign – smothered it at his feet. Jota tried in vain to get a shot away at the end but his effort was blocked. And that, inexplicably, was as good as it got for Wolves on a dreadfully poor day for Nuno's team.

So in match 46 of 46, Wolves arguably saved their worst performance for last. If ever there was the epitome of an 'on-the-beach' display, this was it – bizarrely it was a matter of how many Sunderland would score. But it'll all be forgotten today with the city paying homage to their promotion heroes. The 45 games that preceded this are all that matter, not this end-of-season friendly on the beach. Now for a summer of celebration!

NUNO

We were not as intense as we should be. It's due to a lot of things. We were promoted a long time ago. We pushed until the last moment – we wanted to achieve a victory but the game didn't go well. It's not a question now to look and deeply analyse, but I think we should do better. We need to rest also. I cannot take anything away from my boys, what they've done this season is fantastic. It won't take the shine off the season. We did a fantastic job, the boys worked really hard throughout the season, had fantastic moments and we achieved what we wanted. We are champions and should be very proud. We are looking forward to tomorrow to celebrating with everyone in the park. It's important for us to finish the season celebrating with our fans.

FAN VERDICT - RUSS COCKBURN

Well that was more like the Wolves we know and love. Snatching defeat from almost certain victory, genuinely looking like they can't be bothered and conceding soft goals, it was almost refreshing to end the season in our traditional way. A couple of players will have played their last games for us after and there was only really Diogo Jota and Ruben Neves who can say they performed at anything like their usual levels. Norris, who I rate highly, had a nightmare. Anyway enough about the game, the 90 minutes were just the filling in the weekend sandwich.

LINE UP

SUNDERLAND (4-3-3):
STEELE; MATTHEWS, O'SHEA (MUMBA, 87), WILSON, OVIEDO (HUME, 71); MCNAIR (EMBLETON, 75), ROBSON, EJARIA; ASORO, FLETCHER, LUALUA.

SUBS NOT USED: CAMP, MAJA, CLARKE-SALTER, MOLYNEUX.

WOLVES (3-4-3):
NORRIS (BURGOYNE, 70); BATTH (C), COADY, MIRANDA; DOHERTY, NEVES, SAISS, DOUGLAS; COSTA (ENOBAKHARE, 56), JOTA, GIBBS-WHITE (BONATINI, 56).

SUBS NOT USED: HAUSE, VINAGRE, N'DIAYE, AFOBE.

STAR MAN

DIOGO JOTA

AS SO OFTEN THIS SEASON JOTA WAS A TIRELESS PRESENCE IN THE OPPOSITION THIRD, CONSTANTLY LOOKING TO CREATE SOME MAGIC WITH A BURST OF PACE, A THROUGH-BALL OR A SHOT FROM RANGE. SADLY ON THIS OCCASION HE HAD LITTLE SUPPORT AROUND HIM, BUT JOTA WAS PROBABLY THE ONLY PLAYER WHO COULD SAY HE CAME CLOSE TO DOING HIMSELF JUSTICE.

TABLE

	TEAM	P	GD	PTS
1	WOLVES	46	43	99
2	CARDIFF	46	30	90
3	FULHAM	46	33	88
4	ASTON VILLA	46	30	83
5	MIDDLESBROUGH	46	22	76
6	DERBY	46	22	75

IF EVER THERE WAS AN 'I WAS THERE' DAY, THIS WAS IT. WOLVERHAMPTON WAS ENGULFED BY A STUNNING SEA OF GOLD AND BLACK AS THE CITY UNITED TO CELEBRATE THIS MOST BRILLIANT OF SEASONS. THEY HADN'T SEEN ANYTHING LIKE IT HERE FOR 15 YEARS – THAT'S HOW RARE THESE DAYS COME ABOUT AND MY DID THEY MAKE THE MOST OF IT ON A GLORIOUSLY SUNNY BANK HOLIDAY MONDAY.

EVERYWHERE YOU LOOKED THERE WAS A SWARM OF GOLD AND BLACK SHIRTS, FLAGS, BANNERS AND SMILES. SOME KEEN SUPPORTERS GOT THEIR SPOT ON THE PARADE ROUTE HOURS IN ADVANCE TO GET THE BEST VANTAGE POINT OF THEIR HEROES AND COME 11.30AM THE PLACE WAS HEAVING. OVER AT WEST PARK THE PARTY WAS STARTING EARLY WITH 30,000 PEOPLE CRAMMING INTO A MINI FESTIVAL AREA COMPLETE WITH STAGE, BIG SCREENS, BARS AND A FUNFAIR. THEN, AFTER A CIVIC RECEPTION, THE STARS OF THE SHOW MADE THEIR GRAND ENTRANCE WITH NUNO ESPÍRITO SANTO, HIS STAFF AND PLAYERS GREETING THEIR PUBLIC TO DEAFENING CHEERS.

THE TWO GOLD BUSES MADE THEIR WAY DOWN LICHFIELD STREET WHERE TENS OF THOUSANDS LINED THE ROUTE. THE MAN ON THE OSS HAD NEVER QUITE SEEN ANYTHING LIKE IT. GOLD FLARES AND HORNS ADDED TO THE CARNIVAL ATMOSPHERE WHILE THE PLAYERS PROUDLY SHOWED OFF THE GLITTERING CHAMPIONSHIP TROPHY. HAVING SNAKED ITS WAY THROUGH TOWN THE BUS STOPPED AT WEST PARK WHERE THE PLAYERS WERE INTRODUCED ON STAGE ONE BY ONE IN FRONT OF AN ADORING CROWD WHO'D BEEN WARMED UP BY MATT MURRAY, STEVE BULL AND THAT MAN AGAIN, ITO JACKSON.

THEN CAME NUNO'S BIG ENTRANCE. THE HEAD COACH WAS SAID TO BE 'COLD AND EMOTIONLESS' DURING HIS TIME AT PORTO – WELL WOLVERHAMPTON HAS TRANSFORMED HIM INTO A PASSIONATE, EMOTIONAL, GRINNING, CHARISMATIC BUNDLE OF ENERGY WHO PLAYS TO THE CROWD PERHAPS QUITE LIKE NO OTHER WOLVES BOSS BEFORE HIM. HE LED THE CHANTS, INCLUDING THE SEASON'S SIGNATURE SONG, 'NUNO HAD A DREAM'. THE GIDDY, WIDE-EYED PLAYERS EXPERIENCED SOMETHING ALMOST ALL OF THEM NEVER HAD IN THEIR CAREERS. FOSUN, NUNO, THE PLAYERS, THE STAFF AND YES, THE FANS, THEY'VE ALL MADE THIS POSSIBLE AND THIS WAS ONE OF THE MANY REWARDS THAT COME WITH SUCH SWEET SUCCESS. WHAT A DAY.

END OF SEASON AWARDS

FANS' PLAYER OF THE YEAR

1. RUBEN NEVES **2.** CONOR COADY **3.** MATT DOHERTY

PLAYERS' PLAYER OF THE YEAR

1. RUBEN NEVES **2.** DIOGO JOTA **3.** CONOR COADY

GOAL OF THE SEASON

RUBEN NEVES V DERBY

YOU CAN EXPECT A LOT MORE FROM US NEXT SEASON. WE HAVE A FANTASTIC CLUB AND ME AND MY TEAM MATES ARE PROUD OF THIS CLUB. WE HAVE TO SAY THANK YOU TO THE FANS. WE HAVE A FANTASTIC TEAM, IT WAS AN AMAZING YEAR AND SEASON FOR US AND NOW WE HAVE TO ENJOY WITH OUR FAMILIES.

RUBEN NEVES

TOP GOALSCORER

DIOGO JOTA

I SAID IN MY FIRST INTERVIEW THIS SEASON I WANT TO CONTRIBUTE WITH ASSISTS AND GOALS, BECAUSE THAT'S WHAT MY POSITION REQUIRES. FORTUNATELY, I WAS ABLE TO PARTICIPATE A GOOD AMOUNT OF GOALS, BUT THE MOST IMPORTANT THING IS WE REACHED OUR GOAL OF PROMOTION. IT WAS AN AMAZING SEASON, NOT JUST FOR ME BUT FOR ALL THE CLUB. IT WAS A SEASON WE'LL ALWAYS REMEMBER."

DIOGO JOTA

YOUNG PROFESSIONAL OF THE YEAR

MORGAN GIBBS-WHITE
(ALSO NOMINATED; BRIGHT ENOBAKHARE AND RUBEN VINAGRE)

I'M MASSIVELY PINCHING MYSELF BECAUSE AT THE START OF PRE-SEASON I WAS ON CRUTCHES! TO GO THROUGH THE WHOLE SEASON TRYING TO GET INTO THE FIRST TEAM WITH NUNO AND HIM GIVING ME A CHANCE JUST SHOWS THERE'S A BIG SPACE FOR YOUNG ACADEMY PLAYERS TO PUSH THROUGH. IT'S AN HONOUR TO WIN YOUNG PROFESSIONAL OF THE SEASON. I WANT TO THANK ALL MY FAMILY AND FRIENDS AND THE FANS AT WOLVES THAT HAVE HELPED ME GET TO WHERE I AM TODAY AND HOPEFULLY THERE'S A LOT MORE TO COME.

MORGAN GIBBS-WHITE

ACADEMY PLAYER OF THE YEAR

RYAN GILES
(ALSO NOMINATED; ELLIOT WATT AND AUSTIN SAMUELS)

IT WAS AMAZING TO COLLECT THE AWARD, I THINK I HAVE COME A LONG WAY. I HAVE BEEN THROUGH A LOT OVER THE YEARS, ESPECIALLY WITH INJURIES, AND I THINK TO COME OUT WITH THE AWARD HAS PUT THE ICING ON THE CAKE FOR ME. IT IS A MASSIVE HONOUR THAT YOU HEAR THINGS FROM THE HIERARCHY, STAFF AND YOUR OWN COACHES AS WELL BECAUSE IT SHOWS THAT THEY BELIEVE IN YOU AND I THINK THEIR BELIEF HAS BROUGHT THE BEST OUT OF ME AND ALL I CAN DO IS THANK THEM FOR THAT.

RYAN GILES

NUNO'S VICTORY SPEECH

I WILL START WITH THE OWNERSHIP, I THINK WE BEGAN SOMETHING TOGETHER AND THANK YOU FOR THE SUPPORT.

THE PEOPLE THAT WERE HERE, LAURIE DALRYMPLE, KEVIN THELWELL, MATT WILD, ALL THE STAFF AT MOLINEUX, EVERYBODY, EVERY SINGLE PERSON.

THE MEDICAL DEPARTMENT, THE KIT MEN, AND ON AND ON. BUT SPECIAL THANKS TO MY TEAM - WE CAME FROM FAR AWAY AND WE LOVE IT.

THEN THE FANS - THEY ARE EVERYTHING FOR US, EVERYTHING. THIS IS WHY WE ARE HERE, THIS IS WHY WE WORK.

HONESTLY, FROM DAY ONE I FELT SOMETHING WAS GOING ON IN AUSTRIA WHEN I HAD PEOPLE COMING TO ME, YOU CANNOT EXPECT THAT, PEOPLE COMING FROM SO FAR AWAY TO SUPPORT YOU AGAINST A POLISH TEAM. I WAS SURPRISED. FROM THEN UNTIL NOW IT'S BEEN INCREDIBLE.

ALL THE STADIUMS IN THE COUNTRY, ON TUESDAY NIGHTS, COLD, WITH THE YELLOW BALL - YOU WERE THERE AND THAT MEANS A LOT, COMING AT THE END OF THE GAME AND CELEBRATING WITH YOU. THANK YOU - AND NOW WE HAVE A DREAM!

FINALLY, I THINK IT'S THE MOST IMPORTANT, THIS IS THE ENGINE, THIS IS WHAT MOVES THINGS - IT'S MY PLAYERS. THANK YOU. I ALREADY MISS YOU! BUT WE BEGIN JUNE 27, I ALREADY SPOKE TO YOU.

YOU KNOW WHAT WE HAVE TO DO - AND WE WILL DO IT.

FOR ME (THE HIGHLIGHT) IT'S DAY ONE UNTIL THE LAST DAY, EVERY MOMENT IS IMPORTANT.

THERE WERE MEMORABLE MOMENTS THAT WERE SPECIAL FOR EVERYONE, BUT EVERY DAY, EVEN WHEN YOU GO TO TRAINING AND IT'S F***ING FREEZING!

WE DON'T HAVE TO THINK WHERE WE ARE (NEXT SEASON) - WE JUST HAVE TO FOCUS ON OURSELVES. AND WE WILL DO. IT'S ABOUT BUILDING AND BEING ABLE TO CREATE AN IDENTITY, IT DOESN'T MATTER THE COMPETITION WE'RE IN.

WE KNOW IT'S GOING TO BE TOUGH, IT'S A BIG, BIG CHALLENGE. EVERYONE KNOWS.

BUT WE ARE READY, NO DOUBTS ABOUT THAT. WE'VE ALREADY STARTED WORKING, THINGS ARE MOVING, THE CLUB IS GROWING. THE SUPPORT OF THE FANS, BELIEVING.

I WILL KEEP MY FEET ON THE GROUND.

WE HAVE TO ENJOY OURSELVES AND EVERY DAY WE'LL WORK FOR IT.

NUNO ESPÍRITO SANTO

STATS

GOALKEEPERS

 21 JOHN RUDDY
APPEARANCES 45
ASSISTS 1

 31 WILL NORRIS
APPEARANCES 7

 13 HARRY BURGOYNE
APPEARANCES 0 (1)

DEFENDERS

 15 WILLY BOLY
APPEARANCES 37
GOALS 3
ASSISTS 2

 5 RYAN BENNETT
APPEARANCES 31 (2)
GOALS 1
ASSISTS 1

 16 CONOR COADY
APPEARANCES 48
GOALS 1
ASSISTS 2

 6 DANNY BATTH
APPEARANCES 20 (1)
GOALS 2

 25 RODERICK MIRANDA
APPEARANCES 18 (1)
ASSISTS 1

 30 KORTNEY HAUSE
APPEARANCES 3 (1)

 32 SYLVAIN DESLANDES
APPEARANCES 2 (1)

 2 MATT DOHERTY
APPEARANCES 47
GOALS 4
ASSISTS 4

 3 BARRY DOUGLAS
APPEARANCES 39 (3)
GOALS 5
ASSISTS 15

 29 RUBEN VINAGRE
APPEARANCES 12 (1)
GOALS 1
ASSISTS 1

 38 OSKAR BUUR RASMUSSEN
APPEARANCES 1 (1)
GOALS 1

MIDFIELDERS

 8 RUBEN NEVES
APPEARANCES 42
GOALS 6
ASSISTS 1

 27 ROMAIN SAISS
APPEARANCES 37 (7)
GOALS 4

 4 ALFRED N'DIAYE
APPEARANCES 17 (20)
GOALS 3
ASSISTS 2

 24 MORGAN GIBBS-WHITE
APPEARANCES 3 (12)

 4 DAVID EDWARDS
APPEARANCES 2 (1)

 19 JACK PRICE
APPEARANCES 4 (5)

 12 BEN MARSHALL
APPEARANCES 4 (5)
ASSISTS 1

 20 CONNOR RONAN
APPEARANCES 1 (6)

FORWARDS

 18 DIOGO JOTA
APPEARANCES 43 (3)
GOALS 18
ASSISTS 5

 33 LEO BONATINI
APPEARANCES 31 (16)
GOALS 12
ASSISTS 5

 7 IVAN CAVALEIRO
APPEARANCES 34 (14)
GOALS 9
ASSISTS 13

 17 HELDER COSTA
APPEARANCES 24 (15)
GOALS 5
ASSISTS 6

 19 BENIK AFOBE
APPEARANCES 7 (9)
GOALS 6

 26 BRIGHT ENOBAKHARE
APPEARANCES 9 (17)
GOALS 2
ASSISTS 1

 11 JORDAN GRAHAM
APPEARANCES 2 (1)
ASSISTS 1

 9 NOUHA DICKO
APPEARANCES 2 (5)
GOALS 2

 9 RAFA MIR
APPEARANCES 1 (3)

 14 MICHAL ZYRO
APPEARANCES 1 (1)
ASSISTS 1

 35 DONOVAN WILSON
APPEARANCES 0 (2)
GOALS 1

144

15800000
AMOUNT IN POUNDS PAID FOR RUBEN NEVES, BREAKING THE CLUB'S TRANSFER RECORD

30239 ATTENDANCE FOR WOLVES' 2-0 WIN OVER VILLA IN OCTOBER – THE BIGGEST MOLINEUX CROWD SINCE 1981

131 SECONDS BETWEEN JOHN RUDDY SAVING GARY MADINE'S PENALTY AND THEN JUNIOR HOILETT HITTING THE BAR WITH ANOTHER AT THE END OF WOLVES' 1-0 WIN AT CARDIFF

6 PORTUGUESE PLAYERS IN WOLVES' SQUAD

6 TIMES NEIL WARNOCK TOLD NUNO TO F*** OFF AT THE END OF WOLVES' TEMPESTUOUS 1-0 WIN OVER CARDIFF

99 POINTS WON, A CLUB RECORD IN THE SECOND TIER

17 LEAGUE GOALS SCORED BY DIOGO JOTA, THE FIFTH HIGHEST IN THE CHAMPIONSHIP

31 CONSECUTIVE MATCHES WOLVES WERE AT THE TOP OF THE TABLE FOR (THEY WERE TOP FROM THE 2-0 WIN AT NORWICH UNTIL THE END OF THE SEASON)

109 MINUTES-PER-GOAL RATIO FOR BENIK AFOBE AFTER HE RETURNED ON LOAN AND SCORED SIX TIMES

---

19 SECONDS LEFT OF STOPPAGE TIME WHEN RYAN BENNETT SCORED THE WINNER AT BRISTOL CITY

14 LEAGUE ASSISTS BY BARRY DOUGLAS, THE JOINT HIGHEST IN THE CHAMPIONSHIP

521 MINUTES PLAYED BY WILL NORRIS UNTIL HE CONCEDED A GOAL FOR THE FIRST TIME

4 GAMES REMAINING WHEN WOLVES WON PROMOTION

28298
AVERAGE MOLINEUX ATTENDANCE, THE HIGHEST SINCE 2003/04

25 MATCHES NEEDED TO EARN THE SAME AMOUNT OF POINTS AS FOR THE WHOLE OF THE PREVIOUS SEASON (58)

6 CONSECUTIVE LEAGUE MATCHES SCORED IN BY LEO BONATINI, JUST ONE SHORT OF EQUALLING A POST-WAR CLUB RECORD

11 OPPOSITION PLAYERS SENT OFF AGAINST WOLVES

---

2 DEFEATS AT MOLINEUX (THE SECOND BEST RECORD IN THE EFL)

CARL IKEME'S SQUAD NUMBER FOR THE SEASON

53 POINTS WON AT MOLINEUX (SECOND HIGHEST IN THE COUNTRY)

67 YEARS SINCE WOLVES HAD WON AWAY AT MIDDLESBROUGH (A RUN OF 25 MATCHES)

11 *POINTS CLEAR OF THIRD-PLACED FULHAM THAT WOLVES FINISHED*

33 PLAYERS USED BY NUNO IN ALL COMPETITIONS

24 CLEAN SHEETS FOR JOHN RUDDY, THE HIGHEST IN THE CHAMPIONSHIP

6 CONSECUTIVE WINS FROM OCTOBER TO DECEMBER, WHICH CEMENTED WOLVES' LEAD AT THE TOP

5626 NUMBER OF FANS WOLVES TOOK TO PRESTON, THEIR HIGHEST AWAY FOLLOWING OF THE SEASON

3 TOUCHES OF THE BALL INSIDE THE PENALTY AREA DURING THE ENTIRE SEASON BY NEVES *(HE SCORED SIX GOALS FROM OUTSIDE THE BOX)*

48 MATCHES STARTED BY CONOR COADY IN ALL COMPETITIONS, THE HIGHEST IN THE SQUAD

13 LEAGUE GAMES UNBEATEN BETWEEN OCTOBER 31 AND JANUARY 20

AUG 5 MIDDLESBROUGH (H) 1-0 (BONATINI)
AUG 8 YEOVIL (H) 1-0 (DICKO) *EFL CUP
AUG 12 DERBY COUNTY (A) 2-0 (DOUGLAS, CAVALEIRO)
AUG 15 HULL CITY (A) 3-2 (NEVES, JOTA, DICKO)
AUG 19 CARDIFF CITY (H) 1-2 (BONATINI)
AUG 23 SOUTHAMPTON (A) 2-0 (BATTH, WILSON) *EFL CUP
AUG 26 BRENTFORD (A) 0-0
SEP 9 MILLWALL (H) 1-0 (JOTA)
SEP 12 BRISTOL CITY (H) 3-3 (BONATINI, JOTA, BATTH)
SEP 16 NOTTINGHAM FOREST (A) 2-1 (JOTA 2)
SEP 19 BRISTOL ROVERS (H) 1-0 (ENOBAKHARE) *EFL CUP
SEP 23 BARNSLEY (H) 2-1 (ENOBAKHARE, N'DIAYE)
SEP 27 SHEFFIELD UNITED (A) 0-2
SEP 30 BURTON ALBION (A) 4-0 (JOTA, SAISS, VINAGRE, BONATINI)
OCT 14 ASTON VILLA (H) 2-0 (JOTA, BONATINI)
OCT 21 PRESTON NORTH END (H) 3-2 (CAVALEIRO, BONATINI 2)
OCT 24 MANCHESTER CITY (A) 0-0, 1-4 ON PENS *EFL CUP
OCT 28 QUEENS PARK RANGERS (A) 1-2 (BONATINI)
OCT 31 NORWICH CITY (A) 2-0 (BOLY, BONATINI)
NOV 3 FULHAM (H) 2-0 (SAISS, BONATINI)
NOV 18 READING (A) 2-0 (DOHERTY)
NOV 22 LEEDS UNITED (H) 4-1 (DOUGLAS, CAVALEIRO, JOTA, COSTA)
NOV 25 BOLTON WANDERERS (H) 5-1 (BOLY, BONATINI, CAVALEIRO 2, JOTA)
DEC 4 BIRMINGHAM CITY (A) 1-0 (BONATINI)
DEC 9 SUNDERLAND (H) 0-0
DEC 15 SHEFFIELD WEDNESDAY (A) 1-0 (NEVES)
DEC 23 IPSWICH TOWN (H) 1-0 (CAVALEIRO)
DEC 26 MILLWALL (A) 2-2 (JOTA, SAISS)
DEC 30 BRISTOL CITY (A) 2-1 (DOUGLAS, BENNETT)
JAN 2 BRENTFORD (H) 3-0 (NEVES, DOUGLAS, JOTA)
JAN 6 SWANSEA CITY (H) 0-0 *FA CUP
JAN 13 BARNSLEY (A) 0-0
JAN 17 SWANSEA CITY (A) 1-2 (JOTA) *FA CUP
JAN 20 NOTTINGHAM FOREST (H) 0-2
JAN 27 IPSWICH TOWN (A) 1-0 (DOHERTY)
FEB 3 SHEFFIELD UNITED (H) 3-0 (NEVES, JOTA, CAVALEIRO)
FEB 10 QUEENS PARK RANGERS (H) 2-1 (N'DIAYE, COSTA)
FEB 17 PRESTON NORTH END (A) 1-1 (COADY)
FEB 21 NORWICH CITY (H) 2-2 (LEWIS OG, N'DIAYE)
FEB 24 FULHAM (A) 0-2
MAR 7 LEEDS UNITED (A) 3-0 (SAISS, BOLY, AFOBE)
MAR 10 ASTON VILLA (H) 1-4 (JOTA)
MAR 13 READING (H) 3-0 (DOHERTY 2, AFOBE)
MAR 17 BURTON ALBION (H) 3-1 (COSTA, AFOBE 2)
MAR 30 MIDDLESBROUGH (A) 2-1 (COSTA, CAVALEIRO)
APR 3 HULL CITY (H) 2-2 (JOTA, RASMUSSEN)
APR 6 CARDIFF CITY (A) 1-0 (NEVES)
APR 11 DERBY COUNTY (H) 2-0 (JOTA, NEVES)
APR 15 BIRMINGHAM CITY (H) 2-0 (JOTA, AFOBE)
APR 21 BOLTON WANDERERS (A) 4-0 (DOUGLAS, AFOBE, JOTA, COADY)
APR 28 SHEFFIELD WEDNESDAY (H) 0-0
MAY 6 SUNDERLAND (A) 0-3

NUNO HAD A DREAM,
TO BUILD A FOOTBALL TEAM,

WITH CHINESE OWNERS
AND A WONDER KID FROM PORTO,

WITH 5 AT THE BACK,
AND PACE IN ATTACK,

**WE'RE WOLVERHAMPTON
WE'RE ON OUR WAY BACK!**

WRITER: **TIM SPIERS**

EDITORIAL DESIGN AND PRODUCTION: **SIMON HILL**

PHOTOGRAPHY: **SAM BAGNALL**

ADDITIONAL PHOTOGRAPHY:
TIM STURGESS
DAVID HAMILTON
JOHN SAMBROOKS

PRINTED BY:
precisioncolour**printing** limited

PUBLISHED BY:
THE MIDLAND NEWS ASSOCIATION LTD

MNA Media

Express & Star

ACKNOWLEDGEMENTS

MANY THANKS TO OUR FANS FOR THEIR 'FAN VERDICT' CONTRIBUTIONS THROUGHOUT THE SEASON.

CLIVE SMITH

ASIDE FROM THE DETAIL, THE SEASON WILL BE REMEMBERED FOR THE PATIENT, PASSING STYLE OF FOOTBALL. FIVE AWAY GAMES WILL LINGER LONG IN THE MEMORY – LEEDS, BRISTOL CITY, MIDDLESBROUGH BOLTON AND OF COURSE CARDIFF.

HEATHER LARGE

WE COULDN'T HAVE WISHED FOR ANYTHING BETTER – I STILL NEED TO PINCH MYSELF NOW TO BELIEVE IT HAS REALLY HAPPENED.

CHRIS HUGHES

IT WAS, BY A FAIR MARGIN, THE BEST SEASON WE'VE HAD IN THE TWO AND A HALF DECADES I'VE BEEN A SEASON TICKET HOLDER. THE HIGHLIGHT WAS BEATING VILLA – PURE, ANIMALISTIC, TRIBAL EMOTIONS.

RUSS COCKBURN

WOW. THIS ISN'T WOLVES. STYLISH FOOTBALL, POTENTIAL WORLD CLASS PLAYERS STRUTTING AROUND MOLINEUX AND A MULTITUDE OF HOODOOS PUT TO BED. THE BIGGEST THING FOR ME WAS THE EMERGENCE OF A NEW UNITY AMONGST THE WHOLE CLUB.

NATALIE WOOD

QUITE SIMPLY A DREAM! WE PLAYED SOME OF THE BEST FOOTBALL I'VE SEEN – AND I WOULD ARGUE THE BEST FOOTBALL EVER WITNESSED IN THE CHAMPIONSHIP. WE'LL SPEAK ABOUT THE CARDIFF GAME FOR YEARS TO COME.

ADAM VIRGO

THE BEST SEASON I'VE EVER EXPERIENCED. IT WILL BE REMEMBERED FOR SO MANY REASONS AND EVERYTHING ABOUT IT WAS SPECIAL.

ROB CARTWRIGHT

I'VE SEEN US WIN LEAGUES, WIN CUPS, EVEN APPEAR IN A EUROPEAN FINAL; BUT ON PURE FOOTBALLING TERMS AND SKILL – THIS WAS THE BEST OF MY LIFETIME.

RUSS EVERS

A TRULY MEMORABLE SEASON THAT STARTED WITH A FANTASTIC TRIP TO AUSTRIA WHERE WE SAW THE SEEDS BEING SOWN. IN TRUTH, IT ENDED AS A PROCESSION AS WE SIMPLY BLEW TEAMS AWAY.